THIS IS A NONPROFIT PROJECT

Proceeds from sales of this book are used to distribute free copies of *What They Signed Up For: True Stories by Ordinary Soldiers* to veterans and their families, veterans' organizations, service providers, and student groups.

Our mission is to inspire other veterans to tell their own stories, and to inform and educate civilians about the veteran experience.

For information on obtaining copies of *What They Signed Up For*, visit blueearbooks.com, or email ecasey@blueearbooks.com.

WHAT THEY SIGNED UP FOR

TRUE STORIES BY ORDINARY SOLDIERS

Edited by Jeb Wyman

BLUE EAR BOOKS

www.blueearbooks.com

Published in 2017 by
Blue Ear Books
7511 Greenwood Ave. N, Box 400
Seattle, WA 98103 USA
www.blueearbooks.com

ISBN: 978-0-9844063-8-8

Credits:

Photo Editor:

Bob Hereford

Cover Design and Book Composition:

Christopher Dollar

Printer:

Scott Morris, Morris Printing Services, Arkansas City, KS,
www.morrisprint.com

*For the veterans who told their stories in these pages,
and for those who are inspired to tell theirs.*

For Tony Muething, who started it all.

*For Adam Cajiuat Posadas
August 29, 1985 - March 7, 2016*

CONTENTS

FOREWORD

ETHAN CASEY

WHAT THE 18 NARRATIVE ACCOUNTS IN THIS BOOK BRING HOME TO US IS THAT EXPERIENCE OF COMBAT IN WAR—like all human experience, but surely even moreso—is unavoidably and ineradicably personal to each individual. There certainly is, and should be, a politics to whether, when, and how a society should or should not send its young people into combat—and, as citizens, we all should be engaged in that difficult politics. But the *personal* meaning of combat belongs to those who experience it.

It's that meaning—or, rather, those meanings—that combat veterans are in a position to bring home to the rest of us, sharing hard-won spiritual nourishment with us who sent them to Iraq, Afghanistan, or both (multiple long combat tours being far from unusual in today's American military). The home-front politics of our wars—whether you or I "support" or "oppose" our country's military involvements—feels awkwardly beside the point, even in bad taste, next to the things we stand to learn if we allow ourselves to be still and listen to the vets in this book and others like them.

What does it mean to say that veterans bring our wars home with them? It's not only about them, but also about us who stayed home. Emmanuel Wright lays it out for us:

> I was back as a corpsman at the Naval Hospital in San Diego and I had a difficult time regulating my responses at work. Everything was intensely serious to me, a matter of life or death. I don't know just how I was acting with my colleagues, all I know is that I was no longer the person I had been. All I know is that the nurses and doctors looked at me strangely. All I know is that I couldn't make sense of people anymore, that life had become incomprehensible, and that the dead children of Iraq haunted the hallways and the examination rooms, the sidewalks of San Diego, the streets and highways, the bars and restaurants, the apartments and houses, and my own bedroom.

The dead children of Iraq haunt the sidewalks of San Diego. The American home front, until recently so stubbornly determined to remain placid and pleased with itself, is intimately and permanently connected to Iraq and Afghanistan, in ways we're only beginning to understand. Veterans bring home a dark thread in our national story. But it's not like a story on TV; these stories are not offered for our titillation, to provide a pleasurable *frisson* of fictional danger or darkness. What they rather offer is something we had better confront and come to terms with and integrate into our collective nonfiction narrative, just as each of these veterans is doing on an individual level. The varying reactions from veterans in this book to the film *American Sniper* are instructive. I thought it was an excellent film, but what do I know? I have no credibility regarding either the depiction of combat or its effects on a human soul, and I'm not sure Clint Eastwood does either. The people who do have credibility are the people in this book and the many others like them who live in your American community and mine. Justin Shults explains it very directly: "PTSD is a reminder of what it is that we did."

Finally, a note on what Jeb Wyman signed up for. An editor is any book's first reader, and as such he or she serves as a surrogate for every eventual reader. That is the nature of Jeb's service to us. Jeb teaches writing at a community college—he describes the genesis of this project in his Afterword—and a very good editor. He also serves us as a representative middle-aged, middle-class, Middle American civilian citizen who signed up, on behalf of the rest of us, to make the effort to know combat veterans and their stories. This book is the fruit of his earned personal education over some three years of hard work and often wrenching emotional involvement. It's my honor to publish *What They Signed Up For*, and I thank Jeb for his service.

Seattle
April 28, 2017

"The Marine Corps put us through classes about combat stress. You hear about Johnny who went on deployment, and Johnny's all messed up now. But I wasn't going to say, 'Johnny's me.' I'd just come home from a second deployment. I figured I could just push the bad stuff out."

WE GOT TO THE POINT THERE'S NO COMING BACK

DESHAUN CAPLES

I CAN REMEMBER IT LIKE YESTERDAY. AL-QAIM, IRAQ. NOON. THE SUN STRAIGHT ABOVE. No shade. We waited on a dirty street in the bright light as occasional rifle fire cracked in the distance. We stood in small groups by a small compound with six-foot stone walls, maybe as big as a living room. Humvees were parked outside. Iraqi civilians huddled in the compound, waiting to get medevaced out. They were grim and their clothes covered with dust and some of them damp with blood drying in the heat. A teenaged girl held a baby. The baby was bloodied and crying.

I was part of the communication detachment team for the battalion commander. We followed the tank men around. We ran the radios and phones for the commander. We were part of Operation Iron Fist, and a tank had fired a 120 mm shell into a house, and out of the destruction came these civilians, shocked and wounded. There weren't any insurgents in the house. There were no bad guys.

The baby looked like it was dying. Our medics couldn't do anything more. We listened to the baby cry. We stood in the heat waiting for the helicopters to come and pick them up. I was thinking about my daughter, Nevaeh, who was about the same age as the Iraqi baby. What if that was her? I started thinking about my family. The baby was crying in the arms of the teenaged girl, and there was nothing anybody could do at all. No one said anything. We waited, all of us, listening to the sound of the dry heat, the occasional report of weapons firing, and the crying of the baby. I don't know if the teenaged girl was the baby's mother, or if the mother was dead or if the mother hadn't been in the house. But she was a teenaged girl holding this badly wounded baby, and they'd gotten whatever treatment they could at this little aid station where the helicopters were flying in, and the baby looked like it was going to die.

I PLAYED BASKETBALL IN HIGH SCHOOL, AND I WANTED TO PLAY IN COLLEGE. I met my wife, Kitearia, when we were both in tenth grade, and in February of our senior year she calls me one day. "I'm pregnant," she says. "And I'm going to keep the baby, no matter what." I wasn't upset, because my whole life I didn't have a father. I wanted to have a family, and I wanted to be that guy who was there for his daughter. Kitearia's mom was livid when she found out, but my mom started laughing.

My mom's a tall woman, seen a lot of hardship. She raised four kids, no man in the house, low income and on government assistance. She nursed me when I was a scrawny kid bedridden with juvenile rheumatoid arthritis, missing half of first grade with hot packs on my swollen knees and choking down orange-flavored pills.

When I told her the news, my mom looked at me. "All right. Well. Now you gotta man up," she said. "Basketball is not going to pay for diapers. You need to realize that. You need to do the responsible thing. If you're going to go to school, focus on that. If you're going to do something else, you can do well at the military."

I felt like I had to prove to myself that I could do something amazing, and I wanted to provide for my kid. So I went with a buddy to the recruiting offices. As we were walking away from the Army recruiter, the Marine Corps recruiter pokes his head out of his doorway. "You want to join the best damn fighting force in the world?" he says. We go inside. He pulls out color brochures of the Marines in dress blues in perfect formation, puts Marine Corps caps and ribbons in our hands to look at.

It was very appealing to me, the idea of being the best. The challenge of boot camp was exactly what I wanted to do. I wanted to be that guy for my daughter that proved himself. That tested himself.

"This is going to be the hardest thing you'll ever do," the recruiter said, "and you'll probably be in Iraq by the end of next year. But I think you can do this. I think you're ready." My daughter was going to be born in August. I was working at Taco Bell. I had nothing. No car, not even a phone. Kitearia hated me for leaving. I was supposed to be there when our child was born. But after I made up my mind about it, I didn't think twice.

WE WERE STANDING IN FORMATION OUT ON THE DRILL FIELD DURING THE FINAL WEEKS OF BOOT CAMP. Captain Black walks onto the field, talks to my drill sergeant, and heads towards me. "Caples," he says. "I need to talk to you." He pulls me out, leads me off the field. *This is bad,* I think. I'm certain I'm in trouble. Captains don't talk to recruits. I'm getting kicked out of the Marine Corps, I think. They found out that I had arthritis as a kid, they found out I lied on my medical forms. The captain turns to me. "Congratulations, Caples. You're a father. Your daughter Nevaeh is 8 pounds, 1 ounce. Mother and baby are fine." He hands me a handwritten slip off his desk with the name of my new child and her birth weight. He leaves me to my thoughts for a few moments, then hands me his cell phone. "Go ahead and say hello to your new daughter, Caples." I call Kitearia and she picks up, her voice whispery and slow. She's medicated. She tells me our daughter looks like me, same eyes. She says she's going to send me pictures. It's a two-minute conversation, and I return the phone to Captain Black, salute, and go back to my platoon.

Three weeks later, my wife and new infant daughter fly to San Diego for my boot camp graduation. I hold Nevaeh for the first time. I remember thinking *Don't drop this tiny baby, my daughter.* They told me I was trembling.

WE TRAINED IN THE MOJAVE DESERT. WE RAN THROUGH FAKE IRAQI TOWNS WITH FAKE MORTARS BOOMING and a soundtrack of automatic weapons fire. Fake IEDs going off. Guys laying on the ground, their cammies shredded and the stumps of their limbs wet with what looks like blood. They're real amputees— I don't know if they're Marines or hired civilians—and it really looks like they've just had their leg or arm blown off. Actors dressed like Iraqis come to you and speak Arabic and touch your weapon and try to shake your hand. "You take your right hand off the trigger to shake someone's hand, to be nice," we were instructed, "because the left hand is disrespectful. That's the hand they wipe with."

We'd clear rooms, kicking in doors and putting guys in flexcuffs. We aimed and shot blanks at bad guys, flame barking from the barrels of our M16s. We played war for three months in the Mojave against Marines who'd grown out their hair and beards to look like insurgents.

Before we shipped out, we gathered in a big unit meeting. We stood in a huge circle. Lieutenant Colonel Alford spoke to us. He'd just gotten back from a tour in Afghanistan with the 3rd Battalion, 6th Marines. If there ever was a G.I. Joe leader, it was this guy. "Look to your left, look to your right," Lieutenant Colonel Alford told us. "Think about these guys. Some of us might not make it back." Everyone looked around at each other. It was a moment. I looked at my brothers. Marlin, Wolf, Roope. Rodriguez. I had no freaking clue about all the politics of the war. At that point, the only reason I wanted to go over there was to bring these guys back home. When it came down to it, that's how we all seen it.

We were scared, but we were confident. And I thought, if I'm going to go to Iraq, I want to do something. I signed up to take care of my daughter, but I was ready to kick some butt. In the Marine Corps, badges show what you've done, and the less you have, the less you're respected. In that culture, when you're at the bottom, you just wanna prove yourself so bad. You thirst for the experience. War stories are trophies.

WE'RE SITTING IN A LONG LINE. WE HAVE NO IDEA WHAT WE'RE IN LINE FOR, we've just been told to get in line, like we have done many times before. Turns out we're all getting our picture taken before we go to Iraq. We're all joking around. We're all cocky, giving each other shit.

"Yo. You guys are laughing? You think this is funny, right?" The sergeant taking the pictures glares at us.

"No, Sergeant."

"You know what these pictures are for, right?"

"No, Sergeant."

"It's for when you get killed. You understand that?"

"Yes, Sergeant."

"You understand?"

"Yes, Sergeant."

We're in uniform, battle dress green digicams. We stand in front of a white sheet for the background. They want you to look like a Marine. Do I smile in this, do I want to look happy? Do I want to look like a serious Marine?

"Caples, your turn."

"All right, Sergeant."

"All right, Caples. Go."

"Yes, Sergeant."

I have no idea if I smiled, scowled, or looked like a serious Marine. I've never seen my photo.

I'M GOING TO WAR. I'M 19. We're landing in northern Iraq by the Syrian border, in a C-130 military transport. The plane plunges down, combat flight pattern, churning our stomachs. They'd give you pills before we took off to ward off the nausea, but some guys said, "Oh, I'm good." Halfway through the flight they take off their helmets and puke in them.

We're given our full combat load. We'd been carrying around empty magazines for weeks, and now we're given live rounds. All the games are over. Before you'd think you're watching a bunch of high school kids playing sports, messing around. As soon as we got that ammo, everybody shut up. All right, boys. Time to wake up. We slept on our weapons and boots and sleeping bags.

We're going to clear the little town on the border next to the Euphrates. House-to-house clearing, busting down doors. Kicking butt. IEDs and trap doors and vehicles with bombs.

THE SAND IS SO FINE IT'S LIKE POWDERED SNOW. A DARK-YELLOW DUST. IT PLUMES UP WITH EACH STEP. Kick the ground, the earth floats like smoke into the sky. We leave the base in a Humvee at 3 a.m. in a convoy in blackout. All lights are out, everything black, like we are blind. The driver's wearing night vision goggles to see the infrared chem lights taped to the back of every vehicle. The dust kicks up, penetrates the Humvee, and we smell the dry earth. The radio is squawking, the driver's peering into the blackness through his night vision goggles, and he's getting frustrated with the lieutenant, who's peppering him with questions about who's talking on the radio as he's looking at maps. We drive in the blackness for what seems like an hour. I'm sitting behind the driver, in my helmet and armor plates, my hands on my weapon.

The Humvee starts to lean. I can feel it in the blackness. We lean more and more, keep leaning, and leaning, until we're almost sideways, and we get to this point of balance that I can feel there's no coming back. I grab on because I know something is going to happen, I can feel it slip, and the Humvee gives way and rolls over and over down into the blackness. We roll once, everything tumbling inside, men and gear and weapons and ammo, and roll again. The Humvee stops on its roof, upside down. I'm underneath the driver's seat, looking up at the steering wheel, laying atop the driver. We're upside down and it's completely black and all this fine sand is raining inside, getting into our eyes and ears. I'm thinking the top of the Humvee is not going to be able to hold the weight of the vehicle, and we're going to get crushed. The sand is everywhere and we're trying to find the door handles.

Then I smell the gas. We're upside down and we have big cans of JP8 fuel strapped to the back of the truck, and the gas is trickling into the vehicle. We're going to burn alive. We're going to suffocate. The lieutenant starts screaming, "Somebody help us! I can't breathe, I can't breathe!" The corporal tells him to shut up, and the corporal takes control of the situation, but we can't get the doors to open and I can't find a radio. The corporal says guys will be coming to get us for sure, maintain operational posture, suck it up, be Marines. We sit in the upside-down Humvee in the blackness and the dust and the gas fumes, and as the dawn is beginning our Marines come. They pry the doors open and pull us all out, the light just emerging. Doc checks us out. One guy has a concussion from his rifle hitting him in the face, and he's sent back to base. Doc looks in my eyes, asks if I feel anything broken. I tell him no. "You're fine," he says. They hand me my rifle, I grab my gear bag that's soaked in JP8 fuel and get in another Humvee. We drive into the city.

WE'RE ON A HILL LOOKING DOWN INTO AL-QAIM. MARINE SNIPERS LAY ON A ROOFTOP directly in front of us, some of them wearing beanies instead of helmets, lightly armored flak vests, unlike the guys who kick in doors. The snipers appear and disappear over the next two weeks, flitting around the city like lethal ghosts.

The snipers lay motionless, one eye fixed to their rifle scopes. You don't see the pull of the trigger, only hear the sharp crack of a high-velocity round. You think: somebody's dead. Another crack. Somebody else is dead. I imagined, with each crack of a sniper's rifle, there's another bad guy dead. Bad guy dead, bad guy dead, bad guy dead. We're Marines. We're trained to fight bad guys.

White flags hang from some buildings indicating they've been cleared of bad guys, or they're friendly, or the occupants are surrendering—I don't know. A house blasted into rubble. Next door, another house pocked with bullet holes. Next door to that, a pristine white marble mansion with a satellite dish on top and a cow outside and goat nosing in garbage. Laundry on a line.

Days where nothing would happen, just the dull heat of the sun, the sounds of chickens or a donkey braying or a car with a bad muffler. Days when it was a constant shoot-off, *t-ttt-tt---tt, t-ttt-tt---tt ttt-tt---tt, t-ttt* —nothing but rounds, rounds, rounds, rounds, rounds all day. And then again quiet for a long time. Who are these guys? Where are they at? All we're seeing is muzzle flashes. The day the tank fired a shell into the house full of civilians, we're in the compound where the medevacs are staged. Enemy rockets start coming in. They hit maybe a half mile away, and they get closer. They get closer yet. The guys start talking that the insurgents are going to bracket in on us, adjust their aim, zero in on the compound, shred us with shrapnel. Another rocket hits, closer yet. We're all standing against a wall, all the protection there is, standing with our rifles, waiting. But the rockets stop coming in, and it gets quiet again.

Cooper, he was a tough Marine. A badass guy. I looked up to him. I tell him, "Man, first time out of the wire, I fucking get in a Humvee rollover." He nods. "Dude, guy shot an RPG at me today," he says.

Wolf is one of the wiremen guys like me, communications detachment. He'd been in the thick of it when his Humvee was ripped by an IED. He comes in on a stretcher, a chunk of metal sticking out of his leg, gauze wrapped around it. He's waiting for a medevac helicopter, and by the time I see him he has so much morphine in him, he doesn't give a shit about his leg. "Deshaun, I haven't seen you, man," he says. He starts laughing. "Where you been at?" He talks like we're back home running into each other at the 7-11.

A jet drops a 500-pound bomb a few blocks away. *BA-BOOOM.* A roiling cloud of gray dust leaps into the sky, chunks of a house or cars or body parts rocket outward and fall to the ground. You feel the shockwave, feel the invisible fist punch your chest and thrust out your back. BOO-OOOM. "Holy shit," a guy yells. "*Fuck yeah!*" Fuck yeah, we all think, bring it on. I don't think twice about the people that are killed. Or if anybody is killed. Or what it is for. It's a big fucking explosion and a *fuck yeah* moment. What else do you expect from 20-year-old amped-up Marines in a different country?

Hooded prisoners crouch in the back of an open-bed truck, guys caught with weapons or IEDs or just in the wrong place at the wrong time. Three of us take pictures next to one of them, flashing two fingers.

Later, it bothers me, mugging for photos next to hooded prisoners cowering in the bed of a truck. It bothers me a lot, so I delete the photos. I start thinking about everything I'm seeing, and I come to think it's just fucking wrong, the killing and the war. The ugliness. *The evilness.* Prisoners. The crying bloody baby. The body bags of men I know.

I can't stop thinking about a pair of feet we find in the road, two feet blown off a man now surely dead. By us? Dusty and wearing sandals, the stumps crusted over in the sun. Just a pair of human feet. Standing stupidly like someone forgot them and crawled away. Whose feet were those? We left them in the middle of the road.

At first, coming back home is like falling in love again. But that fades, and after the welcome home sign is packed away, normal life begins. We got an apartment on lance corporal pay, $800 every two weeks. We saved, I took brown-bag lunches to work every day. I bought a car with deployment money. The fruits of labor, the fruits of deployment. I joined the Marines so we could be a family. We wanted to be the American dream.

"Are you okay?" she'd ask.

"Yeah. I'm fine."

"Tell me what it was like—over there."

"No."

"Baby, please help me understand. What're you thinking all the time?"

"No."

"*Please* talk to me."

"Why would you understand?"

"Please, baby. *Please, please.*"

"Leave me the fuck alone."

She thought our life would be perfect when I got home. I was just glad to be out of that goddamned sandbox.

I didn't know how to tell her about Wolf who had a piece of metal sticking out of his leg, or about the pair of dead, dusty feet in the road. I didn't know how to tell her about the Iraqi baby, bloody and crying, in the arms of a terrified teenager in Al-Qaim. I couldn't talk about a lot of things with my wife, and I couldn't stand to hear about everyday problems. It's like I spoke a different language.

A lot of our fights were about money. I saw us as well off. We had food, a house, our daughter had diapers. I was quiet, I kept to myself. Her side of the house, my side of the house. My wife took it to mean I was uninterested in our marriage. She pushed on with her life, kept up a social life on Facebook. I didn't feel like I should be having a good time. For me, it was a matter of respect for the dead and wounded. For my guys still over there. For the Iraqis who lived every day in fear and filth. Respect for our safe, comfortable lives.

My baby Nevaeh was a year old. When she cried, a trigger was pulled inside me. My emotions boiled up, filled me and overflowed, paralyzing me. Grief, anger—I was overwhelmed.

My wife tried to carry on with the relationship she thought we had. But I wasn't a high school boy anymore. I wasn't that happy, skinny, carefree, shy kid she had married. I had lost my youth and my innocence. I was different. At the time, I didn't know how different I was.

AL-TAQADUM AIR BASE, NEAR HABBANIYAH. There's the Euphrates, fields of grasses by the river edge, vendors on the streets with melons and oranges.

I dream about Van Parys. In the dream, he strolls on our base in Habbaniyah, along the flight line and the rusting hangars and massive concrete bunkers. The slumped wrecks of Iraqi Sukhoi jets, the shooting range. Van Parys walks around, somebody touches him, and they collapse and die. He walks up to a sandbagged guard shack or a blue-green port-a-potty or a pallet of shrinkwrapped MREs. He touches it, and it smokes. It catches on fire. Wherever he goes, whatever he touches, either dies or catches on fire. In the dream, everybody runs from him. Everybody is trying to get away from him.

Van Parys was on a security detail for some higher-ranking officers. He was taking them on a tour of forward operation bases when he was hit with an RPG, a rocket-propelled grenade. Not much of him left, I was told. He had been in Iraq for twenty days. Corporal Brandon Joseph Van Parys. From New Tripoli, Pennsylvania. Age 20.

We didn't talk about it. We didn't really talk about any of them. A little memorial on base, and that was pretty much it. You lock it in the basement, put it away. Hide the key. Guy dies one day, fucking wake up and eat breakfast the next.

Loggins killed by a sniper. Phillips crushed by a Humvee. Lindsey, he took his own life while on guard post.

The incoming rockets land randomly, sometimes a mile off, or they can fall right where you sleep. Or you could be eating or you could be sitting on the toilet and be blown up. They were loud and they shook everything.

We'd be on the roofs on base running wire and we were warned about snipers. I thought it was a bunch of bullshit. Like, no fucking way. No sniper is going to shoot me from way over there. But how this guy tells the story, he's sitting there, and he gets thirsty and bends down for a drink of water. Right then a sniper round grazes the back of his neck. If he hadn't taken the drink of water, it would have been straight through his neck. He takes off the gauze to show us the huge fresh crevasse on the back of his neck, pink and weepy.

I was mad about that. Really? That too? I have to be running and dodging even on the rooftops so some guy doesn't shoot me in the neck? Because you're always looking for bad guys. IEDs everywhere, cars blowing up. Anti-personnel mines. A woman looks pregnant but she's carrying bombs instead of babies. Rocks on the side of the road that might be hiding wires. Any middle-aged man's a threat, that's how we seen it. When that truck gets blown up in front of you, that Iraqi sitting there, watching, he pulled the trigger—or was he just watching? So we talked sick humor all the time, weird optimism. You might die, man. Who gives a fuck about that?

This three-star general comes in for breakfast with the troops. Before he comes, we get a little crash course from the lieutenant. "Make sure you don't ask nothing crazy. Make sure you don't mention *blah blah blah.*" The general sits down with a forkful of scrambled eggs. "How's the fight, men?" he says. "You guys taking it to the bad guys out there? Let's go get some insurgents." He sounded like CNN. *Insurgents, insurgents, insurgents. Bad guys, bad guys, bad guys.* This dude was so out of touch. He had no idea—

or maybe he *did* know—that we weren't fighting bad guys most of the time. Yeah, lots of people dying. But they were innocent people that shouldn't be dying.

My worst fear is that Van Parys died for nothing. That he died for fucking *whatever*. Guys from my unit told me they originally called it "Operation Iraqi Liberation." *O.I.L.* Why did these people have to die? Politics? We're just over there for each other. We fucking didn't care about the politics.

IN THE MOVIES BACK HOME, I'D SIT IN THE LAST ROW. I WAS AFRAID SOMEONE WOULD COME BEHIND ME AND CUT MY THROAT. I told myself I was fine, but I didn't tell anybody about it. Nobody thinks like that in a movie theater.

Driving and craning my neck to look for bombs on the side of the road. Crossing a street to avoid a trash can, which might explode at any minute. Looking around the car for immediate threats, moving your eyes out. Searching for overturned earth, obstacles that shouldn't be there. Across from the Taco Bell, what's that guy doing there, on his phone? Watching windows and doors. In a restaurant, I sit in the corner so I can see everybody.

It starts with a trigger. Maybe my daughter crying about a toy. The emotion comes out of nowhere. I'm going to weep—why, I don't know. I can't speak, I can hardly move. My breathing becomes heavy. It feels like good and evil are pulling on my soul. I sit on the corner of the bed, and I just want to be alone. I'm supposed to be the tough Marine, a Superman, and the crying of a child is like kryptonite.

I'm better than this. I'm ashamed. I'm a fucking Marine, you know? The gung ho culture starts in boot camp. If you're going to be sick today because you don't want to train, you're a piece of shit. You're not a real Marine.

My wife and I legally separated for a while. I convinced her to let me have our daughters during the school year. I was a full-time dad, a platoon sergeant, and had two little girls. I was at Camp Pendleton by myself and had base housing set up for us. I'd take my daughters to school in the morning. I started getting mad when they'd do things that kids do. Fight with each other. Who gets in the car first. Putting on their shoes. Normal stuff, but I'd lose it. "Shut up. Get in the car, get your stuff. Get in, *now.*" And their faces, they looked scared of me. My own little girls, afraid of their father.

I went to see a counselor at the deployment health center. I told her, I'm a dad getting mad. I'm getting angry at my kids. I need to do something. We figured out crying was a trigger, bringing me back to my first deployment. The sound of a child crying took me back. When I heard my daughters crying, I heard the crying of the baby in Al-Qaim, and the helplessness and anger and horrible sadness consumed me.

A friend of ours died, and that woke us up to how fragile life is. We began our marriage anew. We've got another child, a son Deroi, named after our friend. When I get overwhelmed, my wife steps in. Daddy needs to take a time out, she says. But I'm still fighting with myself about the idea of therapy, the idea of you-need-help. I don't want to be that crazy guy who went to Iraq. It's a stereotype, but it's real. No one wants to be the Vietnam vet, sitting on the corner with a sign, crazy.

Was I part of something that's going to be a black eye on the United States? Something dishonorable? That's important to me. That's important to my kids. They look on me as a superhero. My dad's a *Marine*, they say. But when they grow up, are they going to see me in a different light? As they get older, are they going to be proud of their dad and what he did?

"I saw the movie *American Sniper* a month after it came out. It took me right back to Iraq. I walked to the parking lot afterward and just broke down. I stayed there for an hour until I could get myself together."

LET ME GO BACK

DOMINIC WILKERSON

MY GRANDFATHER AND I DROVE OUT TO THE AIRFIELD ALMOST EVERY DAY WHEN I WAS LITTLE. I WANTED TO SEE THE BIG PLANES. We'd watch the C-141 Starlifters take off, their four engines roaring down the runway until the huge aircraft lifted into the air. One of those C-141s could have brought POWs home from Hanoi, I realize now. My grandmother has a videotape of me as a five-year-old singing about how I was going to become a soldier and go fight the bad people overseas in the desert. All I wanted for my birthday presents were toy airplanes. I wanted to be a pilot in the military, but I didn't know that I wasn't going to grow up tall enough.

My grandfather was an old-school tech sergeant in the Air Force. My mom was just 16 years old when I was born at Keesler Air Force Base in Mississippi. My dad was some 21-year-old guy she'd met. "Listen," my grandfather said to him, "either you marry her right now or we're charging you with statutory rape." The other option was signing over custody rights to my grandparents, which my dad did. My grandparents raised me much of my life. I never met my dad. He's not listed on my birth certificate, and my mom doesn't even seem to remember his last name. My grandfather said he died in an oil rig accident, but he never would tell me my dad's last name.

When my grandfather died in 2009, I'd been in the Air Force for five years. I was an Air Force cop stationed at Andrews Air Force Base, where Air Force One is based. We worked with the Secret Service to lock down the airfield when the president flew in. Bush shook my hand. Obama said hi. I saw the First Lady and Malia and Sasha all the time. It'd be a dreary day, Air Force One would be waiting on the flight line, and I'd see a red dot and yellow dot running across my security monitors. That was the two little girls running across the tarmac to Air Force One.

I originally enlisted in the Navy. High school wasn't working out for me, so I was in Job Corps. A Navy recruiter came every other week to give us ASVAB tests, the Armed Services Vocational Aptitude Battery. Most of the kids got seventeen or eighteen points out of fifty. I scored a thirty-seven. The recruiter did not leave me alone for the next six months. He convinced me to go into the Navy for four years with a $20,000 signing bonus. Electronics specialist. I was in the delayed entry program.

A couple months in, the deal changed.

"You signed an old contract," they told me. "The new signing bonus is $7,000."

"Seriously?"

"Also, the new contract is for six years. And you're going to be stationed on a submarine, not on a helicopter or aircraft carrier."

"Nope, not doing it," I said. But they wouldn't let me out of my contract. They had me by the balls.

I was working the front counter at Burger King. In comes an Air Force chief master sergeant and his wife, both in their service dress blue uniforms. I stand with military bearing when they come up to order two Whoppers with fries. I tell him my story. "Sir, I wanted to join the Air Force," I say, "but I got fooled into joining the Navy. Now the Navy won't cancel my contract. I want to join the Air Force instead, sir."

"Son, give me your Social Security number and your name."

"I don't know if I should do that, sir."

"Listen, I'm the Air Force recruiter in charge of the entire West Coast. Let me see what I can do."

He pulled strings, and my Navy contract was cancelled. I enlisted in the U.S. Air Force. My grandmother said it was divine intervention. God had sent the recruiter into Burger King that day.

THE AIR FORCE WOULDN'T GIVE ME ANY FLYING JOBS. THEY CLAIM I HAVE POOR DEPTH PERCEPTION. I think they're wrong. I must have great depth perception—I can shoot like nobody's business. I scored 800 out of 800 during the marksman course. I loved the live fire exercises in Yakima, Washington. The MK-19 automatic grenade launcher, pumping 50 or 60 high-explosive rounds downrange per minute. The .50 cal, bullets as thick as your thumb and long as your hand going *chucka chucka* out of a four-foot-long gun barrel. Two heavy weapons you just walk the rounds in. I certified in every single weapon of the Air Force security forces. I became a heavy gunner.

We pulled sixteen-hour days at Nellis Air Force Base in the desert outside of Las Vegas. An hour to get your weapons and gear. Twelve hours of patrolling the perimeter and the squadrons. At the end of the day, an hour unloading weapons and ammunition at the armory with 60 to 80 other security force guys before going home. M4 machine gun, two hundred and forty rounds of .556 ammunition, armor plates, Kevlar helmet. Seventy-eight pounds of gear.

I had a girlfriend. She had worked at Jiffy Lube and come in for lunch every day when I was working at Burger King. After basic training, my emotions were running high. "Let's take this to the next level," I said to her.

"Oh my God, are you asking me to marry you?" she replied.

We were married while I was in police tech school at Lackland Air Force Base in San Antonio. But after a year at Nellis, we started having problems. She moved out. Then she cheated on me. That's when I pushed to get a deployment as soon as possible. I wanted to get my ass out of there. They needed heavy guns to go to Iraq.

That was one of the main reasons I signed up for the security forces—it was almost a guarantee you'd deploy. You join the military to defend your nation, defend your loved ones, to defend everything. Why do you join the military if you're not going to go to war?

I LOAD UP FORTY OR FIFTY BOTTLES OF WATER IN THE HUMVEE. I INSPECT THE HEAVY MACHINE GUN IN THE TURRET, the .50 cal, and arrange the belts of bullets that feed it. That's my position—with the big gun up top. I'm the guy that reaches down and touches someone with the .50 cal if a suicide car bomber drives too close to our convoy. Gloves on, sleeves down, face wrapped against the intense sun and constant dust. Some days the thermometer hits 132 degrees.

It's my third day on patrol out of Camp Bucca, Iraq, just across from Kuwait. It is a detainee facility like Abu Ghraib. Twenty thousand prisoners live behind coils of concertina wire and sandbagged guard towers. An oil pipeline hugs the border. There's an anti-tank ditch, a relic of Desert Storm. The local town is Safwan. We're in a "tier 1 hotspot." Troops in our twenty square kilometers are hit with thirty to forty IEDs each month.

I check the communications system in the Humvee, the "coms." The instant I switch on the radio, I hear screams. An Army unit has been hit by an IED. Two American casualties, one KIA. The bomb disabled the Humvee, and it needs to be towed back to base. We push out to the scene. By the time we get there, the casualties have already been evacuated. The Humvee leans awkwardly in a ditch, where it rolled to a stop after the IED blasted through its thick steel floor and severed the driver's legs.

Our staff sergeant gathers us new guys, six of us. He walks us down to the Humvee and shows us the ragged hole beneath the driver's seat and the delicate traces of copper on the mutilated armor. The copper came from the bomb. The bomb was a type called an EFP, an explosively formed penetrator. EFPs don't just explode, they hurl a molten slug of copper at a thousand meters per second. EFPs slice through our steel armor like a cutting torch.

Staff sergeant makes us look at the blood pooled in the Humvee. It's still wet, still bright red. The driver had bled to death before the helicopter arrived.

Staff sergeant stares at us. "This is why you gotta take your job seriously," he says.

The first three days on patrol, I was always scared, always nervous. But my training kicked in after that day. I had a different mindset. Something clicked. I wasn't scared on patrol anymore. I was still scared of being severely maimed, so injured I couldn't live a normal life, but I was not scared of dying.

I knew I had to do my job. I knew it was *game on*.

First the Iraqis wave at us strangely, then four black armored SUVs whoosh past us on the road. Then the huge explosion. A plume of black smoke rises into the air a hundred meters down the road, towards Bridge 1. We're unrolling coils of concertina wire on the hot concrete in serpentine curves. A few weeks earlier, in exactly the same spot, the IED had severed a soldier's legs and killed him. Now we run a 24-hour choke point.

I'm the driver for bravo truck. My sergeant is delta truck. Alpha and charlie trucks are about to go swoop the city below by themselves. They're .50 cal gun trucks, and .50 cals can handle themselves. They were approaching Bridge 1 ahead of us when the black SUVs raced past them.

The armored black SUVs are private contractors. British, South African security guys, ex-military. We'd see them in the dining hall at Bucca. They drive at breakneck speed to outfox IEDs. We used electronic jammers to foil the IED triggermen, so the IED makers switched from key fobs and TV remotes to motion detectors, like the ones for household security lights. Or devices that detected the heat of an engine. The jammers didn't work on them.

I was lifting our tailgate when the bomb exploded and the ground trembled. Everyone freezes in motion, a sharp intake of breath, eyes and ears straining. "Get in the truck, get in the truck, *get in the truck*," my gunner yells. I jump in, shut the heavy door. I see the plume of smoke drifting near the bridge. My squad leader calls alpha truck on the radio, but they don't respond.

The Iraqis that had just been waving at me—I don't know them. I'd been working the area for six months, and I know most of the locals. "Hey, American," one guy had said, an odd smile on his face. *Why are you waving at me?* I'm thinking. I tell my squad leader these Iraqis are waving at me strangely. He tells me to ignore them and we uncoil more concertina wire. Then the black SUVs almost hit me as they fly down the road at 70 miles an hour, and I'm really pissed off because they almost fucking kill me.

Alpha truck finally comes back on the radio. "IED hit a civilian truck. We got people running on the ground, people with guns, right now." *Ambush.* Adrenalin spikes in everyone. *Oh fuck, oh fuck.* Do you see anything? My gunner up top hunches down and swivels his gaze frantically. We don't see triggermen running, can't get a good eye to engage anyone. The Iraqis that had been waving have disappeared. I can feel my pulse throbbing. We drive towards Bridge 1 and the other trucks.

A black SUV lays on its side at the bottom of a hill, windows shattered and its tires shredded. The IED had launched it over a four-lane highway. The air stinks of burnt oil and engine coolant and charred flesh. The guys in the other SUVs are out of their cars and bristling with guns and menacing the area, but there's no ambush.

The British guy in the front passenger seat is ripped in half. Their Iraqi driver is the nephew of the local police chief of Safwan, the city on the other side of the bridge. One of his legs is gone, a bone protruding from the stump. The guy in the back seat, a quiet South African—a big guy, three hundred pounds and all muscle—has lost both of his legs. Our medic puts tourniquets on their shattered limbs, starts IVs. The Iraqi dies of shock on the scene. We load the South African into a Humvee. He survives for a week but dies of infection before he's able to be medevaced to Germany.

By the time we've got our guys back inside and get on the road, we're a mile behind the rest of the other trucks. One lone gun truck in the middle of Iraq, all by ourselves. We're scared shitless. "Gun it. Gun it. Gun it," my squad leader is yelling, but in 130-degree heat, your truck is slugging, maybe going thirty or forty miles an hour, like slow motion in a bad dream.

WE HAD A LOCAL INFORMANT. HE WAS A KID NAMED ALI. HE RIDES UP TO ME ON HIS BICYCLE while I'm stopping traffic at Bridge 1 after the IED blast. "Oh, you guys didn't get hurt?" he says. He's got a coy look on his face. I can't tell if he's pretending to be happy or hiding that he's disappointed.

"What do you mean?" I say. He takes off without answering.

The next day, Ali comes up to my truck commander. "That

bomb was meant for you," he says. "Not for them. For you."

Ali was maybe sixteen years old. He was pissed off at us, specifically at my truck commander. A week before, Ali had thrown a grenade out in the desert—like a kid screwing around with fireworks—and we arrested him. My truck commander threw him to the ground, flex-cuffed him, heaved him into the Humvee. He hauled the kid back to the base and locked him in a room and interrogated him for hours. We let him go eventually.

We never found out if Ali had planned that IED hit. But he was angry enough at us to try to blow us up.

An IED a few months before had killed an Air Force security forces woman and an Army sergeant. Intelligence learned the hit had been orchestrated by the local police chief. We don't know if the police chief orchestrated the one that blew up the black SUV, but if so, he'd accidentally killed a member of his own family. The Iraqi driver who died from shock after his leg was blown off was his nephew.

I believe divine intervention saved me the day the black SUV was blown over the highway. I almost always rode in the alpha truck, and I would have been the gunner on it that day. Alpha truck was supposed to take that bomb blast. I should have been dead, my body dismembered.

Two weeks later we discovered Ali had been giving information to both sides. Somebody didn't like that. Ali's sixteen-year-old corpse was found rolled up in a carpet.

IT'S MY LAST PATROL OUTSIDE THE WIRE. I'M ROTATING STATESIDE SOON. A CAPTAIN IS IN OUR TRUCK, OBSERVING. He's in his mid-20s. His unit is taking over the patrols in our area because they want some action, and we're showing him the country. He doesn't know about the IED blast that killed the Brit and the South African, or why it happened. He doesn't know about Ali. He doesn't know all the many places we've been shot at. He doesn't know about the night we killed an Iraqi police officer with the .50 cal when the guy ran a checkpoint. He doesn't know about intel reports of suicide car bombers who sidle up to a convoy loaded with four hundred pounds of explosives. The captain doesn't understand that we've dealt with all of this.

A brand-new kid is in the gun turret, manning the M240 machine gun, belts of ammo swaying as we roll down the road. The kid's acting cool in his sunglasses. A white Suburban comes up behind us, closing the gap. It's Iraqi. The Suburban gets closer and closer. The kid is staring at it, his hands on the machine gun. He's supposed to fire a shot to warn them off, but the kid's frozen. I look over. Now the Suburban is right alongside us, the driver grinning at us. The Iraqi waves. Then he drives on.

I'm out of the Humvee and up to the gun turret before the captain can even open his door. I get right into the face of the kid. "You don't fucking *ever* let an Iraqi vehicle get that close." He can feel my breath against his face. I'm so pissed off my spit is hitting him when I speak. "You do *not* fucking freeze up like that. You fire a warning shot. If they keep coming, you *fucking shoot* that gun at them until they *fucking stop*."

The captain has gotten up to the gun turret now. He tells me to calm down. He tells me to lay off the kid. I tell the captain to shut the hell up. I don't care if you're a captain. Don't tell me how to take care of this kid.

I grab the kid by his uniform. My hands are clenched hard. I'm almost touching his face with my face. I'm lifting him off the ground by his body armor. "Don't fucking *ever* freeze up like that again, do you know why?" He's wincing, afraid of meeting my eyes. I have this overwhelming desire to beat the living shit out of him. He needs to remember why he's getting this ass-chewing. "Do you know why? Because it's life and death, you stupid fuck."

THEY WOULDN'T LET ME GO ON VACATION UNTIL I TOLD THEM ALL THE STORIES. THEY WANTED TO MAKE SURE I WAS MENTALLY WELL. "I'm fine," I said. "I'm totally fine." I just wanted to see my family, so I told them everything was okay. But I felt an uneasiness. I was waking up randomly in the middle of the night. Loud noises freaked me out. A semi truck tire blew out next to me and I spun out my car. My first time back at the shooting range unnerved me. I didn't let it show. I pushed it down deep, pushed it down hard.

I had an intense urge to go back as soon as I possibly could. Working the system to get deployed again quickly was going to be a challenge, I knew. Normally you have to be home a year before they let you go back out again. But I was relentless. I went back again and again. "Listen. I'm trained on all my guns. All my weapons certifications are still good. I know what it's like to be out there. Let me go back. Let me go back. *Let me go back.*" Then one day I received orders to Kuwait. I'd be back in the desert again eight months after I'd come home from Iraq.

That night, I start having the nightmares again. I replay the IEDs in my dreams. I hear the BOOM, float into the cloudless sky with the black smoke. I'm on Bridge 1, walking towards the overturned black SUV. All the pieces of human beings in there, the air tasting like iron from fresh blood. The copper splatters inside a Humvee. A man standing in the sun. A shadow on the road.

I start having flashbacks. I'm awake, but I disappear into a memory until that memory eclipses the present. I'm in Las Vegas and trying to focus on my job at Nellis Air Force Base, but right now I'm remembering one afternoon during prayer time for the detainees at Camp Bucca. Hundreds are huddled in tawny robes on prayer rugs, on their knees, heads bowed to the ground, rows of men nearly touching each other. A single mortar arcs from somewhere two kilometers away. It lands in the middle of the mass of men praying on the ground in Camp Bucca. The dense geometry expands outward. Men run away from the single point of the blast, a shockwave of bodies. Some men run towards the chaos in the center. Cries and groans. Some of the bodies don't move. Some roll or crawl awkwardly. Fifty detainees are injured. Six are dead. Clumps of agitated prisoners form, some shaking fists, some talking in low tones. A sense of menace permeates the camp. Command is worried the prisoners might charge the wire in a mass escape attempt. We're ordered to form a perimeter of heavy weapons around the compound. If the prisoners attempt to escape, we are to engage. We are to mow them down. I'm looking down the barrel of my .50 cal at hundreds of men behind the coils of wire. I try to imagine what it will feel like if I have to shoot. What I will be thinking the instant my finger squeezes the trigger.

"How are you supposed to come back and be normal? How can you be told it's okay to do what you did, and then come home and act like everything's all right? How can you come back from war and take walks and go to the grocery store and get cupcakes and do whatever it is people do?"

THE BOY ON THE BRIDGE

ROBIN ECKSTEIN

I HAD LEGAL CUSTODY OF MY YOUNGER SISTER, I WAS WORKING THREE MENIAL JOBS, AND I WAS STRUGGLING TO PAY THE BILLS. I was taking classes at a community college and going to drop out because I couldn't afford tuition. That's when I was spammed by a National Guard recruiter. Free college if I enlisted. I never would have chosen the military, but I knew that college was my way out. I didn't want to end up living in a trailer with three kids and a shitty marriage, like so many people I knew. Nobody in my family had gone to college, not a single one.

"What happens if there's a war?" my friend Jessica asked me. "If there's a war," I said, "I'll let you run over my leg with the car. That way I won't have to go." That was my plan. I wasn't going to war. I joined the military so I could go to school and take care of my sister. It was 1999 and peacetime. I was 22 years old.

I left for basic training on my 23rd birthday. Suddenly I felt I had a place in life. I belonged. I was part of something bigger than myself. I was serving the United States of America. I loved the military, and I decided to go active duty and appealed to be stationed in Europe. I had a plan—I'd be an enlisted soldier for three years, then get a degree and become an officer. For the first time in my life, I had a future.

After six months at Fort Jackson, the Army shipped me to the 123rd Main Support Battalion in Dexheim, Germany, on a small base among the vineyards. I'd scored high on the aptitude test, so I could have gone into language or intelligence, but the National Guard made me a truck driver. So I drove trucks all over Europe, delivering parts and supplies to American bases, and drove trucks in our war games. Every time I got a chance, I traveled. London, Barcelona, all of Western Europe. One weekend, just for fun, I said, "Let's go to Belgium for waffles," so we did. Where I came from, no one imagined traveling to Europe. Here I was, a piss-ass poor kid, living in a dream.

Everything changed after September 11. I didn't learn about the attack until I got back to base that afternoon. Word went around that a plane had hit one of the Twin Towers in New York City. We all believed it was a horrible accident. Then someone says, "Oh my God, it's a second plane." One of my sergeants was talking on the phone with a friend at the Pentagon. The line went dead.

Command closes the gates to the base. No one is going anywhere. German civilians are trapped inside, American soldiers are locked outside. Charlie Company is ordered to patrol the base in full battle rattle. They're issued weapons but no ammunition and they dutifully walk around our perimeter, a single chainlink fence with concertina wire on top. Besides driving trucks, I'm a gunner too, and soon I'm walking the wire for 12 hours in a flak vest and Kevlar helmet, a 25-pound M249 machine gun slung over my shoulder. I'm issued 10 rounds of ammo, enough for a one-second burst on automatic. One platoon is ordered to set up a .50 cal machine gun position behind the base, a fortification of sandbags surveilling the grapevines hanging with ripening fruit.

The U.S. military has no idea what the fuck to do. No one does.

The day after September 11, hundreds of German citizens appear at our gates. They leave bouquets of flowers and light candles and pin sympathy cards to the chainlink fence. They leave letters they've written to America and lay stuffed animals among the flowers. There are old men with canes and mothers with children and college students. Some come to the gate and cling to the fence and tell us of their anguish for America. They tell us they are with us. They bring sweets and sausages and pans of *Käsespätzle* and *Kartoffel*, but we are ordered not to accept any food for security reasons. Many of the Germans stand silently outside the gates, some holding each other, weeping.

WE SIT INSIDE A C-130 AIRCRAFT EN ROUTE FROM KUWAIT TO BAGHDAD INTERNATIONAL AIRPORT, HIGH ABOVE THE IRAQI DESERT. We've got all of our gear on, battle digi-cammie uniforms and helmets and flak vests, and I'm sitting on a cargo net with my rucksack in front of me and another bag stuffed between my legs. We're pressed against each other like sardines. The cargo bay is stark and loud with the dull roar of the engines. Soldiers are falling asleep. I'm nodding off when I jerk awake as the plane bucks and heaves. A *BOOM* outside rattles the aircraft.

Everybody wakes up. We're freaking out because we're all crammed in there, you can't fucking move, and the plane is banking and plummeting like a rollercoaster, making evasive maneuvers. We know what's happening, someone out there is shooting at us, and there's nowhere to hide, nothing anyone can do but ride it out. "Welcome to Iraq," someone says. That was the first time they tried to kill me.

I was following my battalion into Iraq, which had arrived in the country over a month before. Our first soldier was killed before I'd even left Germany. He was a fueler. Their convoy was ambushed, and his truck had been crippled by an IED and the blasts of grenades. A female solder had unhooked the trailer under fire to escape the kill zone. I went to his memorial in the little chapel on our base to pay my respects. He had been promoted from specialist to sergeant after his death. You can talk about war and you can play war video games and watch war movies, but it's not real until you see the boots and the M16 and the photograph of the fallen.

I wanted to go to Iraq. I didn't want to go because I wanted to *kill hajis.* I didn't want to *get revenge.* It wasn't that at all. I had to go to Iraq because all my friends were there, my brothers and sisters in my unit, and I needed to help protect them.

SIX DAYS A WEEK WE DROVE CONVOYS OF GREEN MILITARY TRACTOR-TRAILER TRUCKS OUT OF THE GATES OF BAGHDAD INTERNATIONAL to bases all over the city, ferrying MREs and ammunition and weapons and hundreds upon hundreds of pallets of plastic bottles of water. We unloaded medical supplies and engine parts, grenades and flares and mail. We delivered the matériel of war to the troops.

We reported in the morning and waited to be given the SOPs, the Standard Operating Procedures. The SOPs were always changing. One day you can shoot at Iraqis, but only shoot if you can see them shooting at you. The next day you can run people over with your truck if they are in front of you on the road. Today's SOP is fishtail your vehicles when you pass under bridges. Hey, now they're putting fucking IEDs in dead animals. The SOP is don't run over dead animals on the road. Don't even drive close to them.

As soon as the trucks were loaded, we'd roll out, sometimes with just three trucks, sometimes up to twenty. We always went out with a gun truck, usually a 5-ton with a .50 cal machine gun mounted in the bed, heavy firepower usually placed in the middle or towards the end of the convoy. A Humvee was always the lead vehicle, with the officer and communications. We were to get to our objective, unload the trucks, and get back.

As soon as you're out of the gates, it's on. The road's been blocked with boulders. A personnel carrier is on fire. You hear rounds go off, but you don't see anything or anybody. Men appear from behind buildings and shoot at you, then disappear. IEDs are everywhere, and Iraqis stand on the side of the road watching you, maybe waiting to trigger them or maybe just mesmerized by the spectacle of the U.S. Army—you don't know.

You just stuff all that fear down because you can't be scared. You just can't. When bullets start flying, when a piece of garbage on the road looks fishy and the fear bubbles up, you have to be even more alert. You run at 120 percent, shaking with anticipation, watching *everything*.

Back on base, there's no sanctuary. Mortars rain down from the sky and there's nothing you can do. They're going to hit wherever they're going to hit. It's randomized death, a lottery. So you just let go. Okay, you decide, I'm going to die in Iraq. And there's a certain release when you realize that death is going to come anytime it wants. Accepting your death makes life a whole lot easier, because otherwise, how do you function?

You can't do your job if you're terrified. So you stuff it all down.

CONVOYS OF TRUCKS AND SQUADRONS OF C-130S DELIVER THOUSANDS OF BOXES OF A-RATIONS to the base to feed the troops in iraq. The A-rations contain giant cans of peaches and baked beans and corn. There are institutional-sized pans of lasagna that are warmed in vats of hot water. Eventually the Army decides it can't use the bags of flour and No. 10 cans of green beans. A group of us is assigned to haul the sacks of flour and the green beans to the burn pit. We're going to burn the surplus food.

"Why don't you guys give it to the Iraqis?" I ask.

"We can't do that," they say. "What if an Iraqi gets sick?"

"What's going to happen? They're going to hire a lawyer and sue us?" I can't let it rest. "Listen, roll up a 5-ton truck, stack all the food on that, and I'll personally drive it outside the gates and give it to the Iraqis."

My sergeant tries to persuade me to turn away, forget about it, suck it up and move on. I can't, though. I'm starting to get in trouble, but I just can't stand to see sacks of unopened flour and giant cans of green beans burned like garbage. Every day we go outside the gates and see Iraqis on the streets begging for food. People are fucking starving, and we're burning perfectly good food.

"Listen, let me do this. If I'm going to get shot, I'd rather get shot giving food away than hauling shit to forward operating bases."

I'm finally called into command. They tell me to put a lid on it or I'm going to regret it. I'll be assigned to the shittiest job on base, maybe I'll get busted in rank. But I just don't care anymore. I'm *fucking* pissed off. "If you're going to keep doing it," I say, "I'm going to take pictures of it and send it to CNN." The officer narrows his eyes at me.

They still burn the food. But I never get in trouble.

Several Iraqi civilians walk about the base with garbage bags, picking up trash. They've been hired by the U.S. Army and are paid three dollars per day. I get to know two of them. They speak perfect English and have master's degrees. They come to work in short-sleeve button-down shirts, dress pants, and leather shoes. They look like professors, and they're picking up gum wrappers and cigarette butts.

They tell me the war disrupted everything. Their world went haywire. Buses stopped running, highways closed, schools shut down. They couldn't go to work, so now they have to find a way to make money so they can feed their families. Now they're picking up American trash. No, they said, they didn't like Saddam Hussein. They were happy to be free of Saddam, but their lives were in chaos. "Why isn't the water getting turned back on?" they asked me. "Why isn't there electricity?" They brought their lunches to the base each day, bread and rice and dried fruit bundled in a cloth sack. They shared their food with me one day. *You've got hardly anything,* I thought, and yet you're still sharing your meal with me, an American soldier. We had chow tents. We had dining hall trailers. We even had a shack on base that served Burger King burgers and fries. We had so much food we burned it.

I knew soldiers who hated Iraqis, all Iraqis. Iraqis were *hajis*. Iraqis were somehow less than human to them. Some soldiers thought that way because they had to. They're going on missions outside the wire, they're getting shot at, they have to kill, and they dehumanize the enemy so they can pull the trigger. I get it. But I could never do that. I always saw Iraqis as people.

The command sent down orders about the use of the word *haji*. "The U.S. Military does not condone the use of the word *haji* or any other derogatory terms."

Bullshit. *Everybody* said it.

Your whole life, you're told right from wrong. Respect other people. Help other people. Don't kill, don't even *hurt* other people. All of a sudden you live in a world where it's free game. Right and wrong are out the window.

THAT MORNING, WE GET THE SOP TO SHOOT IRAQIS ON BRIDGES. If our convoy route takes us beneath a highway overpass, and if an Iraqi on that overpass could drop something onto our convoy, we're supposed to shoot them.

We load up the trucks. We do our pre-mission briefing, discuss the details about the base we're supplying, the route we're taking through the city. We determine the order of the vehicles, who is driving each truck, who is sitting in each seat, who is in command, who is manning the .50 cal, who will be scouring the roadside for IEDs to the left and to the right, who will point their weapons out their windows, safeties off. We check our radios, confirm call signs. We check our gear and check each other. Kevlar helmets, flak vests, ammunition, rifles.

We head out through the gates of the base, weave through the concrete barriers, into the city. I'm the truck commander, in the passenger seat with my M16 out the window. We turn right and all the semi trailers follow each other at intervals, like ducks in a row. A thin plume of black smoke rises in the distance. Laundry hangs from a wire. Stray dogs turn their heads at the sound of the trucks. The yellow sun is halfway up the dusty sky.

I'm looking at everything, scanning the apartments to the right, watching the concrete highway ahead. About half a mile farther down, the highway passes underneath an overpass. I can see that something or someone is on the bridge. We drive on, moving closer and closer to the bridge. It's a person. There's a child on the bridge.

"Iraqi kid on the bridge. You see him?" my driver says.

"Roger." I've got my rifle shouldered. I'm leaning out the window, my weapon aimed at the bridge.

"You got a lock on him?"

"Roger that."

He's a boy about five years old. He's facing us, his little arms dangling over the concrete side of the bridge. He's staring at us. The convoy is going to pass directly underneath him. It looks like he's holding something in his hands.

My driver says, "You got a lock on him?"

I've got the boy in my sights. Rifle against my shoulder, one hand gripping the stock, index finger just touching the trigger. Safety off. I'm waiting for the boy to flinch. We approach closer and closer. The boy is looking at us. I'm concentrating on him as hard as I can, staring at his hands down the barrel of my rifle.

We go under the bridge.

After we get back to base, we debrief about the mission. One of the other guys in the convoy says he fired a warning shot and the kid ran off. He was just some kid on a bridge, looking down on the convoy, fascinated by a parade of big green American Army trucks. If I had pulled the trigger and killed him, no one would have batted an eye. It was our SOP.

The boy on the bridge wasn't supposed to live and, later on in my deployment, maybe he wouldn't have. Maybe I wouldn't have hesitated. Maybe I would have followed orders and pulled the trigger. Because you can only see so many people getting blown up and dying and all the shit around you for so long before you just fucking want them dead, too.

THREE YEARS OF BEING GONE. THEN YOU COME BACK TO A SMALL TOWN IN AMERICA. I'm surrounded by civilians. I'm in a fog, and all I want to do is watch television. I just sit there and flip through the channels and watch the commercials and laugh and laugh. A few friends visit, but I don't want to go out of the house. My friend Julie bugs me and bugs me until I agree to go out to a bar with her. "Don't tell people," I tell her. "*Do not* tell people I came back from Iraq, right?" I'm having nightmares about our convoy coming under fire in Baghdad and I've run out of ammunition.

We're at this bar and everybody is laughing and having a good time. I can't laugh and have a good time, because I'm thinking about my friends. My friends, my family, are in Iraq, and I'm supposed to be with them. The people in the bar flirt and shoot pool like no one's getting killed in the desert half a world away. Everybody's getting smashed on cheap beer and shots of tequila.

I'm standing next to Julie and some of her girlfriends. People are dancing, raising drinks in the air. A guy snorts loudly at another guy's joke. I'm trying to pay attention to our little group, and that's when I think I hear someone say *baby killer*. I look over and see a guy looking straight at me, a drunken half-cocked smirk on his face. I don't think, I don't say a word, I immediately go for him. I lunge on top of him and go for his throat. I'm going to fucking kill him. He tries to wriggle away from my fists, but I'm full of rage. I'm going to kill this fucker. Then I feel hands clamping my shoulders and arms, a tangle of bodies. They pull me off him. We get out of the bar, and when we get back home, I don't feel anger or grief or giddiness. I'm completely numb. I have no feelings about anything. I'm empty inside.

I'm still in the Army, and I have plans. I'm going to finish my degree and become an officer. I've got the right stuff, the smarts and the guts and the grit. I'm going to stay in twenty years, move up the ranks, be a career soldier. I'm assigned to a local unit of the National Guard and get a shiny "officer in training" insignia that I get to wear on my uniform. Because I've got prior service, I'm tasked as acting lieutenant of the headquarters platoon. It's an honor. My dream of a career as an officer in the U.S. Army is happening.

A weekend of training out in the woods in Wisconsin. We're equipped with "rubber ducks," dummy M-16s made of hard rubber. We're out in the oaks and pines and scrub playing fucking Army. We're practicing ambush techniques, everyone laying low in the leaves, hush-hush, watching for the enemy. Each of us is responsible for destroying the enemy in an arc in front of us called a "sector of fire." The sectors overlap. If the enemy comes into the ambush, there's no way he's surviving. We lay there in silence, trying to be invisible, and wait and wait.

I'm watching my sector of fire. I'm laying there in the woods, quiet and stealthy, waiting. And I start thinking about Iraq. I start thinking about the boy on the bridge. I'm trying to block it out and stuff it down, but it keeps surging up inside me like bad water. The feelings grow more and more intense. They're about to gush out of me, almost like I'm about to be sick, and I can't stuff them down. I'm trying so hard, but nothing is working. The tears start flowing. I'm thinking, *fuck, FUCK, you CANNOT be fucking crying in training. DO NOT FUCKING CRY.* I'm trying and I'm trying to stuff it, muffle it, I clamp my hand over my mouth, but the weeping swells out of me. It gets louder and louder. Guys start looking over at me, but I can't stop and now I'm just so far gone. Everybody is laying in the woods, being still and quiet like they're supposed to, and suddenly I stand up. *I can't do this!* I hear myself screaming. *I can't do this!*

First Sergeant runs up to me. He wants to know what's going on. Everybody is looking up from their sectors of fire, staring at me. I've lost it. "I can't do this. They can't go. They can't go to Iraq." First Sergeant is trying to talk to me, but I can't understand a word he's saying. "The boy on the bridge," I tell him. "I almost shot the boy on the bridge." He walks me down the hill, talking softly to me, and eventually I calm down a little. "I think you're having a flashback," he says. No, Sergeant, I say to him, that can't be. That's only Vietnam vets.

I'm trying to recover and get back into the training and cover my sector of fire. I'm composing myself hard. Because I want this. This is my future. I'm going to become an officer in the U.S. Army.

But I had just fucked it all up. The officer dream was *over*. The U.S. Army does not tolerate weakness in an officer. Everything I wanted and everything I had worked for was gone. In a few days, they started the paperwork to kick me out.

"When I was over there, I didn't think the Iraqis were bad people. I was just trying to protect my Marines. I was fighting to keep them alive. I was fighting to keep myself alive."

GOODBYE LETTERS ARE BAD LUCK

MIGUEL ESCALERA

I WANTED TO MAKE MY DAD PROUD. WHAT BETTER WAY THAN TO SERVE FOR THE MARINES AS A NAVY CORPSMAN? Being a corpsman is one of the most honorable jobs in the military. I don't mean the corpsmen who treat sprained ankles and VD cases on a base. I mean a *grunt* corpsman—out in the field, in combat. It's the most highly decorated outfit in the military. More corpsmen have been awarded more honors and awards than any other branch of the service combined. Hands down, the most decorated people in the military.

You know Mount Suribachi? The famous photo from Iwo Jima? The statue of the Marines planting the flag? Everybody thinks it's only Marines planting that flag. But there's also a corpsman in that photo. John Bradley. He's the third one in.

When I finished Field Medical Service School and got to my first command with the Marines, I saw the news on TV. George W. Bush announced that we'd won the war, that major combat operations were over. I was thinking I'd missed my chance. I was disappointed. I didn't want to go to war as payback for the Twin Towers; I'm not an eye-for-an-eye kind of person. I just wanted to go to war with the Marines and see if I could handle it. I liked medicine and wanted to see if I could do the most extreme medicine one can do. To be part of war.

I wanted to test myself.

THE FARM COUNTRY OF EASTERN WASHINGTON. AN OCEAN OF WHEAT FIELDS. Rows of radishes and potatoes converge on the distant horizon. It's a huge blue sky, a Sunday morning. I'm ten years old, in fourth grade, about to drive a tractor for the first time. The tractor's tires are enormous, twice as tall as I am. I'm helping my dad, who's the foreman of a large farm. Here's the throttle, he tells me. If you want to go fast, push it forward. To go slow, pull it back. Here's the red button. You hit the red button if you need to kill the engine. If you ever get into trouble, you hit that red button. Now, grab that steering wheel. Wherever the road goes, you follow it. You keep on turning the wheel.

Okay, I say. I got this. It's a huge machine, but in farm country this is what kids do. I'm going to drive this tractor down the road to the next field. He's going to follow behind in his pickup.

He tells me to turn the key. The engine lights up with a few coughs of black smoke and the tractor comes to life beneath me. Put it in gear and let off the clutch, my dad tells me. I take my foot off the clutch and we lurch and then roll slowly forward. He jumps off and runs back into his pickup.

The road is straight for about half a mile. I'm not going very fast, maybe a fast walk, but I must be ten feet off the ground and

I'm feeling more like a man than I ever have in my life, looking out over the fields. Then the road bends to the right, a long, sweeping curve, and I gently push on the steering wheel. But I'm barely turning it at all. I'm not turning it enough, and the tractor's front wheels slowly leave the road and angle toward the shallow ditch. I'm going off the road into the field.

I turn around and look over my shoulder and see that my dad has stopped his pickup and jumped out. He's run up alongside the tractor. He climbs up the ladder to the cab of the tractor, reaches in, and puts his strong hands on the steering wheel. *You gotta turn this wheel!* he says. He cranks the steering wheel hard and gets me back on the road. You gotta make sure you're turning the wheel. Don't baby it. *Turn* it. If you wanna go, *go.*

My dad is out of the house before the sun comes up every day. I've never known a day when he's slept in. He's a loyal employee. He was my role model growing up. I helped out if a worker didn't show up. He'd need someone in the field for the afternoon, and he'd pull me out of school. I'd go gas up the truck, run equipment around the farm, drive the tractor that pulled the digger. I was a teenager in charge of big machines. Growing up on a farm, you're allowed to do anything just as long as your dad says it's okay.

But that day I first drove a tractor is burned in my memory. Drive it like you own it, my dad told me. Don't be timid. If you want to do something, be intent about it.

My dad would tell me stories of how proud he was of his brothers because they'd gone into the Marine Corps and the Navy. It was his goal in life to become a Marine himself and fight for his country, but the Marines have strict rules if you're going into the infantry. Before you go to boot camp, you have to jump off a three-foot step and keep going, like you're jumping off a truck or the back of an airplane. My dad had been a champion wrestler in high school and in one of his matches he had busted out his knees. My dad can jump down three feet, but because of his bad knees, he always stumbles. He was damaged goods. The Marines wouldn't take him.

I sat in the truck as he told me these stories one day. I was maybe twelve years old. That's when I decided I might go into the military. I liked farming, but I didn't want to be a farmer. At that age, I just wanted to make my dad happy. I wanted to live that dream for him and join the military.

You land at night. It's dark. You don't know if you're by a beach, you don't know if you're in the middle of the desert. You don't know anything. You drive for hours.

When you finally arrive, it starts. You better listen up, they say. It's gonna come fast, and it's gonna come hard. This is the start of a change. A change in you. Get your stuff! *Run, run, run!* Stand in line! Do exactly what you're told. We get off the bus and stand in rows. Then we file into a big room.

Take off your clothes, they tell us. Get down to your skivvies. Your civilian clothes go into this mailing bag. This bag will go to your parents or your home of record. Take off your underwear. We are all standing naked.

We're instructed to fold our clothes nice and neat and then jam them into the bag. You tape it shut and write your address on it. They take it away. You don't see that bag again while you're at boot camp.

They issue you smurfs, the all-blue Navy sweat pants and sweat shirt. The Navy logo on the leg, Navy crest on the chest. Tighty whitey BVDs for everyone. Sometimes you're a small but they give you an extra large. Whatever they have, you get. Navy PT shorts, white PT shirt, shoes, the smurfs. They issue you a sea bag, your boots, your stencil kit. They issue you your Crackerjacks sailor uniform, like what you see on the Crackerjack box. Bell bottoms, Dixie cup hat.

Everything's checked off, one by one. Hold up your boots, everybody. They go down the line and make sure everybody has one pair of boots. Okay, you've received boots. Hold up your PT shorts, everybody. They go down the line and make sure everybody has one pair of PT shorts. Hold up your Dixie cup. Hold up your tee shirt. You do this for every item. You jam it all into the sea bag and stencil your name on it and padlock your bag.

It's seven in the morning. You've been up all night, but you don't sleep, you go to breakfast. After breakfast, they shave off all your hair. All I wanted to do was sleep, but I was too scared to sleep.

You fill out your GI Bill paperwork, your life insurance paperwork, your military record paperwork. Now it's lunchtime. You still haven't slept yet. It's a sack lunch, but the Navy calls it a bag nasty. You eat together.

Everything has to be done together. Everything has to be done in the same manner. Even the way you throw away your trash has to be done exactly the same way, every time. Everybody does it the same way, every time.

Sixteen weeks of boot camp. Naval history, major battles.

American history, 1776 to the present. Sailor's creed. How to do watch standings. How to write into a log book. How to properly dress. The ranks of all the armed forces. How to fight fires. First aid. Navigation. Cleaning the heads and mopping the floors.

After boot camp, I attend Corps School. Lung anatomy, immunizations, IVs, blood draws, medical records. Pharmacology, emergency medicine, preventative medicine. I take my oath and am sworn in. I am a corpsman in the U.S. Navy.

I'm assigned to Naval Medical Center, Portsmouth, Virginia. I'm 22 years old. I'm working at Family Medical Clinic. One day, I'm resupplying a crash cart—it has a defibrillator and meds for quickly treating cardiac arrests. I'm coming back from the pharmacy with a med tray and I look up to the television. CNN is reporting that a plane has crashed into the World Trade Center. I hold the tray and stare at the burning tower. As I watch, a jet appears from the side of the screen and smashes into the other tower. I feel my blood leave my body. I look around, and I can sense the gut-churning fear and anger everywhere. Everyone has deadly serious faces. The hospital locks up. The MPs close the gates. Nobody goes in or out. K9 units patrol the perimeters. We hear F-18 jets circling the airspace above the hospital.

We're going to war, my lead petty officer says to me. You better be ready.

IT'S PITCH BLACK OUTSIDE. WE'RE BUCKLED INTO HARNESSES IN THE BELLY OF THE C-17, THE AIRCRAFT PACKED WITH MARINES. The engines scream at full throttle. We're thundering down the runway and the pilot pulls hard on the controls, the wheels jump off the ground, and we leap into the air hard, heading skyward at ninety degrees. It feels like we're blasting to the moon, and everybody slides aft. Everybody's stacked, stacked, stacked on top of each other. No one talks, no one looks at each other. The engines are pumping away, the roar hammers inside your chest, and the pressure change causes a balloon to inflate inside your head. Your ears are exploding. Your face flattens against your skull. The engines are going like crazy and it's intense and then right when you reach cruising altitude, the pilot comes over the speaker. We're leveling off, he says. We're going weightless. Get ready.

The aircraft slows its mad ascent, arrives at the top of its arc. For about fifteen seconds we are released from gravity. The engines cut back, the aircraft becomes nearly silent. My sixty-pound sea bag floats off my lap. It's jammed with uniform parts and ammunition magazines and my corpsman supplies, but it hovers in my hands. It's peaceful, surreal. Then you feel your body gradually sink back into the harness, your sea bag settles on your legs. Gravity returns. Reality kicks back in.

We've left Kuwaiti airspace and fly over Iraq at night towards a smaller airport east of Baghdad.

Downing sits across from me. As the flight drones on, he digs into his ammo pockets and pulls out an envelope. It's sealed and has a name and address written on it. He looks at it for a few minutes. A Marine next to him has also pulled an envelope from his pocket. They exchange the envelopes.

"Yo, Downing," I say. "What are those?"

"These are our letters, dude."

"Letters for what?"

"Our good-bye letters."

"That's bad luck, Downing."

"No," he says, "this is what you've got to do. This is for my girlfriend. I don't make it, my brother Marine is gonna mail it to my girlfriend. He don't make it, I'm gonna mail his letter to his girlfriend."

"You guys shouldn't be doing that. Good-bye letters are bad luck."

"Nah," he says. "This is what Marines do."

"Don't do that, Downing. You're jinxing yourself."

"Dawg, this is what Marines do."

We're actually not expecting much action in Iraq. Back at Camp Pendleton, as we were training up for deployment, we're told that we're going over there for security and rebuilding. We're going to walk the streets and make sure nobody gets hurt. It's not a combat mission, boys. We're going to train for combat, but that's not our goal.

"We're not going to go out and engage?" one guy asks.

"Nope, we're just going to say hi to everybody and win the hearts and minds."

"Dang. That sucks, you know."

We fly on for several hours, everyone lost in themselves, until the pilot comes back on the speaker to tell us we're going in for a combat landing in five minutes. Get ready, guys, he says. Then the aircraft plunges straight down. Everyone's stacked, stacked, stacked on top of each other and you're pointed to earth all the way down and right before the ground comes up to meet us, he pulls back, all the way back. The g-forces load you, gravity claws on every molecule in your body. Your face is melting. Your heart and lungs drop into your pelvis. Your sea bag crushes down on your legs. Then gravity eases up, the pilot aims ahead, and the huge aircraft hits the ground hard with a bark of the tires. The engines howl in reverse thrust, straining us against our harnesses. Everyone scrambles to unbuckle, grab their sea bags, grab their weapons. The ramp lowers and it's pitch black outside and the jet wash is ferocious. Marines line up and leap off the tailgate one after the other.

But the plane is still moving slowly on the runway and it's a three-foot drop to the pavement. I've forgotten that. I step off the tailgate and I hit the ground like a sack of potatoes. I do a somersault. My rifle smacks the concrete, my helmet slams onto my head. It's all pitch black and all you see are Kevlar helmets bobbling in a line. Let's go, let's go, sergeant's shouting, so I haul ass after those guys. We run into a makeshift airport.

The next morning, as we wait to load up our vehicles, I go over my corpsman's kit: battle dressings, rolls of gauze, muslin bandages, five yards of adhesive tape, scissors, tourniquets, plastic airway, thermometer, scalpels, forceps, tweezers, morphine injectors, atropine injectors, hydrochloride, eye wash, bottles of iodine.

We're going to Al Anbar Province in the middle of Iraq, fifteen miles east of Fallujah. We're heading to Ramadi in a huge convoy. It is February 2004.

We were relieving the Big Red One, and we thought we were going to hand out candy and soccer balls to the locals. Win the hearts and minds. We thought we'd keep the roads safe, make sure Route Michigan was free of IEDs. We'd help out the local farmers, build a couple schools. We didn't plan on looking for a fight.

OUR COMPANY COMMANDER HAS OTHER IDEAS. LET'S GO FIND THESE FUCKERS, HE SAYS. LET'S FIND THESE FUCKERS AND KILL THEM. Our combat outpost in Ramadi is mortared every few days, and our company commander orders us to go out and find the mortar sites. Kill them first before they kill us, he says.

We don't know how we're going to find where the mortars are coming from. They're firing mortars with a range of 1300 meters. That means the mortar sites could be any point a kilometer and a half out from our combat outpost, in any direction. We're just not going to find them in the labyrinth of streets and alleys.

We're driving in the Humvees on the streets of Ramadi, looking for the mortars or the guys who fire them. Iraqi men in *dishdashas* ignore us or stare icily as we pass. It's a warren of low concrete buildings and snarls of electric wires overhead. We're scanning the building tops for snipers and doorways for rifle barrels.

"How are we going to find these hajis?" one Marine asks. "It's like finding a needle in a haystack."

"Can you call 'em?" Vergara says. "Like you do that call to find pigs?"

"You mean *soo-wee*?" I say. "Yeah, I can do that. I grew up on a farm." I lean out the window, cup my hands around my mouth, and yell *SOOOO-WEEEE* as loud as I can. *SOOOO-WEEEE! SOOOO-WEEEE!*

It's a loud, loud hog call. Seconds later, something goes *ting-ting* off our windshield. I'm wondering if someone threw a rock at us. We all look at each other, mystified, and then a wall of bullets just slams into the Humvee. Bullets fly into the dirt, smack into the sides of the buildings. A constant chatter of weapons, the crack of rounds striking steel, the pop of lead into cinderblock, explosions of dust and powdered concrete. Bullets upon bullets. RPGs and bombs. We clamor out of the Humvees and get behind the vehicles and squeeze and squeeze our triggers. Just shooting away, just shooting away.

The gunfight is very, very fast. Ten minutes. In that ten minutes, we take four casualties. Gunshot wounds. One of my Marines is also run over by a Humvee. I set up a triage point, stop blood flowing with Quickclot bandages, dull their pain with morphine, start saline IVs. We load the wounded, casevac them to base for a chopper ride to Baghdad. We've killed four of the insurgents, and three more end up in the hospital.

I earned my first combat action ribbon, one of the signature aspects of being a Marine. I was awarded the Bronze Star for the events of that day.

It was a taste of what was to come. From then on, we were in contact with insurgents religiously. Eventually we cordoned off the entire city. We worked our way through one side of the city to the other side. We went through every house looking for weapons caches. We flushed a lot of people out. We took a lot of people in for questioning.

We went there to be a security mission. Keep the roads safe, that's all. Win the hearts and minds. We intended to do no combat, but we killed and died for months. Eventually, Marines whispered they were scared to go out because we were losing Marines on every patrol. Every time we leave that wire, we come back with one less Marine.

IT'S APRIL 6, 2004. A PLATOON ON PATROL IN THE CITY RADIOS THE COMBAT OUTPOST. We're being overwhelmed, they say. We need backup. They've been hit by IEDs and a storm of small arms fire. They've got casualties and have moved through the ambush zone. My squad piles back into our Humvees, still sweaty and dusty from the last patrol we'd done, and haul ass back out there. We link up with the platoon, who are patrolling on foot. Doc Mendez, my fellow corpsman, is with them. We get out of the Humvees.

"Mendez, you got wounded Marines," I say. "You head back to base and take care of them there. I'll take over."

"My Marines are still out here, man."

"I have fresh legs, Mendez," I say. "I should be the one out here."

"You take my wounded back. I'm staying."

"Better for you to get some rest, Mendez. You're no good if you're too fatigued to give care."

Doc Mendez is getting really pissed off at me. "No fucking way. These are *my* Marines, dawg. My Marines are still out here. I'm staying with them."

I pull rank. "Get in the Humvee, Mendez. *Go.* I need you to get some rest."

I hate saying this to him, but this is what's best for our Marines. A corpsman with fresh legs can save more lives.

"All right," he says. "You win."

Mendez reluctantly gets in my Humvee. I tell the driver to take him back to the base. The Humvee with Mendez and the wounded goes to the left. I shoulder my pack and take the safety off my M-16. Me and the rest of my platoon start walking down the road to the right.

Five minutes later, the radios start crackling again. *Contact*, somebody says. *Contact.* I hear the whoosh and boom of an RPG. It's a good fight, I'm thinking. They're getting something, and we're headed the wrong way. We break into a run towards the sounds of battle. It takes about 20 minutes to get there, and it's all-out war. Every Marine on the base has converged on the scene, and every one of them is shooting, shooting, shooting.

A Marine runs up to me. "*Doc! Doc!* Doc Escalera! It's you, it's you. I can't believe that's you."

I look at him, baffled.

"You're alive," he says.

"Yeah, I'm alive."

"No, dawg, you're not. You're *dead.*"

"Who says I'm dead?"

"Doc, seriously, they said you're fucking *dead* right now."

"I'm right here. I'm pretty sure I'm not dead."

"Ah, fuck, man. If it's not you, then who's dead?"

After the shooting stops, we make our way to a courtyard ahead. A silent Humvee is parked amidst broken glass and brass casings. Its windshield is shot through, spider-web fractures surrounding bullet holes. There's blood inside, blood on the cobblestones.

Seven Marines are dead. Some Marines have died with their fingers still poised on their triggers as they tried to escape the vehicle in a hail of bullets.

One of the dead is Jerabek. I'd watched him exchange goodbye letters with Downing on the flight into Iraq.

Doc Mendez is dead, too. My corpsman. He had been sitting in my seat in the Humvee. I had technically been dead for almost two hours, but instead it is Doc Mendez who is dead.

That was supposed to be my spot in the Humvee. I had ordered Mendez back to base. And so, in a way, I caused Doc Mendez to die.

Navy Petty Officer 3rd Class Fernando A. Mendez-Aceves. He had grown up in Mexico City. He was twenty-seven years old.

The moment that one of you passes away is terrifying.

BY EARLY APRIL, OUR PLATOON WAS CONSIDERED "COMBAT INEFFECTIVE." After your unit suffers so many wounded and so many dead, you are no longer an effective fighting force. Out of thirty Marines in my platoon, fewer than twelve men were still fit to fight. The Marines that came to fill the spots were drawn from battalions elsewhere in Iraq. They'd seen action. They were combat ready. They were seasoned Marines. And they were short-timers.

"I have two months left," says one.

"Dawg, I have one month left."

"You have a month left and they sent you here? That's fucked up, man."

"Yeah, that's fucked up," he says. But a lot of Marines were already on their second or third tours. Even some of those Marines didn't make it back home alive.

THE HUMVEE HAS BEEN BLASTED BY AN IED EXPLOSION. INSIDE, SPRAWLED AMID GLASS AND BLOOD AND THE DESERT SAND, is one of my Marines. He'd been sent to our platoon as a replacement. His face is swollen and disfigured. I can't recognize him. I turn to the other Marines who've secured the area. Who am I working on? I ask. We don't know, they say. We didn't get to see his dog tags.

The Marine is still breathing. Bubbles and blood gurgle from his face or throat. He is in bad shape. *Where do I start?* His body is so destroyed. I don't know where to begin. *Get his pulse.* If you can feel a pulse in the feet, you have good blood pressure. If can you feel a pulse in the wrist or arms, you have okay blood pressure. You're in bad shape if you only have a pulse in the neck, but you might live.

I check his wrist, pressing my index and middle fingers on the artery. No pulse. I move them slightly, press deeper. No pulse. *Maybe just readjust his arm.* I lift his arm to adjust. To feel again for his pulse. The Marine's arm separates from his body. It had remained attached only with small filaments of tissue. The Marine's arm falls into my lap.

I have treated many Marines, but an unbearable weight descends on me. I am trying to draw air into my lungs, but I feel like I am a thousand feet under the ocean. *This is too fucking much. This is too fucking fucking fucking much.* I look up into the sky for a moment, bring my hands to the sides of my head and press hard, press until my fingers are white. Then I look at the Marine and I go back to work. As I'm trying to remove his clothing, to reveal his wounds, his necklace comes off. It is a locket. Inside is a picture of his wife and kids. At that point, I know who it is. I know that locket. I know who that locket belongs to.

I know the Marine, and I know his wife is pregnant with their child.

THE ARMY DIVISION BEFORE US, THE BIG RED ONE, HAD TRAVELED IN ARMORED PERSONNEL CARRIERS WHEN THEY PATROLLED RAMADI. Mostly they took small arms fire, pop shots here and there. Their mission was to keep Route Michigan, the road that connects Falujah to Ramadi, free of IEDs. Let's just do our job, they figured. Let's not get too involved. We'll fight 'em as they come.

We took another approach. If we kill the bad guys, we'll get rid of the problem. It'll be cake after that. But we all know that wasn't how it worked out. The Iraqis we killed were from the area. You kill one, two more come to war against us. Sometimes we found out the Iraqis we killed were people working on our own bases. Oh, that was the guy who did our laundry. Oh, that was the guy who took care of our water supply. We were supposed to be winning hearts and minds, but I think we pissed them off too much.

I did a lot of things I wouldn't choose to do. But you're a Marine first, so I was shooting with the Marines next to me. A Marine goes down with a bullet wound, then I'm patching them up and doing whatever I need to do as a corpsman. When I've stabilized that Marine, I go back on the gun. I was doing it to save my Marines. I shot back. I shot back at people. There's some very tragic stuff we did out there that I've never told anybody. I'll probably take that stuff to the grave.

I still have my issues. I'm dealing with multiple traumatic brain injuries. My doctor says I've got "sub-threshold PTSD." I'm functioning well, but I still have symptoms. I get bad dyslexia. I have panic attacks that are just insane. I don't sleep very much at all. But I've been successful in school, and it has taken a lot of self-dedication and self-thought to keep me going.

I was in the Yokosuka Naval Hospital in Japan this past summer. In one of the hallways I came across a mural. It was a wall of portraits. They were Navy corpsmen who died in Iraq.

I stood and stared. A young corpsman came up to me. "We're putting up this memorial for the corpsmen who fought in Iraq and didn't make it back," she said. "It's not finished yet."

"I know almost every one of them."

"Wait—you know these people?"

"Yeah, I fought with them."

I looked from face to face of the corpsmen in the mural. Doc Mendez was one of them. The artist had done a very good job. I stood there for a long time and looked into his eyes.

I thought about the responsibility I carry for the rest of my days. My responsibility to Doc Mendez. You see, I have to lead one life for the both of us now. I have to live Doc's life, too. I have to live a good life *for him*, since he no longer has his own.

"You do dumb shit and get away with it, and they pin medals on your chest. You're not thinking that you might actually make it out of there alive. You're just thinking, 'Well, if I'm going out, I'm gonna go out on my own fucking two feet, on my own terms.'"

PART 1

WE WERE FUCKING GREAT AT IT

KEVIN CHOSE

WE WATCHED AS THE DRUNK-ASS JORDANIAN REAR-ENDED THE PICKUP TRUCK, HEARD THE IMPACT AND THE SHRIEKS OF THE PASSENGERS IN BACK. It was packed with Iraqi civilians. He killed a little Iraqi girl. The little girl's father lived right across the street. The whole family lived there in a compound—grandparents, daughters, kids. They saw it happen, and they were fucking pissed. They wanted this guy's head. They wanted him *dead*. So we had to run the checkpoint and at the same time guard this motherfucker from all these people demanding blood vengeance for the little girl he had killed.

It was a 24-hour mission that turned into four fucking days. The Army had cordoned off a sector of Baghdad, and we were on the outskirts at this checkpoint going through the cars of anybody leaving the city, checking their shit. They stuck us on a bridge on Route Tampa, which is like an interstate, two lanes each way, but one side had been bombed out during the invasion. A lot of those bridges were blown. If we didn't blow them, the bad guys did.

Eight soldiers fifteen kilometers from the nearest friendly forces and a radio that only reached maybe ten kilometers. We didn't have a bunker to hide in, or a tank, or a plane flying overhead to cover our asses. It was just squat and hold for four days. Eight, ten, twelve hours we'd be out there, full battle rattle, 120 degrees, hauling people out of their cars and looking under their seats and through their trunks.

We didn't have an interpreter—I didn't see one of those until we were in Afghanistan. We used rudimentary hand signals. I remembered a little bit of Arabic. I could say "Open your door" and "Open your glove compartment" and "Hurry up" and "Shut up." They knew what we were telling them to do, and a lot of them spoke English. Worst case scenario, everybody speaks the same fucking language when you got a gun pointed at your face.

We found large stacks of dinar, Iraqi currency. The Iraqis were trying to give it to us. They didn't understand. They thought we were out there taxing them. "No, we don't want your money," we'd tell them. "Take it back. I don't want it." We found hiding holes. False trunks and empty stash places in the cars. And I'm thinking, the guy probably left his shit on the side of the road before he hit the checkpoint. Bomb-making materials, weapons, ammo. Whatever contraband they had in their car, they dumped it a mile down the road—IEDs, guns, bombs, you name it.

Bombs and ambushes were shedding a lot of blood in that part of the city. So the Army was kicking in doors, and the bad guys were trying to get out of there. They were being pushed right into us. Kind of a hammer-and-anvil operation. We were there as a deterrent.

I'm sure that drunk-ass Jordanian kid had come to Iraq to play war. He probably stuck it out for a few weeks and decided he didn't want to play no more. Got a little too real for him. Got drunk and drove home. Killed that poor little girl. Wrecked his car trying to get out of the country.

We managed to raise command on the radio. "When are you guys going to come pick up this drunk Jordanian and get him out of here? There's a lot of people who want him dead. They probably want us dead too at this point." Command said they were on it, but a day and a half later, nobody had come to pick this dude up. So, at three in the morning, I kicked him loose. "There's the road, bro. Stick that thumb out, homey. It's called hitchhiking." We had to show that motherfucker how to hitchhike. He starts walking towards Jordan, down the highway. He thanked us for saving his ass. I don't think he had any guilt or remorse over the little girl he had killed, none at all.

We were only supposed to be out there 24 hours, and that's all the supplies we'd brought. After 96 hours, we're out of food and water. Everybody was really fucking thirsty. So I taught my guys that you can consume your own urine three times before it becomes toxic. That's Army survival manual tactics. We filled a small jug with our urine, tied a piece of cord on it, and dumped it in the river for a half hour to cool it off, make it a little more palatable. Half an hour later, the truck shows up to pick us up, and he's got bottles of water for us. The guys were just filling their canteens with cooled piss to quench their thirst. They gladly dumped them out.

It was early on in the war and the start of a year-long deployment in Iraq. I never fired one round when I was there. Not one.

WE DROVE A CONVOY FROM KUWAIT WHEN WE WENT INTO IRAQ. HARDLY ANYTHING WAS ARMORED IN 2004, so we retro-fitted all our aluminum-skinned trucks. They were designed for airborne drops, not for stopping bullets. We combed through Field Manual 5-105 to find out how much wet sand it took to slow down a 7.62 mm bullet like the insurgents were shooting. We figured 16 inches wouldn't stop a bullet, but it probably wouldn't be going fast enough anymore to pierce our body armor. So we made wood framing and sheathed the trucks with plywood and packed the 16-inch voids full of wet sand. Filled sandbags with our E-tools down there on the ground of Kuwait, dumped the sand behind the plywood, poured in water, and packed it down to get it as dense as possible.

Three days straight, all the way to Baghdad, in fucking plywood trucks. We rode to war with plywood armor. That's combat engineering—adapting, overcoming, and fucking getting over the situation as best you can. Doing the impossible with literally nothing.

I trained to be a combat engineer at Fort Bragg. I spent almost eight years in Bravo Company, 27th Engineer Battalion. It's the only airborne company of its kind in the entire U.S. military. One hundred and twenty combat engineers trained to jump off the ramp of a large aircraft at eight hundred feet, usually a C-130 or a Chinook helicopter, and parachute into a forest canopy. We wear special Kevlar-reinforced suits with a nylon strap sewn between the knees to keep you from catching a branch in the nuts. Special helmets with face masks. The 'chutes snag in the trees, we rappel down to the ground, and we bust out the chainsaws and C4 explosive. We start blowing, blasting, and cutting trees to clear an airstrip. We slingload in bulldozers. Within 72 hours, we've built a combat landing strip in the middle of nowhere. While people are trying to kill us.

It takes a special breed to volunteer to train harder, to train more often, to take on those tougher missions. To be more competitive and to surround yourself with people like that.

I joined the Army in 1998. I grew up rough. Arrested several times. Partied a lot, did a lot of drugs and drank a lot. Somehow I didn't end up in prison. Seems everybody I knew back then is either dead or in prison. I dropped out of high school, breezed through a GED. I worked as a cook. Construction labor. Telemarketing. I even did small engine repair. I was the manager at an indoor shooting range when I noticed a flyer for the National Guard taped to the counter. One weekend per month. Two weeks per year. Education. A little bit of monthly pay. I walked into a recruiter's office and told him I was hoping to enlist.

"What do you want to do?" he asked.

"I wanna blow shit up and get paid for it," I said. I always liked explosives as a kid. The 4th of July is still my favorite holiday.

I figured I could be a soldier without actually having to do the whole soldier thing. But I soon realized I really liked being a soldier. I wasn't back from basic training two days before I was down at the recruiter's office signing up for active duty. I wanted to go full-blown from the beginning. Airborne. Ranger Battalion.

Whatever I could do to move up and be at the top of the game. I was twenty-one years old and my girlfriend was pregnant.

I became a combat engineer, a 12 Bravo. My job was to place a precise amount of explosive on a target and detonate it with instantaneous effects. But when I went to war, we didn't make bombs. We looked for them.

WESTERN BAGHDAD. THE WORST FUCKING PLACE EVER. WE DROVE DOWN THE WORST PART OF THE CITY in broad daylight, with big-ass vehicles going 10 miles an hour, scrutinizing the side of the road for a little wire or some telltale sign of an improvised explosive device, an IED, carefully hidden and intended to kill and maim as many Americans as possible.

The only way you were going to find IEDs was to memorize every tiny object on the side of the road and think like a terrorist. Wherever you'd hide a bomb, that's where you find something. "Hey, that tire? That wasn't there yesterday... back the fuck up. Check that shit out. Sure as shit. There it is. A wire." Iraq was a fucking trash dump. Garbage everywhere to hide bombs in.

Route clearance was finding the IEDs on the roads, and it was the paramount mission in Iraq at the time. The four-star general in charge of it all got up every morning, and while he was taking a shit, the first page he'd flip to was his reports on his route clearance. We were fucking great at it. We reduced IEDs in our theater of operations by fifty-four percent. We'd find them. And if we didn't find them, they'd find us. *BOOM.*

We finally got a vehicle capable for that mission, something that was meant to absorb a big blast. It's called a Buffalo, a big six-wheeled sucker with a deep V-shaped hull to deflect the destructive pressure wave of an explosion. We're behind two inches of glass and steel. It has a 21-foot articulated arm that swings out and telescopes. The arm has a little pinching fork on it to pick through debris piles and animal carcasses and wherever else they hide the bombs. It's controlled by a joystick. It's pretty hard to pull a blasting cap out of a bomb with that mechanical arm, but I had guys that could do it.

If you saw us driving that Buffalo down the freeway, rolling real slow, necks craned as we search for roadside bombs, it was a bad idea to tell us to get the hell out of your way and pass us. A minute down the road, you go *BOOM*. Fucking told ya so.

American units came up behind us after we'd been blown up and thanked us for taking the blast for them. "If it wasn't for you guys, that'd been us. *Fuck*. Thanks." These were guys in soft-skinned vehicles with all kinds of people in the back. They'd have become pieces of meat scattered on the roadside if they'd taken that bomb instead of us.

We find an IED, we pull back to a safe stand-off distance. And in a crowded city, there ain't no fucking safe stand-off distance for a piece of ordnance like the bad guys were using. A rigged 155 mm artillery round is about as high as your waist and six inches in diameter. That thing goes off, that's fuck city for everybody within a block. We'll probably survive inside our Buffalo vehicle, go home with a little traumatic brain injury, but we'll live. The civilians out there, shopping for their families in the Abu Ghraib marketplace in the middle of the day, they're torn to pieces.

Used to be we find an IED and the infantry dismounts from their vehicles behind us, unrolls concertina wire and hustles the Iraqi civilians out of the blast area. The terrorists see that's what the Americans do, so they start putting in IEDs where the Americans are probably going to dismount. They put a real obvious IED out there for you to find, and they hide one where you're probably going to get out of your trucks. You find the bait IED, your guys dismount to protect civilians, and they trigger the secondary. *BOOM* goes your infantry guys.

You start showing a pattern, the bad guys pick up on that shit. Then you change tactics. They change theirs. Move, countermove, move, countermove.

Five-dollar car alarms and key fobs used to trigger the bombs. Long-range cordless telephones, Motorola radios, garage door openers, anything, anything you could think of that would send a signal, that'll flip a switch and detonate the bomb, detonate that artillery shell or mortar or mine, they used it. *BOOM.*

Earlier in the war, if you didn't see anybody on the streets in the middle of the day, that meant shit was about to happen. Your eyes were peeled. You knew a bomb was in the ground and it was about ready to find you. *BOOM.* Then the terrorists just quit warning the civilian population because they knew we keyed up on that. They just quit warning them. They put out bombs in crowded areas and they didn't give a fuck.

THE SUN HIGH IN THE SKY, MIDDLE OF THE DAY, HOT. THE MARKET IS PACKED. Iraqis buying tomatoes and lemons and rice and fabric and pirated DVDs and cheap sandals and deodorant and everything else.

We're creeping along in the Buffalo on an offshoot road of Route Iowa. The road surface is completely bombed out.

Not one piece of concrete is intact. It's been completely shattered by IED strikes. Garbage everywhere. Plastic bags, water bottles, ratty clothing, rotten food, just dust and shit all over the place.

I've got this strip of road completely memorized. I can tell you if a tire shifts six inches, if there's a bottle there that wasn't there the last time we passed, if a plastic bag has suddenly appeared, if anything's moved.

We get to the end of the street and pause. I'm thinking, thinking hard. I'm trying to think like some terrorist asshole trying to bomb a convoy of Americans. If I'm that terrorist asshole, what would I do?

I do a U-turn. We drive the Buffalo a couple kilometers back down the way we came, do another U-turn, and drive along the same exact garbage-strewn stretch of road again. I'm looking at the same broken concrete, the same junk and crap, every inch of the way.

Stop. That wasn't there fifteen minutes ago.

It's just a piece of concrete curbstone. Except it wasn't there fifteen minutes ago.

We go in for a closer peek. There's a wire. It's a 155 mm artillery round encased in concrete to make it blend in with the curbstone. It's a fresh IED, it's a big fucking bomb, and it can go *BOOM* at any moment. The market is thronged with Iraqi civilians. My arm operator says, I got this shit, he reaches down with the claw and grabs the wire. He pulls on the wire and the blasting cap comes out of the bomb. It dangles there for an instant, like a fat spider on the end of a line, and then it pops. *POP.* It sounds like a firecracker.

The bomber is probably 100 yards away, and he's just

triggered the IED. But he's half a second too late. The blasting cap just pops harmlessly. It's not inside the bomb anymore, it doesn't set it off. No *BOOM,* no blast, no shattered buildings, no marketplace strewn with the bodies of women and children. The trigger device was an electric doorbell. Just *ding dong.*

The Iraqi civilians freeze in their tracks when they hear that *POP.* They look over at us, think *Oh fuck,* and stampede out of the market area.

Move, countermove. Move, countermove. The bombers knew our route. They waited for us to pass, and then they placed the 155 mm artillery round in the curbstone behind us. We performed a countermove on the fly. That's the only reason we found it.

We adapted and came back and took that IED away from them. Just one bomb that some fucker didn't get paid to set off. It was a small victory.

That's what we did every day.

I HAD A STEADY GIRLFRIEND WHEN I FIRST ENLISTED IN THE NATIONAL GUARD. HER MOM WAS A FILIPINA BAR GIRL IN VIETNAM, her dad was in the Navy during the war. I found out she was pregnant just before shipping off to basic training. It had a huge effect on me. Despite all the bullshit I'd pulled, run-ins with the law and troubles with drugs, I still had good stuff in me. Virtuous. Kind. Responsible. Always looking to take the hard right over the easy wrong. That's the attitude I had about being a father. Be responsible and do the right thing.

I had a three-day break between basic and advanced individual training. I'd squirreled away a few hundred bucks and flew her down to Fort Leonard Wood, Missouri, where I'd just gone through boot camp. We went to the Pulaski County Courthouse, right off base, to get married. That way my son would be born legitimately.

The court clerk looks at me in my uniform, lean and shorn, and at my half-Asian bride-to-be. She's five months pregnant. She's showing.

The clerk is straight-up about it.

"Sorry. We don't marry interracial couples." She says this matter-of-factly, polite.

"C'mon, really? Them days are over. Ya'll need to get with the times."

"I'm sorry, sir, but we don't do it."

"Do you know anybody that does?"

"No, sir, sorry."

She gave us a phone list of justices of the peace who would facilitate a ceremony. I worked my way down the list.

"So, both parties are white?"

"Mmm, no."

"Sorry."

We got to the last name. "Who gives a shit what color you are, obviously," he says. He's a doctor. He's the only non-white person on the list, apparently. He's on his way out of town. He swings by the courthouse, family waiting in the car, and he's half-shitfaced. He marries us—*I do, I do*—hops in the car, and drives off.

That was November '98. Two years later, I re-enlisted in the Army and was sent to Jump School. Next they sent me to Korea for a year, then back to Fort Bragg. I was a seasoned leader by this point, a noncommissioned officer, and ready for war. I was at the top of the game. One day the brigade gets the big news. "Heads up. *You guys are going to war.*" The Iraq invasion was impending, and we were going to be part of it. But the Army is pockmarked with fucking bad decisions and bad decision-makers. It's almost like somebody has it in for you. The same day that the brigade gets the news, five of us seasoned leaders are shipped to Korea for a year. We watch the Iraq invasion on television from the DMZ.

The war in Afghanistan had been on for a couple of years, and quite a few young guns were walking around Korea with combat patches on their right shoulders. These guys were respected, the guys you talked to. None of us wanted to be sitting there in Korea. Everybody wanted to be in Iraq. I re-enlisted in Korea so I could get orders to Fort Bragg, pretty much for the express purpose of going to war. I had an agenda. All they do at Fort Bragg is train people for war. I didn't tell my wife about my plans.

My first day at work at Fort Bragg, I walk down to Bravo Company. "Get your desert shit," they said. "We're going to war." I come home with eight different duffel bags full of gear. My wife unzips one of them, pulls out my desert-pattern camo uniform, and starts crying. She doesn't say a word.

She was gone at that point. I could see it in her eyes. We fought a custody battle over the kids. She moved back home. I was in Iraq by August. By December, I was calling home to talk to my kids, and some other guy was answering the phone. It was Christmas Eve.

WHEN THEY INVADED IRAQ, IT WAS A RACE TO BAGHDAD. EVERYBODY WANTED TO BE THE TIP OF THE SPEAR. Everybody wanted to be the first one to pull down a statue of Saddam in downtown Baghdad. Dick-measuring was the order of the day.

You had some good commanders on the ground, and then there were also some sawed-off Pattons with pearl handles on their Beretta M9s. The 82nd Airborne wanted to parachute in and take Baghdad International. That's one division of troops on foot against two divisions of Iraqi tanks. They had already drawn parachutes to jump into a bloodbath before somebody with another star on his shoulder said, "That's the dumbest fucking thing I've ever heard. *We're not doing that.*" There's no shortage of dumbasses trying to get people killed by the thousands to make a great name for themselves. Modern-day leadership and munitions and military technology should have prevented bullshit like that. Fortunately, it did—at the last minute.

During the big race to Baghdad, no one secured the captured munitions bunkers. The Iraqi munitions bunkers were stuffed with mines and mortars and 155 mm artillery shells and everything else that blows up. While everyone was obsessed with being the tip of the spear, a lot of bunkers were picked clean by the locals and insurgents and anyone trying to make a buck. All that shit ended up stashed all over the country. Thousands of mines and mortars and artillery rounds that made great IEDs. Then we had to find them all again, one by one. If we didn't find them, they found us. *BOOM.*

It's another example of the butt-fuckery of combat. Just the butt-fuckery of it all. Race for glory, but leave the munitions bunkers free for the taking? You want us to shoot bad guys, but now that we got bad guys in our gun sights, you don't want us to shoot 'em? We're here to help these people, now you want us to leave them to get massacred? They were ordering patrols to hunt for IEDs in aluminum-skinned vehicles. By the time we got there, our visions of what the war was like, our illusions, had been shattered. They did not know what the fuck they were going to do after the invasion. It'll leave you in tears, either from laughing or crying, or both.

We knew we were deploying again before we even got home from Iraq. Eight months after we got back Stateside, they sent us to Afghanistan. I laid it out for my guys before we left. This ain't gonna be Iraq, I said. This is gonna be a fight. We're not going to have transient wannabe-warrior college kids from Jordan coming into the country to pop a few shots off at Americans and then run. The people in Afghanistan have been fighting for 2,500 years. They don't give a fuck about dying for their cause. My men were no stranger to the countryside and the enemy, but they weren't ready for that kind of war.

PART 2:

SOMEBODY ELSE CAME BACK

"You were in the shit and you didn't have anybody to come rescue your ass. You were
100 clicks into Indian country, where if you got a flat tire and you didn't have a spare
or the tools to change that bitch, you're digging in. You're making a firebase right
there. Nobody's sleeping until that shit's fixed. Until then, you're out in the open,
waiting for attack. Afghanistan was a totally different war."

WE HAD BEEN CLEARING IEDS ALONG RUTTED, DUSTY ROADS AND
DRY RIVERBEDS IN SOUTHERN AFGHANISTAN ALL SUMMER LONG. We
had busted trucks and battered equipment. We'd been back on
base a week when we get word that we're moving out again.
The Canadians are getting their asses handed to them by the
Taliban in a huge firefight. They've got KIA and their trucks
have been shot out from under them. Everyone and everything
is being thrown into the battle. It's a big fucking deal.

We get briefed at a rickety table in a plywood shack. The
captain's best plan is to dump 200 men by helicopter and have
them march house to house, village to village, and fight diehard
Taliban on their own turf for two weeks. Clear 20 kilometers of
enemy who've been dug in and fortified for centuries. On foot.

I'm the lowest-ranking guy in the room, but right then and
there I said, "No, sir. They'd get massacred. Look, I've got
a ninth-grade education, I'm not a tactician, it's just experience."
It took me right back to the story about the 82nd Airborne
Division wanting to jump in for all their glory against two
divisions of Iraqi tanks and get their little gold stars on their
wings. You don't do that shit.

Some of the Special Forces guys in the room are nodding. They're hearing what I'm saying.

The commander is a colonel in the Special Forces. This guy's got that look in his eye. He's been there. He's seen some shit. "Scratch that helicopter bullshit," he says.

I pull out a map I got from the Canadian engineers. We had been clearing bombs with the Canadians in the same area a month before. The map shows every route in and around where the fight is raging, color-coded to indicate what vehicles can go where. "Holy shit, where'd you get that?" The captain's got no idea there are roads into this place.

"Right across the street, from the Canadian Royal Engineers."

Everybody's scrambling over this map. Everybody's under the impression you couldn't drive trucks into this place. I explain you can get vehicles in there, but there's 15-foot mud walls alongside a lot of the narrow roads. If one of your trucks gets blown up, your convoy is trapped. They start writing up new battle plans using the new map.

The base gears up. Guys repair equipment, load ammo pouches and canteens and medic kits, program frequencies on their radios. Guys make phone calls home. We're not coming back until the job's done.

I'M LAYING IN MY BUNK. I'M TAKING A NAP. WE'RE READY TO GO, WE'RE HEADING INTO THE SHIT IN A FEW HOURS, so I get down while I can. I fall asleep and I have a dream. I'm in the middle of a firefight, a battle. There's a tree line and there's dirt and there's the *snap* of sniper rounds. The enemy is real close. It's deadly. We're trying to kill the enemy, but they're hidden, they're protected, they're shooting down on us. We have wounded soldiers. For some reason, me and my men have to cross a field. We're crawling across this field, dragging the wounded with us. And then, in a flash, I'm shot in the face. The bullet enters above my cheek, just below my eye. I don't feel pain, only the shock of being killed.

I bolt awake in a dead sweat. I spring up and almost hit my head on the top bunk. My clothes are soaked. I've been shot in the face in a dream. You're not supposed to die in your sleep, but I just did.

It's a ghost town, at least it looks that way. Army psychological operations had flown over two days before and pushed pallets of leaflets off a helicopter. The leaflets stated it bluntly: We're coming in, and if you're still here, we're fucking gonna kill you. There wasn't any discussion of rules of engagement. There wasn't really any point.

We're walking through the middle of an open field. It's me and my guys alongside an Army infantry platoon. We're also with a platoon of Afghan National Army guys and their two American trainers. A lieutenant is in charge. Our interpreter is listening to his radio, monitoring the chatter on all the frequencies. "The Taliban is talking on their radios!" he says suddenly. "They're— they're watching us right now! They're waiting for us."

The lieutenant keeps walking us forward through the field. The dream I had of getting shot in the face is haunting me, and what's before me is starting to look real familiar. I've never been here before, but I know this place. It's right out of my dream. I'm looking at the same field, from the same angle, as I saw in my dream. I start looking for a place to dive when the shit happens, because I'm damn sure it's going to.

The first shots of the ambush erupt—*zzzippp! sssnappp! POOM!*—one breath later. I grab my guys and plunge into a shallow irrigation ditch. We crawl up a ways and the ditch gets deeper. I yell at the infantry to follow us and get the fuck out of the middle of the field, and they start crawling towards us. The Afghanis, however, turn and run right down the middle of the field. Their two American trainers chase after them, yelling for them to stop, when the Taliban open up from both sides and cut them down. Mike, one of the Americans, is shot in the face. Half a platoon of Afghanis lay wounded and dying, some already dead. Some try to crawl back and are picked off when they move.

The lieutenant takes his radio guy and his medic with him, pushes out of his ditch towards the Afghanis, and makes it 50 yards into the middle of the field until they get pinned down. Now his platoon is separated from him with no leadership and no radio. The senior squad leader's with us in the ditch, and he's already cracked. He crawls over to me. "What are we gonna do! What are we gonna do!" We're being shot at from the west and the north, and we're pinned down.

A few of the Afghani soldiers have managed to crawl back and fall into the ditch. Some have taken multiple shots. The infantry guys are saying they're not our guys, we only got enough first aid shit for our guys, we're not gonna treat them. My guys always had two or three kits' worth of first aid on us. We had hemcon bandages, which are quick clot in a patch. You slap them over a bullet wound and they adhere to it like glue and seal the hole. We've got pockets full of these, and it pays off that day. We save a lot of Afghani lives.

The Taliban are firing at us from mud buildings two stories tall. The buildings have thatched roofs and slits about a yard long and a foot wide for them to shoot through. The Afghan farmers hang grapes and marijuana in the buildings to dry—that's how they cure their harvest, in these grape huts called *qalats*. The walls are three feet thick and solid mud and rock. Whatever we fire at those things bounces right off. We launch an 84 mm rocket, enough to take out a light tank—*pfhwwwwww BOOM!*—and it hardly dents the grape hut.

The lieutenant and his radio man are still in the middle of the field, hunkered face-down in a shallow ditch, bullets whizzing inches overhead, probably trying to dig a hole with their dicks to get even lower.

The lieutenant can't do anything but try to stay alive, so I use our radio to call for air support. When the Warthog arrives, you don't even hear the aircraft. You just feel the impact of thousands of high-explosive rounds thudding into the earth and exploding on impact. It's so fucking close. You feel the roar before you hear it, and the sound of the gun on an A10 Warthog is not like any other gun. It's one long, continuous *BBBBBRRRRRRRR*. It is loud beyond loud, louder than imagination, like the roar of a god. Me and my three guys run out of the irrigation ditch as the Warthog strafes the orchard behind the grape huts. We run forward and find cover behind a small dirt mound.

An Apache attack helicopter follows the Warthog. He's 50 feet above the battle. The Taliban are lighting him up, bullets sparking off the Apache, and the pilot is waiting for somebody to tell him where to shoot. He can't risk American lives. We've left the radio behind with the remains of the other platoon, so I grab a bright pink signal panel out of one of my ammo pouches and wave it in the air frantically. I'm on my knees waving and hearing *zip! snap!* because the Taliban are shooting all around. I can see the pilot, and he's nodding vigorously *Okay, Okay, Okay!* that he's seen me and needs to know where the enemy are. I tell my guys to light up the grape huts with tracers, and we all stand up from the mound and blaze away with tracer rounds, green light streaking into the grape huts. The pilot roars up and away to circle around for an attack approach.

It's then that a Taliban fires an RPG at us. It whooshes just overhead and explodes a hundred yards behind us. Joe is one of my guys, and the RPG flips a switch in him. He's entered another state of mind, rage and darkness. *Fuck you,* he yells hoarsely. *FUCK YOU.* He stands up in the middle of the firefight with his grenade launcher and draws a bead on the Taliban who shot the RPG. The Taliban is sprinting behind a wall, and Joe is aiming at him with the grenade launcher. *I got this motherfucker,* he says. The body of an American is still laying out there between us and the Taliban. We can't risk that grenade landing short and desecrating his body, but before I can stop him, Joe pulls the trigger. The grenade arcs 200 yards and lands on top of the wall the moment the Taliban arrives there at full sprint, as if the man were racing to meet it. The blast of the grenade cuts him in half. We can see the spray of blood and organs, see his torso separate from his legs. The war stops. For three seconds, everyone stops shooting. In the middle of Armageddon, everyone is too stunned to breathe.

Like clockwork, as if it were planned, the Apache has come back around for an attack pass. He's lined up. Everybody's still shocked by Joe's grenade shot, and then the fucking Apache comes in, one pass, 30 mm gun belching, rockets smoking into the grape huts, one pass, all of his firepower expended in one orgy. He dips his rotor and lifts up to go reload back at base. He's *Winchestered*, he's an empty aircraft. The Apache's navigator fixes a grid coordinate for the grape huts during the attack, and not long later shouts go up from the platoon behind us. *Hey! the shit's coming in, it's coming in danger close.* Danger fucking close. Shut your eyes, plug your ears, and fucking open your mouths. We're that close. We don't hear the jets, we don't hear nothing, it just gets quiet. The F16 drops a 1000-pound bomb from high above. It strikes right on the grape hut. We're 100 yards from the detonation. The explosion lifts our bodies clear from the ground, the earth ripples like a giant angry fist has slammed down. The pressure wave sucks the air from our lungs. The only thing that saves us is the little hump of dirt we're clinging behind. Everything's a blur. Smoke, dust, blood, body parts everywhere. Six hours after the first bullet was fired, it's nearly over.

We recover Mike's body. He'd caught his Afghani troops smoking hash before the battle, and that angered him. He was an islander, a light-skinned black man in life, but now his face is drained of all color, ghastly white in death. I cover him up with a poncho because I don't want to look at his face and the bullet wound that had killed him. I tell the infantry platoon to evacuate his body to the rear. They start moving his body roughly, like he's a piece of meat, and I fucking go off on them. You fuckers treat him with the proper dignity and respect, I scream, or *I'll fucking kill you.* He was an American soldier. He had a wife and three kids.

You drink some water, puke, cry, smoke, jerk off—whatever you gotta fucking do—and get your shit back together. You push on. You expose yourself to the enemy so they can light you up. You find out where they are and then you fucking light them up and drop 1000-pound bombs on them. Then you keep pushing. We got our gear back on and walked deeper into the valley.

That night, we circled the wagons and set up our perimeter. It's quiet. We can hear a tiny hum in the dark sky. We don't see any blinking lights, but we know Spooky is five or six thousand feet overhead, circling in long, slow arcs. Spooky is an AC 130 gunship equipped with infrared targeting. We get the word to make sure everyone's inside the perimeter, Spooky's on station. A couple minutes later, we hear *boom...bah-BOOM*. The first sound is Spooky firing its cannon. The second is someone dying in an explosion far below. *Boom...bah-BOOM. Boom...bah-BOOM.* Spooky doesn't miss. The whole valley—nothing makes it in and nothing makes it out. If you're not American forces, you're dead.

For almost three straight weeks, we went village to village, mud hut to mud hut, killing and being killed. I went home on leave shortly after we left the valley. I'd lost a lot of weight. I don't remember much of leave. I was drunk the entire time. I stayed that way. There was no way around it.

I had gone to Afghanistan six months before.

Somebody else came back.

My entire adult life was spent in the army. Sixteen years. I excelled. I went places. *I was somebody*. There are some great moments in all those years, but a lot of it is overshadowed by despair. A lot of us who have been to war and come home know the struggles with depression. You don't come back from war and not have a scratch on you.

Two weeks ago I went to the VA to get examined for traumatic brain injury for the fourth time. "What caused it?" they asked again. "Look at my medical records," I said. "Airborne operation. IED strikes. How do you think I got concussed so many times?" Every time I go to the VA, I have to explain it over and over again.

When I got home, I looked at my wife with tears in my eyes. It was the worst day in a long time, a come-to-Jesus moment.

My life was spared, but I lost my soul in Afghanistan.

It's a wake-up when you come home and realize nobody gives a fuck what you did. After all I've done, I don't know why I have to stress about going to college and finding a job. I spent 16 years in an institution and came out just dumbfounded on the tail end. Life was a whole lot simpler—life was a whole lot *better*—when all I had to worry about was staying alive and keeping my men alive. Ask any combat vet. They'll say the same.

I get so overwhelmed by all the bullshit of day-to-day life. Some days a part of me just doesn't want to play anymore. Do I want to live anymore, or not? You get to that precipice. Then you have to make a decision. You analyze your life and how you can fix it. And then you either put that plan into action, or you swallow your pistol.

Sometimes the reasons I want to stay around aren't so clear. But, I think, if you end it all now, it was all for nothing. And after making it through all that, I recognize a higher power. My life was spared not by anyone or anybody, but by a higher power. There's got to be some meaning why I lived through all that shit and can talk about it.

I try hard to have compassion for my fellow human beings. I try to be virtuous. I pull over to the side of the road and change people's tires for them. I carry a lady's groceries to her car. That's my method of fighting the battle up here in my head. I have good days and I have bad days. Most days, I'm the sheepdog. I'm the *protector*. I help others and I do the right thing. But on some days, I'm the wolf. I should be in a cage. That's the fight that goes on now for me. The fight's not over there anymore. It's right here in my own head.

SOMEBODY ELSE CAME BACK

"I heard stories about my grandfather sleeping with a gun under his pillow all the time, waking up screaming and yelling. But he didn't talk about his war. My grandfather was a combat legend, but nobody knew his story. I watched my grandfather hold that stuff in for all those years."

MY JOB WAS TO DESTROY THE ENEMY

DENNIS ELLER

WE SPENT THE FIRST TWO WEEKS ON ROUTE IRISH IN BAGHDAD. A COUPLE GUN BATTLES, NOTHING BIG. Then we got sent to Sadr City—that was July 2004, when Muqtada al-Sadr called for his Mahdi army to rise up. We ran and gunned for two straight weeks in that fucking shithole. We were patrolling an area and we're told to set up a blocking position just north of where we were. We start hauling ass there when the world just started exploding. All of Sadr City erupts into gunfire and RPGs, mortars are dropping, and suddenly the vehicle in front of me explodes, there's a giant smoke cloud, and I can't see what was going on. The IED heaved the vehicle sideways. One tire blows out, but they keep driving. Three RPGs come whizzing at us. One of them bounces off my hood, the other one hits my door and rings our bells, and another one skips right in front of us. We'd just entered a kill zone and a mile-long ambush.

Flashes come from a mosque and every window in the buildings on our left. I look at Radar behind me. He's my radio guy, or RTO. "Radar!"

"What?"

"Can you fucking believe this?" We'd been hearing stories about how Al Jazeera reporters were always next to the insurgents, filming when they started shooting at us.

"What, sir?"

"Fucking Al Jazeera is already here taking pictures of us."

The Humvee window I'm looking through goes *POP POP POP*. The inside of the two-inch ballistic glass blossoms with eggshell-shaped craters as the bullets impact.

"Sir, those are muzzle flashes, they're fucking shooting at you."

We rolled through the ambush. The Humvee was good enough to drive. The gunner was good enough to gun. And that's all I cared about—to get out of the kill zone.

We had left Kuwait a few weeks before. We crossed the border and drove up to Baghdad in a Humvee with kevlar doors. It was crap. The guy who'd been in the Humvee before me took an IED right to his chest. He'd been completely blown away. He'd been in the commander seat where I sat. I put plywood over the hole in the floorboard and sandbags to cover it up. We rolled into Camp Victory North in Baghdad in the nighttime, and the mortars start dropping on us and rounds flew overhead as soon as we went through the gates. It was like the insurgents were welcoming us to the fight. We park the Humvees and my company commander, Roy Tisdale, jumps out and tells everybody to get to the bunkers and fast. We thought, *This is war. This is the shit.*

Looking back on it, we were a bunch of cherry-ass bitches. Eight months later, I was back at Camp Victory North again, and a seasoned veteran by that time. The rounds start popping and mortars start dropping in, and the mechanics I'd been talking to dive underneath a table. "Dudes," I say, "those rounds aren't going to do shit to you. Get outta there." But they'd never left the wire, never been out there. They didn't know.

The 1st Cavalry was in charge of Baghdad when we arrived, and they'd gotten hammered. When the insurgency cranked up, they lost a lot of guys in less than a month. They made us Baghdad QRF, the quick reaction force, so whenever something bad happened in Baghdad, my company was sent to take care of it.

I experienced my first RPG on the second day. We're rolling up and down Route Irish, and they're showing us all the spots they've had issues with, where they'd been hit with ambushes. "Yeah, we just had a guy get blown up here the other day," the staff sergeant says. "And we had this happen over there, and that happen over here." As he says that, we hear a POP! and I see a flash a couple hundred yards in front of us. I watch a trail of sparks dance down the road, kind of like a fuse burning, as the RPG rocket skips over the pavement directly towards us. The RPG goes *WHISHHHHHH* and misses me and the truck by a yard or two.

For a year straight, my guys and I went on 275 raids. We did over 332 active combat patrols. On every combat patrol, someone was trying to kill us, anything from a single sniper shot to a four-hour gun battle. The battle in Sadr City lasted two straight weeks, and we stayed out there for five days. Watched tanks obliterate houses. My platoon was hit by over 25 IEDs. Six of those IEDs hit my vehicle. We saw some shit. When we came back, we probably all had traumatic brain injury, but the Army didn't think about TBIs back then.

When I stepped foot in Iraq, I was a dead man. From this moment on, I thought, my life does not matter. I am dead. I am nowhere near alive. I will not make this tour. But as long as my guys do, that's all that matters. As long as I accomplish the mission and my guys survive, that's all that matters. I told my guys that if somebody is going to do something a little too dangerous, it's going to be me. Because if I get killed, big deal. I'm already dead.

My wife at the time, she probably felt a little differently. She was six months pregnant when I deployed.

I was born in Tahlequah, Oklahoma. It means "only two" in Cherokee. Three tribes originally left from northern Georgia and agreed to link up where the Illinois River meets Flint Creek. One tribe never arrived. I think it's not so much historical fact as a story to explain that the Cherokee lost a third of the tribe on the Trail of Tears.

I'm a member of the Cherokee Nation. Fully registered in the tribe. I grew up on the rez until I was about ten, then I moved up to Washington with my mom and stepdad. We still have the family farm, all hundred acres still, and have had it since 1839. We all grew up on it. My kids are the first generation of our family that hasn't grown up on the farm. We raised beef cattle, 150 head, for a long time. Then my granny got sick and we sold them all to pay for her surgery. We used to go fishing all the time on the bend of the Illinois River, down by Stillwell and Watts, by the border of Arkansas. Every summer, all through high school, I'd go back and work on the farm with my grandparents.

When I got back from Iraq, my grandfather finally opened up to me about his war. He finally felt like he could tell me stories and I would understand. And I did. "You always listen to a machine gun," he said. "There's always a natural pause. That's when you move." He was 82nd Airborne. He jumped into Sicily. He jumped into Italy. He jumped into Normandy. He jumped into Holland. He fought the Battle of the Bulge, he crossed the Rhine. He told me that in Italy, when they were moving up to their positions in the mountains, they were approaching a M*A*S*H unit between two hilltops. The Germans waited until they got to the M*A*S*H unit and dropped artillery on them. He said he walked on top of American bodies for a mile. He was one of five men to make it back from his original company. My grandfather saw some shit. He died six months after I got back from Iraq.

I joined the Army when I was 18. I was a private. Straight-legged infantry. Eventually I became a Ranger. Airborne. I received a commission as a first lieutenant. It was the peacetime Army. Life revolved around training. You trained for the big show you never thought would come.

WE PATROLLED FOR A WHILE OUT OF CAMP BONSAI IN THE NORTHWESTERN CORNER OF BAGHDAD, across the river from Adhamiyah and Sadr City. They mortared us from Adhamiyah every day, three or four or five times per day. They got very good at mortaring us. One day a whole platoon was out exchanging weapons, gear, refueling the trucks. One team of fourteen or sixteen guys would come in, swap out Humvees with another team, and the next team would go out. And the mortars dropped right on 'em. We had fourteen wounded to evac and every other guy in that platoon was hit. I ran out during the middle of the explosions to carry guys away and watched them just get their legs taken off right in front of me.

It was a rough tour. A couple of other guys lost legs. One guy had his face scraped off, but he survived. Brown, who was in my recon platoon before we left, took an IED to the neck. He got killed. Sergeant Swank was burned alive. His vehicle hit an IED, and we couldn't get him out. His door got buckled in and he was knocked unconscious. When we went and grabbed the door, the whole thing went up in flames. We finally got a hook on the door, jacked it open, pulled Swank out, and got him evaced to the hospital. But he was badly burned, and he didn't survive.

When we worked in Sadr City and south of Baghdad International Airport, we lived in sector, as we called it. That was probably the roughest part of the tour—we stayed out there for three, four weeks. Patrol base to patrol base to patrol base. And when you're out on the streets, you have to keep moving. You can't hunker down, stop and rest. You can stay awake maybe 48 hours, but you can't keep active the whole time. Those were the roughest times. It put a strain on you. Forty-eight hours in the city. Forty-eight hours just driving and watching and waiting, and around every corner you might get into a horrific gun battle or you might run into schoolkids throwing rocks at you or trying to give you flowers.

SAW A LOT OF DEATH. KILLED A LOT OF PEOPLE. WHAT WE DID, THOUGH, THAT'S WHAT WE WERE SUPPOSED TO DO. We shot a guy one time with a .50 cal machine gun, and it took off half his head. What was weird about it was, when you saw him from his eyebrows down, he looked normal. He looked like he was just driving with his hands on the steering wheel. But when you looked from his eyebrows up, there was nothing. Gone.

One night we were on guard duty at our Traffic Control Point. A car approached. It curved between the serpentine barriers, headed towards us between the coils of concertina wire. It doesn't stop. We fire warning shots. It still doesn't stop. It keeps coming and coming towards us, and finally I and my gunner open up on it, fill the windshield with bullets. We blast the car. We fire until the car creeps to a halt. But it's not a suicide bomber inside, it's a family. Mom, Dad, and a six-month-old baby. The whole family is dead.

My first daughter was born when I was in Iraq, and when I came home, she was a six-month-old baby. Every time she fell asleep, all I saw was that dead baby and the bodies of her parents and broken glass and blood at the Traffic Control Point. I checked up on her constantly, making sure she was alive every minute. I didn't sleep for three or four months.

WE WERE ABOUT TO COME IN FROM WEEKS OF PATROLS, GET BACK TO OUR MAIN BASE, AND EVERYBODY WAS SUPER EXCITED. Back at base you take showers and there's little haji shops where you can buy movies and restaurant food and you can relax a little.

We get a call over the radio. We have an American casualty. We have mass civilian casualties. And we have a bomb that just went off.

It's about ten in the morning. It's February 19, 2005.

First platoon heads out in the Humvees. First platoon sergeant was known for making false reports over the radio. You always knew when he was really in combat, and when he was faking it. When he was faking it, he's all calm, cool, collected. When he was in actual combat, he couldn't get his words out.

I call him up on the radio. "What's your situation?"

He's stuttering. "*Ah…bah…it…uh.*" He can't tell me what's going on.

It was the Ashura festival, a major holy day, when tens of thousands of Shiites go to the enormous mosque in Kadhimiyah and perform their pilgrimage. Pilgrims were streaming in on packed buses.

I'm not getting anything out of the sergeant, so I launch a patrol to investigate. I roll up on the scene, and there's a stack of bodies. There's a bus, and the bus is shredded. I mean *fucking shredded.* A suicide bomber had blown himself up on a bus full of pilgrims.

That had been the first explosion.

My buddy Adam Malson of Alpha Company had arrived from another patrol base shortly after the bus was blown up. When he walked in among the wreckage and gore, an Iraqi police vehicle next to the bus blew up too. It had been rigged with an IED. Adam's interpreter was killed. Adam—he was cut in half.

I knew all the guys, but Adam was a guy I would go talk to. We'd go have cigars and whenever something stupid would happen in the battalion, I'd come in and ask him what was going on. He calmed me down. He was a good dude. He was 23 years old. He was from Michigan.

When I rolled up on the scene, I set up a cordon. I called in the battalion QRF. And I looked at Adam's body. Adam was missing his left arm. On his left arm he'd worn his dad's watch from Vietnam and his wedding ring. He'd gotten married just before he deployed. The body parts blasted off the Iraqis on the bus had been stacked into a pile, and I spent an hour going through the arms and legs looking for Adam's arm. And finally, I just couldn't do it anymore. I couldn't find his arm. We bagged what we could find of Adam's body and sent him home.

That's the second time I've ever talked about it.

Adam's death was the worst for me.

WHEN WE CAME BACK HOME, WE WERE FUCKED UP. WE WERE REALLY FUCKED UP. My platoon was the worst. One of my guys got into an argument with his wife, pulled out his handgun, shot her dog. Another guy tried to commit suicide in the barracks. I had daily occurrences of guys beating their wives. Daily occurrences of drunk driving. A lot of drug abuse.

We were fresh in the war at that time, and the Army didn't care about PTSD or the effects of a year of intense urban combat. We were expected to come home, train, and go back out again a year later.

I had taken over as company commander, and I was supposed to charge my guys with Article 15 offenses for drunk driving and all the rest. These guys that I just went through hell with, I was their leader in combat, and now we're back in peacetime and I'm supposed to prosecute them for crimes against the Uniform Code of Military Justice. It was bullshit. I wouldn't do it.

I was really angry all the time. Really numb too. My first clue that I had problems should've been when I went to buy a truck with my wife. We negotiate with the salesman, agree on a price, but when we go to sign the papers, the price magically goes up an extra $10,000, just like the bad clichés about car salesmen. I flip the table, jump on him, and start choking him out. "You fucking lied to me, you son of a bitch!" I yelled in his face. "You're no better than a fucking Iraqi." My wife grabbed me. "Hey, hey, hey. You're not in Iraq," she says. "Calm down. Calm down. You go take a walk." She smoothed things over, and when I got back, I signed the papers as the car salesman looked on warily.

I saw myself as normal. I figured that's how to deal with somebody who lies to me, because that's how I dealt with Iraqis. But it wasn't normal, it wasn't normal at all.

They brought in a new captain to take over as company commander. He started to prosecute my guys, and I got into a fistfight with him one night. The next day I found myself at battalion headquarters with a combat officer who'd been in the shit and understood what I was going through. "Eller, I'm going to put you in charge of our airborne operations," he said. "Then you're going to Special Forces. Just get out of this place. You'll only burn up if you stay here."

EVERYTHING AROUND US IS ALIVE. EVERYTHING HAS A SPIRIT. I'VE SEEN TOO MANY THINGS IN THIS WORLD that I can only attribute to having my ancestors watch out for me. I left the reservation when I was young enough that I didn't get really wrapped up in the culture aside from understanding who my ancestors were and understanding that they'll always be with me.

I can count at least six times I should've died in Baghdad, and all I can say is that an ancestor was looking out for me. I shot the triggerman for an IED wired to explode mere feet from where I stood. If I hadn't made that split-second decision, I wouldn't be here. One time we entered a doorway during a raid, and a guy comes down the stairs and snatches the weapon out of the hands of the guy in front of me. If I hadn't had my weapon up and aimed where his head appeared, I wouldn't be here. A sniper missed me by three inches. If the wind hadn't been blowing the right way, the bullet would have hit me in the face. There's so many things that I can't attribute to just good luck. Your ancestors are with you.

But that's about the only thing I draw from my heritage. My biological father is full-blood Cherokee, my mom is half. My biological father is a reservation Indian. I remember many things about him. I remember him coming home drunk all the time. Remember him beating our family. Remember him beating me. The only thing I can thank him for is that he prepared me for a hard life in the military. Other than that, he was a waste of human flesh. He was in my life until I was five, and then he was in and out of my life until I was ten. And then, no more. Where he is now, I don't know. Don't fucking care. Not worth the breath.

My dad is white as can be. He's been my dad since I was five. I have a dad, and he's a good man. That's all that matters.

I SPENT A YEAR AND A HALF WITH SPECIAL FORCES IN BURKINA FASO, MALI, ALGERIA AND OTHER PLACES IN AFRICA. I was home for ten days, then sent for another year-long tour to Nigeria to collect intelligence on Al-Qaeda.

My company commander and a chaplain picked me up from the airport when I got back from my third tour. I'd been gone two and a half years that were more stressful than my time in Iraq. You could trust no one. I had almost been kidnapped three times. I had seen corruption in the American military that deeply disturbed me.

I asked why my wife and kids weren't picking me up. The chaplain and my commander said nothing. They drove me to my house. It was dark. The power had been turned off. Everything was gone. I knew exactly what was going on.

I called up my buddy, a weapons sergeant from 3rd Special Forces Group, and he brought over a couple bottles of Jack Daniels. I got drunk for the next year. I started riding a motorcycle and drinking at biker bars, basically being self-destructive. I went through a horrible divorce. I got moved up to U.S. Army Special Operations Command staff, but I didn't really have a job. I was a captain in a colonel's world. The colonel who was in charge of me came up to me a few days after I got there.

"You got a cellphone?" he asked.

"Yeah."

"Okay. You call me, let me know you're alive every morning."

"All right."

"Other than that, don't get killed."

"All right, sir."

I TOOK A LOT OF LIVES IN IRAQ. A LOT. THAT PART DOESN'T BOTHER ME, HONESTLY. IT'S THE REASONS WHY. When I was there I could justify it. Now, after seeing the corruption and the politics involved, that's the part that bothers me. You're just a cog in the moneymaking machine. That's all you are.

We're not at war because we're saving the world from some terrorist bogeyman. Our government is not fighting a war on foreign soil to prevent war from coming here. We're doing it to make money for a small percentage of the population. We're doing it so that the war industry and the contractors who provide the services for the military make money. Corporate America hires lobbyists to go to our congressmen and senators and bribe them to deploy another 20,000 soldiers to Iraq because suddenly ISIS is the new threat. The media pump out stories on ISIS. Then our congressmen and senators justify what they're doing. "Oh, look. ISIS is a big threat. We gotta take care of them, because soon they'll be over here." But ISIS is not a threat to us. They're a threat to Baghdad. Baghdad does nothing for us, so why are we over there again?

Fact is, we don't have a big global threat against us. I've been around the world. Yeah, people don't like us, but people don't like us because we prop up dictators and say that we're supporting democracy. People don't like us because our corporations take their natural resources and destroy their land and don't provide for their people. That's why people don't like us.

If the average American would stop for one second and realize the vicious cycle that is being perpetuated on us, they could vote in place a government that would stop the lobbyists and special interest groups and the corporations. We would have massive change. But the American public cares more about what's on TV and Kim Kardashian's big ass and whether their McDonald's will be bringing back the McRib.

War is not good versus evil. It's not good guy versus bad guy. It's not America versus terrorists. War's not glamorous. It's about making money. That's all it is.

I HAVE ONE FRACTURED VERTEBRA AND SIX HERNIATED DISCS IN MY BACK FROM BEING BLOWN UP. I HAVE HEARING LOSS IN MY LEFT EAR. I have nerve damage on my left leg. They said I likely had a TBI, and I said, "Yeah, probably." They said I had enough PTSD to qualify for 75 percent disability. I said, "I did a lot."

Combat isn't all running and gunning, getting blown up, and shooting people. It is 23 hours of sheer fucking boredom, 30 minutes of sheer panic, and 30 minutes of adrenaline rush. And 90 percent of your day is not wondering how you're going to survive but *how am I going to get through the day doing the same fucking thing over and over and over again.* Chow hall, get my gear, get on my truck, go out into sector, drive the same roads, see the same guys, get shot at in the same place. Go back to base, get some sleep, get up, get some chow hall, get my gear on, go into the sector, drive the same road, see the same guys, get shot at for a little bit. All over again. The same thing. Every day.

The reality of war is that it's not the big, glorious bullshit you see in the movies. The whole *American Sniper* thing? That guy is full of shit. *So full of shit.*

WE'VE LOST A LOT OF GUYS SINCE OUR TOUR IN BAGHDAD. STEVE JENNINGS, A GOOD FRIEND OF MINE, ONE OF MY BEST SOLDIERS from day one, committed suicide about four years ago. He had watched one of the Iraqi Army first sergeants get decapitated, and that really shook Steve up. He had a bad knee from getting blown up in a mortar incident. He went to the VA and got hooked on pain meds. I palled around with him on Veterans Day, and about two weeks later, Steve ran out of pain pills over a weekend, got super depressed, and put a gun in his mouth and blew his head off.

That was the second guy in less than a year we lost to suicide. A guy named White Tree hung himself. Another guy, someone I love to death, is so strung out on drugs right now. He just doesn't want to remember all the shit and how bad the tour was. All these guys who have issues—that was their only tour. One year in Iraq.

I'm 41 years old and starting all over again. I feel like the ultimate failure. There's times I feel like I really fucked up my life. And yeah, there's times when I wonder if it'd be a lot easier if I just wasn't around. But it passes. You keep moving on. You suck it up. You drive on. Life of the infantryman.

It could always be worse. That's the only thing keeping me driving on. *Per ardua ad alta.* Through hardships to heights. That's the motto you have to keep.

At two in the morning, I'm wide awake. It doesn't matter if I have to be up at 5 a.m. or if I can sleep in 'til whenever, every morning I wake up at 2 a.m. The shitty part is, after I wake up at two o'clock in the morning, all I do is think. And I think and think and think for hours. Combat and the tours in Africa reset my body clock. In combat you launch raids and make your hits between midnight and three in the morning, when the human body just shuts down. The enemy is usually falling asleep, so that's when you want to hit them. That's also when you want to be on guard to prevent from getting hit. So as a leader, I'd always be up at two o'clock in the morning, either doing a raid, or walking around and making sure my guys were awake in our patrol base. Checking security. Making sure people weren't sneaking up on us.

I take muscle relaxers at night to try and fall asleep. Funny thing is, the muscle relaxers I take will knock a normal person out for 12 hours. I still wake up at two in the morning. They had me on a really heavy one for two years. And I told them, "It just makes me numb, I can't do anything." I had to come off of them because I couldn't think.

I take a lot of antidepressants, too. They keep the edge off, keep me mellow. Without them, I'll notice myself going into a depression, which builds into anger, which then builds into worse depression because I'm bummed out that I'm angry all the time. And then you start thinking, "Well, you know, maybe it would be better if I was not here." It takes a lot to come back out of that. When you're at that point, what do you do? Do you go back to drinking? Do you go back to thinking about ending it all? Do you go back to thinking it's better in the Army? All those thoughts go through your head. So you take the antidepressants to keep the demons inside. There's a little lockbox down there.

The first time I watched *The Avengers* with my kids, they wanted to assign everyone a character, like kids do. Hannah wants to be Captain America, Emma wants to be the Scarlet Witch. You know what character they assigned me? They said I was The Hulk. Bruce Banner, who's all mellow and calm and, out of the blue, blows up and becomes The Hulk. There's a line in the movie when they ask Bruce Banner how he gets angry so fast. And Bruce Banner says, "My secret? I'm *always* angry."

"Yeah, that's you, Dad," Hannah says.

A YEAR AFTER MY LAST TOUR IN AFRICA, I RESIGNED MY COMMISSION AND LEFT THE U.S. ARMY. I got hired on with a firefighting department as a paramedic. After a couple of years of that, I discovered it was just as bad a mentality as when I was in combat. Eighty percent of your calls as a firefighter are medical calls, and 95 percent of those are cardiac arrests. So every day I'm doing 30 minutes of chest compressions on a dead guy. I stop looking at him as a patient and regard him as a cadaver, and I start making morbid jokes. I realized I was going to self-implode again.

So I applied to a master's in education program to become a high school science teacher. Both my parents are retired high school science teachers.

"You sure you want to do this?" my dad asked.

"Yeah, Dad, I think I do."

"You sure? Because kids are kind of a pain in the ass."

"Look, on my worst day, nobody dies. I can handle a pain in the ass."

I love being a teacher. I love it. I hope some of my students come away with the ability to just think *logically* about things. That's what I want. I hope they look at the world and they say, "Wait a second. Why are we putting in an oil pipeline and drilling into a wildlife refuge in Alaska? Why are we so worried about what OPEC says? Why are we fracking and ruining our groundwater?" I want them to ask those questions. I want them to find out.

I wear long-sleeve shirts because my tattoos are too much of a distraction. I learned that one day when it was hot in the classroom and I took off my sweatshirt. I was wearing short sleeves underneath. The topic of discussion abruptly shifted from ecosystems and the water cycle to *Oh my God, Mr. Eller has tattoos*. For six months, I had only been Mr. Eller in shirt and tie, the teacher who taught them all this stuff about science. Now the kids could only fixate on my tattoos.

"Why you got that tattoo?"

"That's our unofficial motto from Third Special Forces Group."

"What?"

"I was in the Army."

"You were in the Army? What'd you do in the Army?"

"A lot of things. Okay, let's get back to what we were talking about." I start sketching out the rain and evaporation cycle on the chalkboard.

Then, of course, the dumb kid in the back. "Did you kill people?"

They're all waiting for me to answer. I figure I can deflect them, use this to teach them some geography, teach them some science. "I did my job. But what I did over there was see a lot of different ecosystems. Can you imagine what the ecosystem in Baghdad looked like? Or what the ecosystem of Abujah, Nigeria, looked like? All the different types of organisms I saw?"

I try and bring them back to what we're supposed to be doing, but they don't stop. They keep looking at the tattoos and asking about them. They keep asking what I did when I was a soldier in the Army.

I look at them. They're all sitting there, looking at me. I laugh, but it's not a funny laugh. "Okay, guys. What do you think I did? I wasn't a truck driver. I wasn't some cook. I wasn't some pack clerk who got to stay behind the lines. I wasn't some mechanic who worked on engines all day. My job was to destroy the enemy. And I was really good at it. I was really, really good at it."

"We hear about 'civilian casualties' on TV. Yeah, those people are dead, we think. Yeah, that sucks. But there's no emotional understanding of those deaths and horrible injuries. I want people to know what it feels like to witness the deaths of children and innocent civilians."

FIREFLY

EMMANUEL WRIGHT[1]

WE CROSSED THE BORDER FROM KUWAIT ON THE TWENTIETH OF APRIL, THE TIP OF THE SPEAR. We took some small arms fire. "Jesus Christ. Jesus Christ," my driver kept saying. "Jesus Christ, we're gonna die." I was in a Humvee that was our ambulance. I was a corpsman. I was "Doc," and I was in charge of 22 other corpsmen. Our first casualty was a laceration to a guy's forehead. The Humvee jolted violently—we slammed into a sand dune or crashed into another Humvee, I only remember a big impact—but we drove relentlessly on. The next morning, as daylight came, hordes of Iraqis walked towards us waving white rags, trying to surrender. We roared past them towards Baghdad. It was like, *Fuck you guys*.

We paused for a couple of hours. I needed to sew up the Marine's forehead, so I went to grab some sutures. One of the

[1]The author of this story requested that his name not be published. This is a pseudonym.

corpsmen was sleeping with his mouth open, and it looked like his mouth was filled with blackberries. "Dead Man," I said—we all had nicknames, and his was "Dead Man"—"Dude, where'd you get those fucking blackberries?" He's sleeping and doesn't answer, so I lean in for a closer look, and I see that his mouth is coated with flies.

That was Iraq. Blood and flies and wild dogs.

We pushed north nonstop for almost six weeks. Our driver was at the steering wheel for three days straight with no sleep. We'd drive into an ambush, return fire, and just push right through into another one. We'd secure a town. We secured gas and oil plants. North to Baghdad, leapfrogging with other units.

The Republican Guard and the Iraqi Army put up a little fight before evaporating away. Foreign fighters shot at us, too, young men from Syria and elsewhere, jihadists who wanted to fuck with Americans and maybe find martyrdom or manhood with a gun in their hand. The Fedayeen were a special unit loyal to Saddam and wore black pajamas and Darth Vader helmets and were vicious. The word on the street was that the helmets were supposed to be scary and intimidating. We heard that Saddam's son Uday, who commanded the Fedayeen, was a big fan of *Star Wars*.

A few times the enemy lobbed artillery on us. *BABOOM BABOOM BABOOM*. Massive concussions. And what are you going to do? Run around? You're more likely to get hit if you do that than just sit there. So you just lay in your fighting hole, the shallow graves we dug every time we stopped, and tried not to think about it. I was sleeping the second time they hit us with artillery. The first explosion woke me up. But after the next shell landed, I went back to sleep. In my dreams I heard *baboom ... baboom...ba-BOOM*, and then someone shouts *Gas! Gas! Gas!* and we're shitting our pants. I jump up and start going fucking crazy. Everyone's pulling on their MOPP suits, those hot and rubbery full-body suits and gas masks that protect you from chemical or biological weapons. But someone took my MOPP boots, so my suit was worthless, and I was shaking. I was afraid—this sounds stupid—but I was afraid my dick was going to drop off. I know mustard gas and nerve agents won't make your dick drop off, but I felt that I might be writhing as my internal organs melted, or choking as my lungs frothed with yellow bile, but if my dick dropped off, that would be really bad.

The U.S. Air Force bombed us once, the bastards. Infrared blinkers mounted on top of our vehicles were supposed to let the jets sort friendly troops from the enemy at night. We must have looked like a field of Christmas trees from up in the air, blinking like crazy. But for whatever reason, they bombed us. You hear the screams from the jets, and then there's a moment of quiet. And the next instant, a massive wall of flames and heat erupts. Then another scream of a jet, another moment of uneasy calm, and an explosion fills the sky with a cloud of fire. But no one got hurt.

Some days later, we're ordered to secure the Hantush Airfield. Golf Company makes first contact. A gunnery sergeant is hit in the temple by a sniper and killed. His men lay his body on the deck of a half-track vehicle. His skin was white. The Marines stood frozen in a circle around him, their eyes huge, staring at him. As we carried his body down Iraq's Highway 1, gunfire crackled all around, and this time I thought my ass was going to be shot off—I literally thought I was going to get my ass blown off. Then we learn our First Sergeant has been shot through his forearm on one side, and his bicep and tricep on the other. This guy was badass, too. First Gulf War vet, had served with the First Recon Marines. So we lost a gunnery sergeant and our First Sergeant in that one engagement. And then, after we secure the airfield, we're ordered to retreat. We listened to the BBC during the whole engagement, and they're reporting that the Republican Guard kicked our ass. As we drove away, Iraqis stood on the side of the road, clapping, as if to say, *Go on, get out of here.*

One night, as we drove north of Baghdad—we had pushed around from the east, and then moved south towards the city—a light floats by above me. It arcs overhead, and it's beautiful, this glimmer in the night. A *firefly*, I think. Wonder of wonders, a *firefly*.

But then I realize, of course, it's not a firefly, it can't be. This is war. It's the glow of a tracer round fired from an Iraqi AK-47. I shout, "Contact left!" and word goes down the whole convoy instantly and everyone is just fucking firing, sending hundreds upon hundreds of bullets into the darkness. One guy empties the clip on his M16 and then pulls out his 9 mm handgun and empties that too. I grab my M16 from the Humvee and pop up again and aim the barrel into the darkness, but I just couldn't do it. I couldn't get myself to shoot. And that was it. We stopped firing. Silence. We drive on in the darkness. We didn't know where that round came from, or where any of our rounds went. We didn't know who shot at us, or why, or if we had killed a Fedayeen or a Republican Guard or an Iraqi farmer sleeping in his bed. We didn't know what the fuck.

I didn't fire a round during the entire invasion. I felt strongly about my capacity as a healer. I focused on medicine. I made sure I performed my duties as a corpsman. A few times I could have, and probably should have, pulled the trigger. But I never did.

AFTER THE SANDSTORM CAME THE RAIN. The rain fell on the dust that coated our Humvees, our combat boots, our MREs, our uniforms, our helmets, our sleeping bags, our radios, our M16s and M4s, our hair and our skin. Everything was red, everything caked with rust-colored clay. The battalion was running a checkpoint. An Iraqi civilian vehicle approaches. They don't slow down. I don't know why—the Iraqis just kept running checkpoints. Most of the times when a vehicle was shot up at a checkpoint there was no suicide bomber, no guns pointing at us, but the orders were to fire if a car didn't stop, and keep shooting until it did. So Echo Company lights them up. By the time I get there with my medical kit, they've pulled three bloody Iraqis out of the truck. The windshield is blasted away, the vehicle shot through. One of the Iraqis is still alive. He's an older man, shot through both forearms and both legs. There's also a bullet wound in his chest, but amazingly none of the wounds are life-threatening. The other two men, one older and one younger, are dead. The younger man had been a member of the Iraqi National Guard, and the other men were his uncles. They had snatched him from his unit, forced him to desert, and were racing to take him away from the war, to save him from getting killed by the Americans. He made it as far as an American checkpoint.

Everyone was afraid. The civilians were afraid of the Marines.

The Iraqi National Guard were afraid of dying in a pathetic war against American soldiers bristling with firepower. The Iraqi military guys were afraid that if they deserted, Saddam's Fedayeen would find them and kill them, and kill their families too. The Marines weren't afraid, but they sure as hell weren't letting any cars run through checkpoints.

I spent most of my time as a medic cleaning up civilians caught in the crossfire of firefights and the destruction radii of bombs. Firefights in schools and public squares, where the enemy seemed to engage us. I didn't clean up the dead bodies, I tried to sew up the maimed and wounded.

I didn't spend much time treating Marines. Our battalion experienced only a handful of wounded and two KIAs during the invasion. From our perspective, the losses were relatively light.

FARMS AND APARTMENT BLOCKS AND DUN-COLORED STREETS. SMALL ARMS FIRE. The Marines are clearing houses, kicking in doors, weapons shouldered. I'm in an Iraqi house and there's a toilet. And I had to go so bad. So I figure, fuck, there's an actual toilet, we cleared the homes, everything's secured. It's safe. And as soon as I sit down, the whole house gets lit up. The house is being pelted with bullets, puffs of dust everywhere and glass shattering and bits of concrete spraying. But I sit there, shitting, because I couldn't help it. The firing pauses and I finish, and when I go outside the Marines are lighting up an eight-story building. In one window there's a silhouette of a man. I don't know what he was doing in there, but the Marines fire on him. Another man appears in a field near the building, and one of the Marines fires a TOW missile, a guided anti-tank round, and blows the dude up.

One second he's there, the next second he's not. He's just *gone*. Everyone is cheering *yeah, super awesome*, and off to the side are more homes and Iraqi children, men and women. They're watching everything going on. Mortars are dropping randomly, but whoever is firing them at us doesn't know what they're doing. They're not aiming very well. The mortars are popping up in the air and off away from us, and we're laughing. We're laughing at how the Iraqi Army sucks so bad.

SOMETIMES THEY CAME TO US, THE SICK, THE INJURED. A FATHER CARRIED A CHILD, A WOMAN HELD AN INFANT WRAPPED IN BLANKETS. "Mister, you give?" They pointed to their heads. They wanted medicine or a doctor or a miracle. People tried to pawn off sick babies on us. Or their daughters. People would show up with holes in their bodies, broken bones, injuries from car wrecks. Often we had to turn our backs, because we didn't have enough medical resources for everybody. The Marines were the priority.

An Iraqi man drives up with bullet wounds in his back. He wasn't in combat, he was in the wrong place at the wrong time, he didn't know what to do after being shot up, so he drives up to us in his truck full of bullet holes. And he was hit. Fifteen times. The rounds went through two layers of metal through the truck and the bullet wounds are all relatively shallow, and he's not having difficulty breathing. I give him some Motrin and bandage him up and he drives off.

A father is driving a pickup truck full of people. He gets too close to the convoy, and the Marine shoots. The Marine is following orders by shooting, and the Marine is shooting because he will do anything to protect his brother Marines. The Marine is a good shot. The shot goes directly through the driver's throat. It kills him instantly. The truck veers off the road and crashes several feet into the field below.

I go to treat the occupants. The body of the driver is laying on the ground. The passenger's face is cut up from the shattered windshield. I'm sewing him up. The people who'd been in the bed of the truck are farmhands, and they're sitting on the side of the road above the wrecked truck. There's a young boy among them. One of the Iraqis speaks English. "What's going on?" he asks. "How's the driver?" I tell him the driver is dead. The young boy is sitting right next to him, and as soon as I say this—the boy's face contorts in an unimaginable way. So full of grief. I've never seen a face like that before. The boy was the driver's son. The son had watched his father die.

The guy who speaks English tells us that the man's daughter tried and tried to stop her father from leaving the house that day. She did everything she could to make him stay, because she was worried. Worried about the danger in Iraq. But he needed to provide for their family, to work, to get money for food. So he went to work.

We left him there next to the shattered pickup by the side of the road. We left the passengers alone to carry him home.

PASSING BY A SMOLDERING IRAQI TANK AS IT POPPED AND CRACKLED AS AMMO COOKED OFF, or fuel erupted, or a grenade ignited in the flames... a truck blasted on its side, a man chained by his hands to the axles, screaming at us... the bombed wrecks of cars and trucks and tanks in a farm field, black smoke pouring skyward... Marines smoking Marlboros and joking and taking bets as they watch a donkey mount two female donkeys, for hours on end, in a fenced corral...

We paused in an area that had been a garbage dump. Plastic bags, cans, ratty clothes, the waste of the households of ordinary Iraqis compacted into the soil. We parked the Humvees and half-tracks and five-ton trucks, and we dug our fighting holes into the dirt and the garbage. We had had a long night before, the firefight at the Hantush airfield, a Marine dead with a bullet to the temple, our First Sergeant shot through his arms, the demoralizing retreat. We went to sleep on the garbage and one of the Marines digs up the corpse of an infant. It had been buried in the dump, in the garbage. There were no markings of a grave site, just the decomposed remains of a baby.

We were constantly surrounded by death. Everywhere were bloated bodies and freshly killed corpses and pools of dark blood and flies and wild dogs, every single day, until the fall of Baghdad.

WE WERE ENCAMPED SOMEWHERE IN THE MIDDLE OF IRAQ. I HAD WALKED OFF INTO THE DESERT TO RELIEVE MYSELF. And I came upon her. She was a child maybe ten years old. She was all alone, and she was badly burned. From what, I don't know. I thought at first that I could treat her and help her. She kept saying *ma'an*, the Arab word for water. *Ma'an. Ma'an. Ma'an.* I didn't understand— I thought she was saying *Why? Why?* Why are you doing that, I thought, why don't you shut up? *Ma'an. Ma'an. Ma'an.* Her lips were burned. I tried to perform a cutdown on her, when you directly access a vein by cutting through the skin and isolating it and inserting a catheter into the blood vessel. *Ma'an. Ma'an.* Her skin was like leather, it was so burned. I couldn't find the vein.

And I was afraid... I was afraid of causing her more harm... I was afraid of being a fraud, afraid I didn't know what I was doing. *Ma'an. Ma'an.* I wanted her to shut up. I didn't want to hurt her anymore. *Ma'an. Ma'an.* I gave her morphine as she looked at me and I stayed there with her and watched her until she died.

AFTER THE FALL OF BAGHDAD, WE WERE SENT TO THE SOUTH OF IRAQ. Fox Company was stationed in Rumaitha, garrisoned in a soccer stadium. Golf and Echo were barracked in a train station in a town called Samawah.

Major combat operations had ended. Our priorities were shifted. We conducted missions to root out lingering Republican Guard elements or search for someone on our deck of cards. Some Marines were tasked with digging up the mass graves of Kuwaitis or Kurds massacred in the First Gulf War and cataloguing the remains. They exhumed rotted, desiccated bodies for months.

One of the battalion surgeons was removed from duty after he was caught in a sex act with another corpsman. Our other battalion surgeon was drained of his will to perform medicine by the heat and the dust and the barbarism of being a doctor in a war. He refused to treat Iraqis. That left it up to the corpsmen, who did procedures they couldn't legally do in the U.S.

We had spent six weeks turning our back on the civilians, but I still wanted to believe in Iraqi freedom. Iraqis invited me into their homes, shared their meals with me. Most of them labored just to get clean drinking water. I wanted to help people. I still wanted to make a difference.

So I treated Iraqi prisoners and practiced medicine in the hospitals. Iraq had had one of the most robust medical infrastructures in the Middle East, but after the sanctions from the First Gulf War, medical care went down the tubes. The Republican Guard facilities were top notch, but hospitals for ordinary people were filthy and crowded. Cigarette butts on the floor. Stinking toilets. No equipment, no drugs, no sutures or bandages or plaster for mending broken bones. The wards were crammed with the sick and injured. I went to an Iraqi hospital, and a single doctor served the entire hospital on any given night. I wondered if I knew more about medicine than he did. One time he grabbed a laryngoscope out of my hand—that's used to open up the esophagus, so you can insert a tube down the airway—but he tried to use it to look in someone's ear. Maybe he'd lost his mind. Maybe all the death and suffering was slowly driving him mad.

AUGUST. THE BATTALION REDEPLOYED BACK TO SOUTHERN CALIFORNIA. Iraq had been brown and dirty-white and orange, and smelled of shit and diesel smoke and death. On the I-5 corridor through San Diego, billboards for Disneyland, Dunkin' Donuts, women's lingerie, 1-800 diet plan, Wonder Bread, lawyers that get you off for drunk driving, gun shows, abortion services. Flashing neon lights, boulevards strung with traffic lights. Green trees, green lawns. I go to the grocery store and I see someone filling two carts full of shit. A stack of fucking frozen foods. I didn't know what to do.

I was back as a corpsman at the Naval Hospital in San Diego and I had a difficult time regulating my responses at work. Everything was intensely serious to me, a matter of life or death. I don't know just how I was acting with my colleagues, all I know is that I was no longer the person I had been. All I know is that the nurses and doctors looked at me strangely. All I know is that I couldn't make sense of people anymore, that life had become incomprehensible, and that the dead children of Iraq haunted the hallways and the examination rooms, the sidewalks of San Diego, the streets and highways, the bars and restaurants, the apartments and houses, and my own bedroom. All I know is that, at some point, I was admitted without my consent to the psych ward at Balboa Naval Hospital in San Diego. I had been back from Iraq for four months.

I was removed from the battalion, and I was officially retired from the military for PTSD and depression. I lost my profession. I lost everything. I was hospitalized again because I started cutting myself. I had no idea what was going on. I hated my wife, and I was estranged from my daughters. I hated fucking George Bush, and I hated all the flag-waving patriots who wanted vengeance for September 11 and clamored for war against the Arabs. I hated them because so many people died for no reason at all.

I had brought her home with me. I had adopted her, the young Iraqi girl I had found, the girl who was terribly burned, the child I watched die. In my wounded heart, she supplanted my own daughters, and she became my only daughter for a long time. I created a ceremony finally to bury her and to say what I needed to say. I laid her to rest in a sacred place, where she deserved to be, this beautiful child, where she needed to be. But my heart still hurts.

"You don't know someone until you go to war with them. At first you can't tell what they're made of. But you will find out. You will see their true colors."

THERE'S NO REASON TO CRY

ZONG HER

I arrive at Kandahar Airfield, Afghanistan, at the beginning of summer. the sun is painfully bright. The heat is exhausting. Sweat runs down your face and into your eyes. Sweat rolls down your back, your stomach, arms. Sweat trickles between your breasts. Sweat rolls down your butt cheeks, sweat beads on your knuckles. You discover sweat glands you didn't know you had. I ride my bike six miles from work to my room with a bottle of frozen water. By the time I arrive, it's melted. I once was amazed when the thermometer hit 125 degrees. After a while, I stop paying attention.

Red dust covers the mountains, dust as fine as flour, dust that blows through the base and penetrates the cracks of the buildings and alights on everything. Next to the airfield is a citadel everyone calls the "Taliban's Last Stand." The center of the fortress is shattered from U.S. airstrikes in the weeks after

September 11. The concrete is pocked with bullet and shrapnel holes. The walls are plastered with posters showing pictures of corpses. They're to remind us the Taliban are real and they are trying to kill us.

There are no bathrooms in the buildings. There is no sewer system. When they owned this place, the Taliban shit and pissed outside. That's how they do it in this part of the world. We use port-a-potties now. Third World workers roam the base with tanker trucks that suck up the poop and dump it in a pond. The sewage pond is in the middle of the base and was built by the Russians. It's filled with thirty years of human shit, bubbling away, and the smell is everywhere and it is hellish. Biohazard signs are posted every few hundred yards. Depending on the wind, there are times the stench burns in your chest. I stock up on everything I can to combat it: perfume, incense, candles, body spray. When I arrive at my office, I spray a sweet aroma around my desk. I start thinking up gruesome scenarios I would rather endure than to fall into the sewage pond. I stop. It's depraved.

I'm a soldier in the U.S. Army on a NATO airbase. I coordinate trucks and aircraft and freight. I put labels on containers and radio frequency tags on equipment and type up flight manifests. I keep the computers operating in eight offices. I'm also assigned to manage the drug tests, which means I collect urine sample kits. It does *not* mean I watch soldiers piss.

The base feels like the alien ghetto of *District 9*, or the grimy underground of *The Matrix*, or the filthy survivalism of *The Walking Dead*. It's overcrowded. Everything is made of metal and wires. I live with my battle buddy in a steel shipping container 20 feet long and eight feet wide. I ride my bike to work every day, past the sewage pond and the Afghan National Army compound. I wear fatigues, combat boots, and a bike helmet. I wear goggles. My mouth is wrapped with cloth to keep out the sand and dust. Only my hands and nose are exposed. As I ride by, I feel the stares of the men.

We barter for everything. At one point, we have no laundry detergent on the entire base. Or no toothpaste. Or no gum. If you need something, you have to barter for it. If you don't have bartering skills, you better know someone who does. Otherwise you're not getting what you need. You want it, you make it. Or find someone who can.

One evening I'm biking between the concertina wire and steel shipping containers. As I take a turn, the bike's handlebars swivel eerily. The handlebars come loose and flop uselessly. I slam into a cement barrier so hard it knocks me out. When I come to, I'm bleeding from my face and lip. I've cracked my bike helmet and snapped my sunglasses in half. It's 6:30 at night, and I'm on the way to teach my yoga class on base. *There's no reason to cry*, I think. There's no reason not to go teach the class, either. I have nothing else to do except sit in my steel shipping container. So I daub the blood from my face and go teach yoga. As I stretch before we start, I notice a rip in my pants and blood seeping through by my knee.

The class is packed, as usual—maybe 80 people. Soldiers and sailors and Marines and civilian contractors follow my orders: *Okay, everyone, now do crescent lunge.* The class places one knee forward and sweeps their other leg back, sinking deeply into a martial arts fighting stance. *Okay. Now side plank. Like this.* I look to see if everyone has good form. *Okay, dolphin pose. Okay, corpse pose now.* In the back of the room are the bearded guys who don't talk much. The muscles in their arms ripple during the poses, and they move like cats. Americans with beards are probably Special Ops guys, silent killers who go out into the desert at night. But you don't ask, so you don't really know.

I AM A DAUGHTER OF THE VIETNAM WAR. MY PARENTS ARE HMONG PEOPLE WHO WERE BORN IN THE MOUNTAINS OF LAOS. The CIA gave money and arms to the Hmong to fight the Viet Cong. One of my grandfathers died in the war. Another grandfather was a captain in the Army of the Republic of Vietnam. After the U.S. left, the Hmong were massacred by the new regime. My parents fled as war refugees to Thailand, where I was born. They immigrated to the States when I was five years old. My dad eventually returned to Laos.

I grew up a typical American kid. Cheerleading. Campfire Girls. Volunteering at the food bank. I knew virtually nothing about the military. I didn't even know my grandfather had been a soldier. But my best friend Mandy proposed we join the military. I had never thought about it, not even once, but she and I enlisted together in the Army Reserves at the end of summer. "You'll never be going to war," the recruiter said when I signed the paperwork. "You'll just be a reservist." It was a typical recruiter's tactic.

Less than a month later, on September 11, the planes crashed into the Twin Towers and the Pentagon. Mandy dropped out of the military, but I decided to stay in. I had no idea what I was doing, but I had signed up for it. I was 18 years old. I went to boot camp to become a weekend warrior in the Army Reserves.

I learned how to drill and march and salute. I learned to keep my hair pinned up. I became an expert at push-ups.

Shortly after the invasion of Iraq, I was pulled out of my sophomore year of college. With the country at war, reservists were put on active duty. They told us we'd be deploying to Fort Drum in upstate New York. The guys in the reserve unit were all mad—they were keen to go to Iraq. They were *gung ho*. They liked watching *Full Metal Jacket*. They called me "Woman Nazi" and "Ms. Uber Liberal." I had told very few people I was a soldier, not even my father, but I called him up when the orders came to deploy to Fort Drum. Even though I wasn't headed to Iraq, he was very upset.

"Can't you somehow get out?" he asked.

"No, Dad, I can't."

My dad knew what war was about. So did my grandfather, who was very worried about me. He knew all about guerilla warfare from the war in Vietnam. He did not want me seeing the things he saw, doing the things he had to do. He did not want to bury his granddaughter.

I spent two years at Fort Drum, one of many thousands of soldiers on base. My job was transportation logistics. Thousands upon thousands of troops flowed through Fort Drum on the way to Iraq and Afghanistan, but I didn't get to know any of them. I put up a wall around myself. I tried hard to ignore the truth that each of them was going to war. I worked in an office managed by civilians. We made sure each unit got its equipment over there— we ran the paperwork that filled containers, ships, and planes with pallets of MREs and tents and weapons and Humvees and five-ton trucks and everything else. I lived off-base. It was a small town in a rural area, and everywhere I went people stared at me because I'm Asian. A man approached me on the sidewalk. "Excuse me, do you know what time the Chinese restaurant opens?" he asks.

"No, sorry."

He repeats the question slowly and a little too loudly. I'm pretty sure he doesn't think I speak English. "The Chinese restaurant. IS—IT—OPEN?"

"I really don't know, sir. I don't even speak Chinese."

I was a good soldier for the first few years, then I began a love-and-hate relationship with the military. I was supposed to deploy again four times, but I always got out of it. I hadn't received certain trainings, I didn't get my security clearance. Finally I decided I had to shit or get off the pot. *Okay*, I told myself. *I'm going to take this seriously.* I had made up my mind. The military was going to be my career.

A week later, I received orders to report for training. I was going to Afghanistan.

SEXUAL ASSAULT CASES ARE ALL OVER THE NIGHTLY NEWS. A LIEUTENANT COLONEL IN THE AIR FORCE IS CHARGED WITH GROPING. An Army sergeant is caught videotaping female soldiers in the showers. Seventeen Air Force trainers are charged with rape or improper relations with female recruits at Lackland AFB. So many ugly headlines that year.

I was sent to Fort Hood in Texas for training to deploy to Kandahar. Morning drill. Weapons training. Cultural classes. Abruptly, command issues a new order. *Females*, until further notice you *will lock yourselves* in your barracks at 10 p.m. You *will remain* in your *locked* barracks until reveille.

They don't tell us why. They don't answer our questions. The next day my boyfriend calls me. "Did you hear about what's going on at Fort Hood?" he asks. "They just busted a prostitution ring there." A sergeant had been pimping out female soldiers to higher-ups for $200 a trick. Some of the girls were told to meet men at a La Quinta Inn. One of the johns drove a Hummer with Department of Defense decals on his license plates. The girls did it because they were broke and had kids. The guy pimping them had been in charge of the sexual assault prevention program on base.

So a prostitution ring had been busted on our base. But we women soldiers are ordered to lock ourselves in our own barracks. We're supposed to make ourselves prisoners.

Do not speak to any media, we are ordered. *Yeah, of course you guys don't want me talking to the media.* Better keep the media far away from me because I'll tell them it makes no sense to lock up the women. Aren't the men the ones committing the sex crimes?

We deployed to Afghanistan in a huge gray military C17 aircraft, twenty hours in the air. Thirty thousand feet over the Caspian Sea, a stop in Uzbekistan. We land in Kandahar dirty and disoriented. Fifteen minutes after I get on the ground another female soldier comes up to me. "Be careful," she says. "Rape is real here."

It's not a joke. It's not funny. We receive weekly reports of sexual assault on the base. Two last week. One the week before. Six cases of sexual assault this week. There's posters in the female bathrooms, posters on the blast walls. The posters give a date, time and location of the assault. Sketch drawings of the perps. Suspect had black hair. Suspect in military clothing. If you have any information, call this number. I rarely hear about arrests.

The base is crawling with men from armies around the world, most of them with guns and knives. Germans, Italian, Spaniards, British, Bulgarians, Turks, Czechs. Canadians, Norwegians, Romanians, Hungarians, Koreans. Afghan merchants selling rusty Soviet belt buckles and Taliban souvenirs. Rugs, sandals, DVDs. Kebabs, doughnuts, pizza. It's an uncivilized city, a rat maze of blast walls and shipping containers. There are secret groups and prostitutes and dark alleys.

My office is near the Afghan base, which looks like a half-deserted village, ramshackle, filthy and harsh. It's sketchy, but it's between my shipping container and office, so I bike through it, face and eyes covered, hiding my sex. One day, there's an eruption of gunfire on base. An Afghan soldier, possibly a Taliban fighter, has sprayed coalition troops with his AK-47. It's called a green-on-blue attack, one of dozens around the country. After the attack, the Afghan base is closed off. It becomes off limits.

You take precautions. Don't make eye contact. Walk into a store or chow hall, you keep your eyes forward. Don't give someone the wrong idea. Don't smile. Don't give someone an inkling that you're interested. Talk only to people you know. Be cautious all the time.

When you go out at night, bring an escort. Always carry your weapon.

I walk into a soldier's room and walk right back out. Pictures of vaginas on the walls. There's rules, but people don't follow them. There's a thin line, they claim. *Oh, that's not pornography.* But it is.

I hear rumors. A lieutenant colonel is hit on the head with

a frozen bottle of water as he showers. Unconscious, he's raped in the shower. Then the rumor changes—no, that couldn't have happened. You would've heard his screams. Now the rumor is the lieutenant colonel got caught having sex in the shower.

There's a lot of hearsay about sexual assault committed against men. Some people think there's more assaults of men than of women. There's an Afghani saying: Women are for having babies. Men are for pleasure.

A close friend I trained with was gang raped in Iraq. But she told me she never said the word *No*. And so, she thought, technically she could not have been raped. It took her almost three years to say something.

General Order No. 1 of the U.S. military is no sex in war zones. No intimate relationships permitted. You get caught with your lover, you're in trouble. I get it. *Sex and war don't mix.* But sexual assault and war seem to get along just fine.

And if you're raped, the rapist probably gets away with it.

The chill of winter. A layer of snow blankets the sand and dirt. I walk the two miles from my office to my room. I need the icy air to ease my heart, soothe my pain.

In less than seventeen days, I will be on my way back to the States.

My body aches. I have tumbled off the tailgates of trucks, top-heavy with helmet, body armor, and weapon, slamming hard to the ground. I have pedaled my bike fifteen hundred miles over rutted dirt roads. I have bruises on my legs. My back is sore, my ribs hurt, and my left arm tingles strangely. Pain has become my normal.

This place has broken me into pieces. I have slept for a year in a steel box. I have wiped red dust from my lips and eyelashes and ears, washed the dust from my hair. I fight every day not to allow the days to beat me down further. I talk to myself, searching for strength stored away in some dark corner of myself.

I had fallen in love.

He was a warm body that helped me stay sane and gave me some sweetness while I spent my life in a metal box and fought to keep alive. I appreciated what we had; it probably got me through the year. He told me he wanted to buy us a dreamhouse on the Pacific Ocean. But that was a fairy tale. I was nothing to him but a pretty trophy he hid on the shelf in the cupboard.

I was a good soldier. I did my job well. I volunteered to have my deployment extended, the only soldier in my unit. I'll stay another three months, I told them. I can deal with this. I wanted to stay so I'd be eligible for full education benefits. But my commander said, "It's not safe enough." And I thought: if any man asked to be extended, you'd never deny them because it wasn't *safe enough*.

I had worked my ass off, and I deserved an end-of-deployment evaluation that reflected how well I'd done my duty. But I was given a searing official evaluation before I left. Someone had written on the form that I was a "meat gazer." "Meat gazer" is crude Army slang for someone who administers the drug tests. It had no business on an official evaluation. It was bullshit. I went all the way up the chain to battalion headquarters to defend myself.

"You're not taking my evaluation seriously," I told battalion command. "This is sexual harassment."

My hands trembled in the meeting. I was challenging the status quo. But I was willing to risk everything to have my voice. If I kept quiet, I would hate myself forever. I had accepted many assaults on my dignity. There was no way I was going to accept any more, especially on my final evaluation. I knew I had to draw my line. There was nothing inside of me that would not revolt.

I stood up to them. I made them fix it.

My lover told me I would lose him if I stood up for myself. Screw it. I didn't care anymore. As I left battalion headquarters, he smirked at me from above, a thick sheet of bulletproof glass separating him and I. He claimed I betrayed him.

The alpha males, the "excellent soldiers," couldn't get things done at Kandahar. No one would work with them. They couldn't build relationships because they weren't kind to others. I got stuff done, because in that primitive, chaotic community, people only helped people they liked. People who were respectful and kind. That's what I had to offer—human kindness. That was my survival skill.

You don't know someone until you go to war with them. At first you can't tell what they're made of. But you will find out. You will see their true colors.

"Everything that I did over there, and everything that my soldiers did, was righteous and noble. I don't regret a bit of it. I'm blessed in that regard. I know a lot of veterans who were forced to make decisions that they regret."

OUR CAUSE WAS JUST

MIKE FARNUM

A YOUNG KURDISH LIEUTENANT TAKES US TO SEE THE MASS GRAVES. We are near the Roman ruins of Hatra in northern Iraq, close to the Syrian border. He walks us on top of a hill and points out lines of bulldozer scars on the desert below.

We pick through the mounds of dirt and pull out clumps of long, black hair. We find a onesie, the infant's outfit that snaps so you can change diapers. We find tattered clothing and buttons and shoes, fragments of human life. It's clear Sadaam's army had machine-gunned thousands of Kurdish civilians and bulldozed over their bodies.

The Kurdish lieutenant takes us to a nearby cave. We shine our tactical flashlights down a hole. Hundreds of human bones appear in the darkness. "Some of my family are in these graves," he says. "But I don't know where they are."

This isn't just about oil, I think. This is about genocide. This was a murderous regime. Human rights meant nothing to them. Saddam needed to be removed from power. The image of the baby's onesie burns in my memory. I'm haunted by that long, black hair of a young girl in a mass grave in the desert.

Now ISIS controls that part of Iraq where the bones of the Kurds lay heaped in mass graves. It's like we weren't even there. We didn't see it through. The same thing happened during the First Gulf War. I was in that war, too. Plumes of inky smoke poured off Kuwait's oil wells after Saddam set them ablaze, and we breathed noxious black air for weeks in southern Iraq. After we left, Saddam swept through and murdered them all.

I don't know if seeing it through is the right answer, either. But I know our cause was just.

H E HAD WAITED FOR US ON THE ROOF OF A THREE-STORY BUILDING. He held in his hands two wires attached to a motorcycle battery, and just as we passed over the bomb he'd planted, he touched the wires together.

The Stryker heaved ten feet off the ground and fell back to earth like a huge, dead beast. The blast tore the engine loose and ruptured the hydraulic hoses. Fuel poured from burst lines. Six of us were inside—my driver, my counterintelligence agent, my medic, my gunner, my squad leader, and myself.

We had passed on that road twice that day—and that was our mistake. Never take the same route twice. He was waiting for us.

If we'd been in a Humvee, the blast would have vaporized us into a pink mist floating over Iraq. The floor of a Humvee is a sliver of aluminum. This was a 40-pound charge buried under the road surface. That's 40 sticks of dynamite. We were in a Stryker, much more heavily armored than a Humvee. Luckily the blast hit just under the front end of the vehicle, where the nose angles up and outward. The blast was deflected, which probably saved all our lives. My driver's leg was broken. That was our most serious injury.

If the bomber had waited a fraction of a second longer, the explosion would've struck directly underneath our belly, probably blowing a hole through the floor. The pressure wave would have taken off legs and arms, liquefied organs, and filled the Stryker with white-hot flames. Even so, the explosion tore into the engine compartment. The Styker was dead and on fire.

We scrambled out of the hatches, dazed and wobbly, and laid down suppressive fire. If there are bad guys waiting, you keep their heads down. We looked for movement. I saw a guy cross the street, slowly and calm, like he was going to go get a newspaper or a cup of coffee. I was using an M14 sniper weapon system. I locked onto him, put him in the crosshairs. I didn't fire. He wasn't carrying a weapon. I couldn't shoot.

The Stryker burned for hours. Since I was the platoon sergeant, all the extra ordnance was in my vehicle. Boxes and boxes of ammunition and grenades and explosives. Hundreds upon hundreds of .556 mm rounds and 40 mm grenades and smoke grenades and cases of C4 explosive—you name it. It takes time for a fire to consume everything, the ammunition and grenades, and they ignite in stages. Rounds would cook off like popcorn for a few minutes, the fire would burn some more, then more ammo would pop off.

A large group of Iraqi civilians gathered on the street to watch the Stryker burn. We're kicking sand on a smoldering tire to put it out. We're watching this crowd, and one of my soldiers points out two men. They're both looking directly at us, and one hands a wad of money to the other. It's obvious what's happening. Standing right in front us, the guy's paying off the triggerman. He's getting paid for destroying my Stryker and trying to kill me and my men. I know what they're thinking: *You Americans are fools.* The next morning, the battalion commander orders the triggerman's building bulldozed to the ground. It's turned into a pile of rubble.

I have the unfortunate honor of having lost the very first Stryker to an improvised explosive device in the Iraq war. That same day my Stryker was destroyed, American forces captured Saddam. In the grand scheme of things, we got the man we were after.

I was born and raised in Florida. My dad started off as a Marine, then went Army, then went Navy, and finally retired out of the Coast Guard. He was a butterfly with his military career and with his women. He left Mom and me when I was an infant. He married another woman, and then another woman. Then he married the second woman again. He left her and married another woman, and then he married one more time. My mom passed away about three years ago. She still loved him.

He's tried hard to make amends. I still love him, too.

When I was 12, we moved to Kentucky. I was raised with a lot of exposure to Japanese culture and honor of the warrior class. I've trained in Japanese, Chinese, and Korean martial arts. I was on the Third Corps taekwondo team, black belt, men's division, and I taught hand-to-hand combat in the Army. One of my first martial arts teachers was a man named Sensei Golden. A power emanated from him. You could feel it when he walked into the room. The gymnasium literally reverberated when he stepped into a fighting stance. Like my other teachers, he was a very impressive warrior.

The warrior class should honor each other. Never underestimate your opponent. Do not denigrate your enemy. Don't assume they are inferior to you. I instilled my beliefs about this in my men. I taught them the Army values—loyalty, duty, selfless service, honor, integrity, personal courage. I told them to uphold all of the values of the Army, always. I never let my men call our enemy a haji.

WE BACKED OFF THREE OR FOUR MILES FROM THE DETONATIONS. We opened our windows and doors and prepared for the blast. Everybody stopped what they were doing. We got up on top of the roofs to watch. The countdown started at 30 minutes. Detonation in 15 minutes. Detonation in 10 minutes. Five minutes. Two minutes. One minute. Thirty seconds. Ten, nine, eight, seven… and then the mindboggling explosion and the mushroom cloud climbing into the sky and into the clouds.

It was a long-term project to destroy Iraq's arsenal stockpile. Saddam's ammunition depot near Hatra was about three miles long and over a mile wide, a vast field of concrete bunkers each big enough to hold four fully loaded semi-tractor trailers with plenty of room to have a picnic in between them. Our guys would bulldoze a hole three or four yards deep, ten to twenty yards wide, and about a football field long. They'd lay down a blanket of plastic explosives. On top of that, they stacked the munitions. One day artillery shells, another day Italian anti-tank mines piled three feet high. They stack this stuff up, then detonate a thousand tons all at once. The blast would literally move the clouds in the sky. The clouds above parted as the explosion ascended into the atmosphere.

There's both an electrical ignition system and an actual burning fuse when you detonate a huge pile of munitions. Once you commit, you can't change your mind. A fuse is burning. It's going to blow.

We had lit a fuse for another thousand-ton detonation and the countdown was on. Then this commander suddenly calls me up and says he's got General So-and-So inbound on a helicopter. The general's bird is arriving in fifteen or twenty minutes.

"You gotta stop that bird," I tell him. "We got a detonation underway."

"No. You don't understand. You got a general coming in. You are going to stop that detonation."

"No, *you* don't understand, sir. The detonation's gonna happen in maybe twenty minutes whether or not you want it to, and you better get the general out of the air or else it's going to be a really, really bad day."

They finally get ahold of the helicopter and tell it to make a forced landing immediately. The detonation goes off, and another mushroom cloud rises like Hiroshima. The pilot thanked us later.

We blew up the ordnance we found, but untold numbers of munitions were looted early in the war. I've got photographs of Iraqis driving away from ammo dumps in motorcycles, their sidecars stuffed with mortar rounds. They went into the abandoned Iraqi army stockpiles after the invasion, snatched away artillery shells and mines and bombs, and they buried them in the desert. Iraq is a giant cat box.

THE KURDS TAKE US TO ANOTHER AREA WHERE WE CAN SEE THAT THE DESERT HAS BEEN DISTURBED. "Iraq's army came and cordoned off the area," says the Kurdish officer. "A bulldozer came and started digging until it disappeared under the earth." The bulldozer had dug a deep trench. Then the Kurds watched as the Iraqis drove a semi truck with a trailer into the trench. A few minutes later, the semi truck emerged from out the other side without the trailer. The bulldozer filled in the trench, burying the trailer.

After the Kurds showed us the site, we start digging. We brought chemical agent monitors with us—they're called CAMs, and they sniff for chemical warfare agents like mustard gas and sarin. We dig down until we hit the top of the semitrailer. We cut a hole in the steel and lower the chemical agent monitors inside. The CAMs go off like crazy. They sniff blister agents, blood agents, nerve agents, a lot of stuff. We jump into our protective suits and masks. But before we can investigate any further, we're ordered back to base.

Later, we're told the trailer contained medical waste. I call bullshit. Medical waste doesn't light up CAMs.

We excavated a fully functional Russian MiG fighter jet that Sadaam had buried on the eve of the invasion. It was carefully sealed in plastic and duct tape, the batteries disconnected, ready to be unearthed and unleashed again. Who knows how many other fighter jets he stashed in the sand? Who knows what else Sadaam hid in that vast country?

The weapons of mass destruction that people say aren't there? They're there. They're still buried in the desert.

When I got back home, I looked at plastic bags stuck in bushes with dark suspicion. Over in Iraq, a plastic bag was a common target line marker. A triggerman waits a few hundred yards away with a cell phone or a garage door remote—anything that can detonate a bomb. When he sees your Stryker cross in front of that bag, he presses the button. You and your men are blasted into bits by the charge that's buried under the road surface or in a concrete curb or dead goat. We saw a lot of that in Iraq, when we weren't dodging bullets.

These days, when I drive past a guy on the side of the road with his car hood up, I get uneasy. I wonder what he's doing. I can't help wondering if he's conducting surveillance, because we saw a lot of that in Iraq, too. Men parked outside our base with their car hoods up. They wanted us to think their car was broken down, that they were just ordinary civilians, but they weren't hunched over their engines. Their eyes were on us. It was obvious they were writing down license plates, keeping track of our personnel coming and going. They were observation posts for people planning to kill us.

Insurgents planted explosives under bridges, especially to attack tanks. Tanks are vulnerable on the top where the hatches are open and the armor is the thinnest. When I drive underneath highway overpasses with my family, I still look up for bombs.

When I hear loud thumps or booms—a dumpster closing, a sheet of plywood falling over—my heart flutters. It's been years since Iraq, but I still have hypervigilance.

I had anger management issues when I was in Iraq. I went to the "head shed," the Army mental health professionals. "You're experiencing stress after stress," the guy counseled me. "You keep dumping stress into your cup. Pretty soon, your cup gets full. When you dump in even more stress, it spills over." That was me.

A call from home once made my cup spill over. My son was in high school at the time, and one of his teachers made the class watch an ISIS propaganda video showing a terrorist cutting off a prisoner's head. I was incensed. I was fucking furious. I called up the school from our base in Iraq and I screamed at them. "I want that guy *fired*, I want that son of a bitch *fired!* He showed my kid a snuff film." But the school district just appeased me over the phone.

I tried to protect my hardened soldiers from seeing crap like that, and here's a guy who makes teenagers watch the most obscene video imaginable. I wanted to choke the living shit out of him. I could barely contain myself.

I was in the grip of an anger that, had I been back in the States, might have turned out really badly. I used to explode. I scared the hell out of my family sometimes. I'm still married to the same woman—I got lucky, she loves me and she's stuck with me—but my younger son holds on to some resentments. He doesn't come by the house much. Dad wasn't a nice guy when he was growing up. I wish with all my heart I could take it all back. But it's too late. He can't hear my apologies. The damage is done.

I was driving home one day after I was back from Iraq, and a guy on a motorcycle raced around me and cut me off. He drives right in front of me and makes me slam on my brakes. Then he pulls over and parks to talk to a guy on the sidewalk. As I drive by, I glare at him to let him know I'm *pissed*. And the fucker gives me the finger. I immediately pull over because I'm going to give him the good news. I'm going to beat the shit out of him. But as I'm getting out of my car, the guy races off on his motorcycle, leaving his buddy just standing there. I get right up in his face. "What the fuck is your friend's problem?" I say.

"I don't know, man," he says. His eyes are wide open. He's afraid of me. "I don't want nothing to do with it."

Then it dawned on me. What if the guy on the motorcycle had had a gun? What if his friend had a gun? What might have happened then? Could I have gotten myself shot? I went to counseling. I needed some tools to empty my cup. Next time it spilled over, who knows what could happen.

ONE OF THE SOLDIERS IN OUR BRIGADE COMMITTED SUICIDE. He received a "Dear John" letter from his fiancée. We knew he was in distress. We counseled him and took him to the chaplain. We did all the things we were supposed to, everything we could think of. He convinced us that he was fine. But that night he wrapped himself up in his poncho and sleeping bag and left a note and he put an M4 in his mouth and blew his brains out. He put himself in his poncho and his sleeping bag to make it easy for us to clean up.

Suck it up, cupcake. Stop being a pussy. Shut up and do your job. That's the military culture. Soldiers take that to heart. Whenever they have aches and pains or issues, they say, "I'm just being a sissy. I'll just suck it up." I work with veterans now on a university campus. Usually they're typical GIs who think they're weak if they seek help. "Hey, those days are over," I tell them. "It's okay to go seek help. You're not being a sissy, you're taking care of yourself. You're taking care of your family. You have to get the tools to help empty out your cup."

If they go get help, they're glad they did. They wished they'd gotten help a long time ago. But you have to move them past that military indoctrination. Soldiers come to me with anxiety issues, PTSD that's causing them to fail classes, suicidal thoughts. So far we haven't lost anyone, but I know at some point in my career it's going to go south. I try not to think about it.

IT'S THE FIRST GULF WAR. I'M IN A BRADLEY FIGHTING VEHICLE. IT'S LIKE A TANK WITH TRACKS, and we're sweeping north across the desert as we push the Iraqi army out of Kuwait. I'm a gunner with my hands on the chain gun. It can pump out 25 mm rounds that shred armored vehicles. Next to that is a coaxial M240 machine gun for killing troops on foot. The battlefield is covered with murky clouds of dust and smoke from the burning oil fields. We're on edge. Iraqi tanks or troops can appear out of the dark haze in a moment. Either we destroy them, or they will destroy us.

"Gunner! COAX troops, 800." The commander is suddenly talking on my headset. Enemy troops 800 meters away. I grip the gunner's hand station controls and select the M240 machine gun.

I hover my finger over the trigger. I'm scouring the battlefield through my electronic gun sight.

I see the enemy. No—I see *something*. I can only make out shadowy forms through the smoke. I see people, I'm pretty sure. But that's all I can tell.

"*FIRE*," he says. I'm supposed to pull the trigger. I'm supposed to spray the shadows with machine gun fire until nothing moves. But I don't know who I would be shooting. I see some kind of target, but I don't know who I'd be killing.

"*FIRE!*"

"Wait," I say.

I'm switching my optics between day sight and night sight, high-magnification and low-magnification—trying to get better eyes on the target, trying to figure who or what it is.

"*GODDAMMIT I SAID FIRE!*"

But I still don't know what's out there. I can't shoot. "Wait!"

He leaps down from his commander's station. He's reaching for the joystick at his fire control station. It's got a switch, and as soon as he activates that switch, he'll take total control of the machine gun from me. When he does, there's nothing I can do.

Just as he's reaching for the switch, the smoke clears and I see the people we're about to annihilate. It's a family. They're huddled by their tent in the middle of this smoke-covered war zone. There's a woman. A child. There's sheep.

"Wait!" I yell. "Look! They're Bedouin! It's a family of Bedouin!" My commander leans in and stares hard through his gun sights. Finally he sees the desert nomads in the chaos, their tent and sheep and children, living like they have for a thousand years. A couple seconds pass. He looks up at me.

"Good thing you didn't shoot, huh?"

A fury burns inside me. I'm trembling with rage.

"Yeah, *good thing* I didn't shoot," I say to him. I can hardly get my words out. "A *goddamned* good thing I didn't shoot, because I could've been living with that shit for the rest of my fucking life. That I had slaughtered innocent women and children."

Maybe I put our men at risk by not shooting. Many soldiers have died because they hesitated. And many soldiers have taken innocent lives because they did not want to take that risk.

I know a lot of guys who struggle with the moral choices they were forced to make in Iraq. They did something horrifying. Maybe it was the right thing to do. They did it to save other lives. My moral choices were all pretty cut and dry. I was lucky.

"I have a bunch of friends who are dead so that this could be a free country. But America's less free now than before I left for Afghanistan. I totally disagree with both these wars. We're there because somebody's getting rich. That's what I think."

TELL THAT DUDE NOT TO SHOOT ME

JEFF RADCLIFF

THEY HAD TRASHED OUR ROOMS, FLIPPED OUR RACKS OVER, YANKED OUR CLOTHES AND TOILETRIES AND PERSONAL POSSESSIONS OUT OF OUR LOCKERS. Everything was strewn on the floor. It was 11 o'clock at night and we had to clean it up. They'd hauled us out of our racks at 4 a.m. that morning and for eight hours we did dips on parallel bars. They'd tell us to get down on our bellies for five minutes and do push-ups as they hosed us down and then screamed at us to get back up. We did PT all day, every day. Some nights they dragged us outside at 1:30 in the morning and shot machine guns loaded with blanks around us. The next night, they'd tear up our rooms again. After you'd cleaned it, they'd produce handfuls of sand out of their pockets and fling it around the room. We cleaned up again and slept for maybe an hour and a half. Then we went running.

I had graduated from Navy boot camp just before Christmas. I went straight over to the Navy SEAL prep course. The Navy was trying to increase the success rate in the BUD/S course, the Navy SEAL selection course, and this was meant to toughen us up for it. Two months of constant PT. Two months of mind games. Two months of dumb stuff to try to make you mad.

I was 17 years old when I enlisted. *I can do anything I want,* you think at that age. Until I got to BUD/S, I never thought I wouldn't make it. I never quit anything in my life. But down in Coronado, soaked by the cold surf, running in combat boots on a soft sand beach, stress fractures in my legs, I didn't run my second six miles faster than my first. The third six-mile run, I still didn't run faster. So I was gone. That's the way it works. I washed out. Out of 386 guys in my BUD/S class, I think eleven finished.

When you get kicked out of BUD/S, you're put in X-Div. You wake up and hate every day. You get into formation in the morning. Ackerson, you're gonna go rake sand. Cutler, you're gonna go paint rocks. Sykes, you're gonna go wash windows. Radcliff, you're gonna take out all the garbage.

They finally gave me two options. One, I could be on the color guard at Annapolis for two years—and then get another crack at BUD/S. Two, I could attend Corps School. Being a Navy corpsman meant emptying bedpans in a Naval hospital or treating seasick sailors on an aircraft carrier. I wanted nothing to do with medicine or ships, so I told them to send me to Annapolis. I'd get another shot to become a Navy SEAL. Come back on Tuesday, they said, we'll have your orders. On Tuesday, however, I was ordered to leave for Corps School in two days. I was really, *really* pissed off about it. But there was nothing I could do.

At least I made them guarantee that I'd be sent to Field Medical Service School. Combat medicine. If I had to be a corpsman, I wanted to deploy to war with the Marines.

If they're bleeding, make it stop. If they're not breathing, do it for 'em. That's really all battlefield medicine comes down to. Morphine is the main painkiller, but it's likely to kill someone who's bleeding out. It lowers your respiration so much that you suffocate. Any kind of chest wound, you can't give them morphine. Any kind of stomach wound, don't let them drink, even if they're begging for water. All the other fancy medical terms in the medical books you just forget.

I'm attached as a corpsman to the 7th Engineers Support Battalion at Camp Pendleton. The battalion builds bridges, purifies water, sets up electrical power at bases, manages the fuel farms. Basically, nothing exciting at all.

The buzz is that we're headed to Iraq, but eventually we learn we're going to Afghanistan. For three months, we train for deployment. The Marines mock up fake fuel farms, purify barrels of water. Charlie company constructs bunkers and builds bridges and stacks up walls of sandbags. The corpsmen take medical classes from guys who've been on combat deployments before. Six of us corpsmen are sent to a piece of private property in California. On the property is a bunch of pigs.

They shoot the pigs with AK-47s. They light them on fire. They lay them on top of hand grenades. You're sitting in a circle listening to an instructor lecture about tourniquets and plasma, and somebody cuts all the pigs' throats. *Hey, your pig's bleeding.* Two corpsmen are assigned to work together on one traumatized pig.

You try to keep the pig alive all day. There's the smell of fresh blood and burning hair. The pigs don't move, don't make any noises, but you feel the pulse of their heartbeats and hear the whoosh of their breath in their snouts.

I'm not expecting the smell. There's a lot more blood than the movies make it seem. I've never been around a gunshot wound or a stab wound. In the movies, the corpsmen aren't elbow-deep inside somebody's stomach, trying to get a hemostat on the aorta or a femoral artery. The pig is dying, and I have to figure out what to do real quick. Whatever I can think of to save the life of the patient, I do it. Maybe there's a better way, but I don't have time to ruminate. We're forced to get hands-on and go for it. It was the first time I learned anything in the Navy.

The pigs are doped up the entire time. They're knocked out, oblivious to what's happening. A veterinarian administers a cocktail of anesthesia and other drugs though an IV. As the day goes on, she injects them with more drugs so they feel no pain. I hate animal cruelty, but you have to get the training somewhere. There's no better option to learn how to save lives in combat.

We all thought we were going up to the mountains in Afghanistan and hang out in the snow. We ended up going to Helmand Province down south. A huge, flat desert and deep ravines and brown mountains scattered across the land. Some people were nervous.

I was totally gung ho. I wanted to go kill terrorists and blow stuff up.

Camp Leatherneck in southern Afghanistan has nine different chow halls spread over 1600 acres. Any kind of food you want, it's always full. Domino's Pizza. Green Bean Coffee. Air conditioning and Internet. Row upon row of telephones for people to call home. Seven or eight huge gyms filled with weights and elliptical machines and treadmills. A bus route system.

When we first arrive, we're put through a week of welcome-to-Afghanistan classes on customs and culture. All kinds of mind-numbing PowerPoint lectures on rules of engagement that everybody already knows. My buddy Hayes and I get pulled out of classes on the second day to go on a mission. We're to accompany a convoy of about 200 trucks headed from Camp Leatherneck to the city of Nawzad, about 30 miles due north as the crow flies. The convoy is manned by Canadians and a few Brits. Hayes and I will ride in the gun trucks. They're armed with MK19 grenade launchers and .50 cal machine guns. If something happens, hopefully we get to do something cool. We hope we get to shoot.

The civilians fled Nawzad over a year ago. If the sun is up, the U.S. Marine Corps owns the town. If the sun is down, the Taliban own the town. The Marines are getting ready to flush the Taliban out of Nawzad. We're driving a fleet of tanks and ferrying a ton of ammo to them.

The convoy zigzags through the blackness, all lights off, the trucks equipped with infrared headlights. The drivers wear NVGs, or night vision goggles. Back in training, they told us if we see rocks stacked on the side of the road, we're going to get blown up. As we drive I see stacks of rocks spray-painted red on one side or blue on the other. We're thinking every stack of rocks means an IED is planted there. The whole time I'm thinking: We're gonna die, we're gonna die. We're gonna hit an IED and I'm gonna be dead.

It's the first night of the convoy. We're rolling slowly along, texting back and forth on the Blue Force Trackers, the BFTs, which is a computer with a GPS map. Some guys are sleeping. Then: *BOOM*. It's a big explosion, but you feel it more than you hear it. It's not loud—it's a deep, ominous THUD. The pressure wave radiates through the air, through our gun truck, through our chests and gut. I feel the pulse in my ears.

The explosion is seventeen or eighteen trucks ahead of us in the convoy. Every truck halts. The radios light up with chatter. I can't see anything in the darkness. Sgt. Tellez and I get out of our truck. He sweeps a combat mine detector in front of us as we walk. It takes fifteen minutes to hike up to the scene.

There's a six-foot crater in the road. The air smells of dust and burnt metal and explosive, and when I see the wreckage of the truck, I think, *Holy shit, there's going to be a lot of blood.* Everybody's looking at me, the corpsman. I have no idea what I'm doing. I'm in country two days, and I have no clue what to do. But the two guys in the truck, both Brits, are fine. One of them is standing up on the truck, which is still smoking from the blast. He's really fucking pissed off, cursing like he can't find words fast enough.

He heaves his helmet into the desert in fury. He's angry that he can't find his iPod.

The convoy grinds along for two and a half days. The area is laced with *wadis*, dried-up river beds. There's no way to cross them, so we drive fifteen miles out of the way and fifteen miles back. The trucks are slow and the tanks break down. All the trucks have to stop and refuel. It takes a lot of time to put gas in 200 trucks.

We hit eight IEDs by the time we arrive at Nawzad. We hit one IED on the way back to Camp Leatherneck. Some IEDs just blow a tire off a truck. We put a new tire on and drive on. Some IEDs cripple a truck. We load the wreckage onto a flatbed. The truckless men climb aboard the armadillo, an empty truck with 20 seats to carry guys whose trucks have been blown out beneath them.

If a truck is blown up and we can't haul it back to base, we destroy it. We place a thermite grenade on the engine block. The thermite roars with purple flame like a road flare, and the fire consumes the chassis and tires and wires and all. We leave the charred wreck in the desert. We melt the sand into glass.

I only heard news about Nawzad one time after that convoy. I heard that a patrol of Marine snipers had been ambushed up in the mountains. The quick reaction force discovered their bodies, but their gear was gone. So we knew the Taliban had acquired awesome sniper rifles, body armor, and Marine Corps uniforms. That's the last I heard of Nawzad.

I made the mistake of bringing my wallet with me. My ass hurt so bad from sitting on my wallet for four days. It's what I remember most about that convoy.

ONE MAN DIGS A HOLE. THEN HE LEAVES. THE NEXT DAY, ANOTHER MAN RUNS A WIRE FOR TWO OR THREE HUNDRED YARDS, UP AND OVER THE BERM. THEN HE LEAVES. The next day, another man will come and hook up an IED to the wire and bury the IED. Then somebody will watch. *There's a convoy coming*, he'll report. *They're traveling this fast, they're headed in this direction.* Another man appears and puts a battery on the end of the wire. Then he leaves. Thirty minutes later, a truck full of Americans hits the IED.

Most of the IEDs are triggered by pressure plates. It's hard for them to use radio-controlled IEDs. Our trucks have ECMs, or electronic countermeasures, that create an invisible bubble around the truck so that no radio signals can come into the bubble. Walkie talkie or cell phone radio waves can't get through that bubble to set off an IED. But ECMs don't stop a simple pressure plate trigger.

There's only one paved road in Afghanistan. Route One. Camp Leatherneck is built right off it. Everything else is dirt, desert, rock, mountains and wadi.

The military came up with mine rollers. It's an axle of ten wheels that sticks out 30 feet in front of the truck. The idea is, the mine rollers hit the IED and blow up, instead of the men in the truck. So then the Afghans started putting the IEDs thirty feet behind the pressure plate triggers. By the time the mine roller hits the pressure plate, the IED is under the truck.

They're smart, crafty people. They figure out a way to do anything. They make IEDs from leftover Russian rockets and mines and artillery shells. They make IEDs out of plastic bottles, cooking oil jugs, Coke cans, stew pots. Everyone in the village pees in a bucket, and after it dehydrates, the urea crystals left behind are mixed with gasoline and aluminum shavings to make explosive. They make blasting caps out of ballpoint pens and gunpowder, pressure plates out of plywood.

I've seen kids put in IEDs.

I'D ZONED OUT WITH MY IPOD AND DOZED OFF AS WE BUMPED AND BOUNCED ALONG FOR HOUR AFTER HOUR IN THE OSHKOSH M-ATV. It's a cross between a Humvee and an MRAP. It's a big, heavy, mine-resistant armored truck. The dude driving is Huntsberry, one of my really good friends. We give him shit because he isn't a very good driver. He always seems to hit the bumps.

I'm jolted awake when the M-ATV lurches hard. *Really* hard.

"What the fuck, Huntsberry?" I figure he's just hit a huge fucking bump.

"No man," he says. "It wasn't me, it wasn't me."

I look out the window. Smoke and dust fills the sky.

My buddy Dejesus—we call him Bernie—is up in the gun turret. He starts yelling. "My leg's on fire! My leg's on fire!" I go up to the turret and pull him down. He's not on fire. I don't see any blood on him, but his eyes are distant, the whites showing. He's muttering, incoherent. He's rubbing his knees.

We've struck an 80-pound IED. We're protected inside the M-ATV, but the blast sent a shockwave through the truck, like we've been smacked with a giant hammer. Two ammo cans that weren't secured flew into the turret and tore ligaments in Dejesus's knees.

Up in the turret, Dejesus was directly exposed to the violent pulse of the explosion. He's got a concussion. I get him out of the truck. I lay him down on the ground, get on my knees beside him. I see a touch of panic in his eyes. "You're good," I reassure him. "You're good." I take off his Kevlar helmet, briefly palm the side of his head. I check his pupils. I start concussion protocol, asking him a series of questions. *Bernie. Bernie! Repeat these words: Chair, apple, table. Chair apple table. Bernie, who's the president? Bernie.*

Bernie! What country are we in? Bernie, answer me, buddy. Bernie, is it morning or afternoon?

He closes his eyes and goes to sleep. He will sleep for four hours.

I check on his respiration and monitor his heart rate while we wait for the Black Hawk medevac. It arrives in under a half hour. We turn our heads as it lands, the blade wash whipping dust and grit into our eyes. After the chopper has disappeared over the horizon, we take photos as I stand in the crater where the IED had been. My head is just above the crater's edge. I stretch out my arms, and I cannot touch the sides.

Dejesus will get a Purple Heart for his TBI, his traumatic brain injury. He'll be walking again three weeks later, without crutches. My own knee is messed up from that IED, too. It's pretty bad, and I'm limping. But I don't say anything about it. I want to go on another deployment after we get home.

When the convoy gets back to Camp Leatherneck, we go to chow with all the Navy guys from our battalion. Our chief tells a story about a Marine who was unloading pallets off a truck. One of the pallets tumbled off the truck and cut him in half.

That's a shitty way to die in Afghanistan, we all agree.

WE ARE RUNNING NONSTOP CONVOYS TO MARJAH, SIXTEEN GUN TRUCKS ACCOMPANYING LOADS OF LUMBER and sandbags and Hesco barriers. Hesco barriers are eight-foot-tall chain link cages lined with canvas. The Marines assemble the Hescos, each one flush against the other, and fill them with earth and rock. They're building the defensive perimeter for a Marine firebase in Marjah.

Most of the world's opium flows out of Marjah. It's the heroin center of the universe. The Marines are going to flush the Taliban from the area and convince the farmers to plant black mung beans, red radishes, alfalfa, watermelon, and corn. They want the farmers to plant these instead of opium poppies.

We've been awake for four days straight, grabbing 30 minutes of sleep when we can. We drive two hours from Camp Leatherneck to Marjah, unload Hesco barriers and lumber and Marine engineers, and turn around. We drive by kids and farmers and donkeys. We drive by brightly painted Afghan trucks and the silent rusting hulks of shattered Russian tanks. We drive by the irrigation canals that line the roads in and around Marjah, smelling the foul, green water. A film of scum floats on the surface.

For four days, we don't stop for anything besides gas.

It's 4 a.m. It's pitch black except for the Milky Way blazing overhead. Our six-wheeled MRAP truck creeps along at 15 miles an hour. Nobody's wearing their seat belts. Nobody's wearing their helmets.

I'm sound asleep like almost everyone else, but if I were awake, I'd hear our turret gunner shouting. He's hollering at the top of his lungs at Lance Corporal Eely. Eely is supposed to be driving the MRAP. But Eely has fallen asleep at the wheel. Our turret gunner up top watches us slowly angle off the road towards the deep, fetid canal.

Eely is a tall, skinny black kid whose white teeth are always showing, like he has a perpetual grin. He's the funniest guy in the truck. He's constantly cracking jokes and making us laugh.

"Eely! Eely! Wake the fuck up, man! EELY! *WAKE THE FUCK UP!*"

But Eely has been lulled by the quiet night and the monotony of the road and the fatigue of round-the-clock operations. He doesn't wake up. The front tire of the MRAP leaves the road and heads towards the dark water of the canal. The second tire leaves the road and down the steep bank. When the MRAP is on the cusp of rolling over, the gunner jumps down into the cabin.

I wake up and realize I'm floating in warm water. My ears are filled with liquid, the world mediated with aqueous sounds of sloshing and creaking. I have no idea what's going on. I don't know shit. The only thing I know is I'm underwater. I figure out the MRAP is upside down. I stand up. Me and the two guys in the back are up to our armpits in warm, slimy water that smells like human shit and dead animals.

You'd think it would be a shock to wake up underwater. But no. *Oh, I gotta get out,* you think blandly. *Commence MRAP emergency egress procedure.* That's all. You just deal with it. Like it's normal.

A lot of things become *normal.* The first time you get shot at, you get real excited. Your heart hammers. No way I'm getting out of the truck, you think. *No fucking way.* But you get shot at again. And again. After the fourth or fifth time someone shoots at you?

Well, I gotta pee, you think. I'm gonna get out of the truck.

So tell that dude not to shoot me.

THEY'RE ALWAYS SO FAR AWAY. IT'S NOT LIKE THE MOVIES. YOU SHOOT HUNDREDS AND HUNDREDS OF ROUNDS AT SOMEBODY AND HAVE NO IDEA IF YOU GOT THEM. At some point, they stop shooting. You have no idea if they're dead or if they ran off. You're not going to hike in just to confirm there's a corpse. You simply go back to work.

Most Afghanis have no clue about September 11. They don't even know where America is. Ninety-nine percent of the people who shoot at us aren't Taliban. They're 16-year-old kids. The Taliban came by their house and said: You're gonna shoot at these Americans or we're gonna kill you. So these kids aren't really trying to shoot us. We drive by in our trucks, and they think we're aliens. When they see us in our trucks, they think, "We'll shoot at the truck a few times and then the Taliban won't kill us."

If anybody came to America with trucks and machine guns, I'd shoot at them too.

My buddy Hayes and I are home from Afghanistan. We're mad at the world. On deployment, you don't have to pay the bills. You don't have to sit in traffic. You put on the same clothes you wore yesterday. You eat food that somebody else made for you. You don't even have to get up on your own—somebody will come wake you up.

You just hang out and try not to get killed.

Life is simple.

You come back to the States, and there's laundry and bills. I gotta cook, I gotta go to the store, I gotta answer this phone call, I gotta put gas in my car, I gotta sit in traffic.

"Dude, I *hate* it here," Hayes says to me. We've been home from Afghanistan for four days.

I tell him I fucking hate it, too.

"I have to leave," Hayes says.

"So do I."

We beg our chief to find a unit that's deploying to Afghanistan.

We're supposed to wait fourteen months before we can deploy again, but we beg and beg and beg. We fill out all kinds of paperwork. We call everyone we can think of. We get lucky. We find out 1st Explosive Ordnance Disposal is short a couple of corpsmen. If you don't hit an IED but you find one, call EOD. We come out and blow it up.

Nine days after we'd come home, we deploy again to Afghanistan. One guy lost his arm on that deployment. Another guy lost both his legs.

Not a whole lot happened.

LESS THAN THREE MONTHS AFTER THAT TOUR, I DEPLOYED FOR A THIRD TIME TO AFGHANISTAN AS A CORPSMAN. We were security for a road construction project. The road never got built. There were IEDs every day, just like usual. We found a huge IED cache in a cave complex, multiple tunnels with about forty freshly made, ready-to-go IEDs inside. EOD had showed up with thirty Marines to blow the cache when a big firefight erupted. The guys who owned or were supposed to protect the IEDs were really fucking pissed, and they had guns. The shooting got pretty ridiculous.

I don't know if we killed any of them. They didn't hit any of us.

When I got back from that deployment, my third deployment to Afghanistan in three years, I was pissed at everybody in the world. For no reason. I had a ridiculous sense that I was better than everybody else. I felt that way, and I thought I was normal. But people who knew me told me I was different than the guy they'd known before.

No way, I'd say. I'm not different. *Fuck you.*

About six months after I got out, I realized I'd been a giant asshole to everybody. I realized I was treating people like they were beneath me. That's not who I am, I realized, that's not the kind of person I want to be. I went to therapy a few times at the local Vets Center. It wasn't really doing anything for me. I figured I just needed to get over it.

I was working a really shitty job that paid thirteen bucks an hour. Four months into it I quit in the middle of a shift. I started driving and a thousand miles later pulled off a long, desolate highway in Arizona in the middle of the desert. I tied a tarp to the top of my Jeep, staked the other end down into the sand, and stayed there.

I checked out from life. Didn't pay any of my bills. Dropped out of contact. All I brought was my guns, my BMX bike, my laptop, and some clothes. I smoked weed for the first time. Sometimes I lay in the sand, staring at the sky and pretending it was Afghanistan. It made me oddly comfortable. I would go into town and get on Craigslist and find people who needed help with moving or taking stuff to the dump for a few bucks.

One day it hit me out of nowhere that I needed to grow up and get my shit together. After eight months, I decided it was time to be an adult again. I drove home to Washington. You can't just hide in the desert forever.

MY BUDDY PAT KILLED HIMSELF THREE YEARS AGO, ON VETERANS DAY. PAT WENT TO IRAQ TWICE. They put his name among the others on the veterans' memorial in Mill Creek, Washington, where he grew up. I was glad for that. I knew him through friends in high school, and they all ended up going into the

Marine Corps. Another buddy, Dan, also went to Iraq twice. Dan's going through some stuff right now. We went camping with him a few weeks ago. He's depressed, talking about suicide. It sucks.

I was thirteen years old when I watched Bruce Willis play a Navy SEAL in the movie *Tears of the Sun*. I wanna do that, I thought back then. My dad's friend was in the Special Forces. He was like Rambo with his Ka-Bar knife strapped to his belt. I wanted to be like him, and that's what pushed me towards the military.

I shouldn't have joined when I was 17. It was an amazing experience, but if I could go back and tell myself things, I wouldn't join the military. You're 17 and you see all these cool action movies and you go talk to a recruiter and you buy the lie. You think you're defending your country, or our freedom. I used to think everybody should join the military, that we should have mandatory service after high school, but my political and world views have flipped 180 degrees since I got out. Everybody I meet these days, I try to convince them not to join the military.

None of those people we shot at in Afghanistan flew the planes into the Twin Towers. I was in no threat from any of them. They weren't going to come into my house or do anything to harm me. They're just trying to live their lives. *Like me.* Everyone has the same goal in life—to make enough to get by and feed their kids. I have more in common with the people of Afghanistan than the people I was with who were trying to kill them.

Those people didn't deserve what happened to them. I think we're over there for the wrong reasons. Somebody's getting rich. There's oil in Iraq and heroin in Afghanistan. I think it's all built on fear, how they control us. I didn't do horrible things, but I feel guilty about stuff I did over there all the time.

"Combat truths are the hardest truths to face, but you can't come home until you wrestle with your own demons. You have to forgive yourself, and you have to forgive others. Telling a false story makes you a prisoner of the past. The guilt and confusion eat you, and ultimately will kill you."

THE HEROES OF THE DAY

TIMM LOVITT

ELEVEN HOURS INTO A TWELVE-HOUR PATROL ON THE STREETS OF BAGHDAD, WE PARK OUR HUMVEES IN A HALF-CIRCLE, 25-yard intervals, pulling over-watch for an Iraqi police checkpoint. It's oppressively hot, the air stinks like human shit, and it's been a really bad day, even by the standards of Iraq in 2005. We're trying to get through one more hour and get back to base safely. A meal, maybe a quick game of cards with the guys, and then some sleep.

I see a car come down the road towards us, watch it slow down. It's a white beat-up sedan, like thousands of other cars in this city. It turns toward us. I see wires snaking out of its front grill into the driver's window. I train my eyes on the driver and shift in my seat.

I'm ready to tell my gunner to light him up, stop the threat with a hail of bullets, but before I can draw in my next breath the Humvee heaves into the air, like we've been slammed by a massive wave. A cloud of orange flame engulfs us. Weapons, MREs, water bottles fly over the seats. The four of us are tossed around inside like dolls in a toy chest, and my head slams against an ammo can. I'm in a daze, not quite knocked out, looking upwards at my gunner's feet. Shane is jumping out of the turret, yelling about something. The rest of the Humvee is quiet and still. I'm aware of a high-pitched whine in my ears, but the world beyond me is muted. Smoke and dust swirl around me. The dust is so fine it fills every millimeter of the air. I can't see anything.

I think the truck on our left has been turned into a charred wreck by a rocket-propelled grenade or a mortar. A profound sense of loss washes over me, unbearable, like it's choking me. I take inventory of the guys that I'll never get to see again. Kelly, Zach, Richie, and Eric. *Fuck, Eric was in that truck.* I kick the Humvee in gear and punch the accelerator—I have no idea what I'm doing, I'm on autopilot or something—but the Humvee just rocks back and forth, quivers, as if it's wounded. I try to open my door. It's stuck. My platoon sergeant appears outside my window. He yells something at me, but I can't make sense of his words. I watch him bend down. I hear squeaks and groans of metal on metal. He opens my door and looks at me.

I get out of the Humvee and immediately look for the wreckage of the truck that Kelly, Zach, Richie, and Eric were in. But it's still there, intact and undamaged, my guys jumping out and looking at me. I can't figure out what the hell has happened. There's a bumper on the ground at my feet, wrenched away by my platoon sergeant. That's what was jamming my door, I realize. It slowly dawns on me. Maybe we were the ones who were hit, not the other truck. I turn and look at my Humvee. The dust is settling.

There's an engine block lodged in the driver's side wheel well. It's a 300-pound hunk of steel that could have easily ripped my legs off. The only thing that stopped it was some minor components in my Humvee's engine compartment, the power steering pump and the steel plate we welded to the floor. I lift the hood, grab hold of the engine block, and drag it out. I'm not that strong, not even close, and later I'll wonder how I did that.

The other Humvees remain in the half-circle formation we'd set up, but my up-armored, 10,000-pound Humvee, with two-inch blast-resistant windows and 200-pound doors, is not where I'd parked it. It's been thrust backwards. The blast has flattened the cinderblock wall behind us. I know the guy who owns it, an Iraqi doctor. I feel bad for him and his family. Their wall just got trashed.

We're all alive, though. Rattled, our ears ringing, our heads throbbing, but alive. My gunner's face is burned, but he's going to be okay. The Humvee is a wreck. The steering is shot. Red hydraulic oil trickles into the dirt. We radio in our situation.

Less than an hour later, we're bumping along in the silent Humvee as a recovery vehicle tows us back to our base in Baghdad. We pass by cinderblock walls and stray dogs and Iraqis staring at us. Wave after wave of emotion surges through me—elation and despair and how funny that shit was and the terror of the blast but mostly, Jesus, I think about how I love my guys. My guys. My instincts kick in, and I recognize that Sosa, Ryan, and Alton are on the edge of the abyss, and I'm responsible for them. I start talking to them, trying to take care of them. I order Ryan to pull out a pack of smokes, and we all light up cigarettes. I don't smoke, never have, but we all smoke those cigarettes together.

We replay the moments leading up to the blast. We talk smack about the suicide bomber. How that dumbshit didn't know how to pack his car with explosives properly. If he did, then he would have known that too many explosives would just tear his car into shreds, pieces just too small to destroy an up-armored Humvee. We're relieved that fucker was ignorant of basic blast dynamics.

Intelligence reports indicated five suicide car bombs were on the streets of Baghdad that day. For eleven hours, we tried to stop them. The first car bomb explodes in the Green Zone. When we arrive at the scene, arms and legs and unidentifiable pieces of human flesh are everywhere. Fifty dead in the blast zone, all Iraqi men and women and children. While we're in the Green Zone, a white van parks on a crowded street two miles away. The driver announces to the milling crowd that he's offering jobs, and the van is mobbed by Iraqis clamoring for work. The suicide bomber detonates. We get there as fast as possible. What we see does not seem from this world. A pond of congealing human blood, shredded muscle and intestines on the pavement, the shops splattered red and black. We watch Iraqis survey the gory remains of what has to be at least a hundred human beings.

A third car bomb goes off at an Iraqi police checkpoint on an overpass, and we mount up and race there. We push the smoking remains of the SVBIED—suicide vehicle-borne improvised explosive device—off the road, and set up a security over-watch a hundred yards away. We park in a semi-circle, tense but exhausted.

The fourth car bomber, what I thought was going to be the white sedan with the wires snaking out of the grill, turns out to be the one that we never saw coming. It's the one none of us saw coming. The fourth car bomber was a red car. The red car was meant to kill me and my men. He intended to incinerate me and my men, dismember our bodies, blast the Humvees into tormented steel. It's the car bomb I will replay in my head over and over and over forever.

Over the next few years I learn, through bits and pieces of drunken stories, that my two gunners, the guys manning the .50 cals, had nodded off before the bomber hit. We'd been racing for eleven hours, dizzied by the gore, cooked by the sun, and after all that, my two guys couldn't stay awake. If they had, maybe they'd have seen the red sedan approach. Maybe they would have turned the driver into hamburger before he detonated. There'd have been no fireball, no thunderous blast tossing our Humvee. Just a bloody pile of a dead suicide bomber behind a shattered windshield.

Or maybe they wouldn't have been able to stop him. We'll never know. It doesn't matter to me. They were good soldiers. We made it home. That's the story that matters to me now.

A LITTLE OVER A YEAR BEFORE, I HAD BEEN A CHERRY PFC IN AFGHANISTAN ON MY FIRST DEPLOYMENT. We were stationed on a small forward operating base in the southeast part of the country, the homeland of the Waziri tribe. Time had forgotten about this land. Villagers drew water by hand from wells dug into the earth and produced electricity with jimmy-rigged portable generators. Generations of human shit dried in ditches just outside each family compound. But the mountains made it a place of solemn beauty. I would go back to look up at them again. Nothing hinted at the brutality of the war.

The wake-up call comes at the end of August. Our Scouts are observing activity from two over-watch positions a few miles out. We're on base monitoring radio traffic when someone near the Shkin firebase calls in a 9 Line, a medevac call for critically wounded. A couple of local goatherds had wandered up to one of the positions, pulled out AK-47s, and raked them with fire. *Shane*, I'm thinking, *Shane's in the Scout platoon.*

Shane had been my battle buddy ever since basic training. Our bunks were right next to each other and we became fast friends. We went to airborne school together and then on to RIP, the Ranger Indoctrination Process. He flew out to be my best man at my wedding. The only thing that separated us was his decision to join Scout platoon. He thought they were high-speed and a sure-fire way to promotion. I thought differently. He joined the group shortly before our deployment to Afghanistan.

Details of the attack and condition of the Scouts slowly unfold. I'm queasy. I don't know if Shane had been out on the mission. The status of the three wounded comes through the command center abstracted into military jargon. One Scout is reported as "urgent surgical," meaning he's in critical need of a lifesaving operation. Two of the Scouts are "expectant." It means they are not expected to survive.

I run to the airfield. Two Black Hawks land after about five minutes. There's not much movement in the second helicopter, but I see Shane moving his arms in the first one. The bird stays on the ground for just a few short minutes, enough to grab some gas, and then heads off for the larger base where there are surgical facilities. The bodies of Riley and Steven will be flown to Kandahar. From there, they're sent on to Kuwait, and then to Dover Air Force Base. Riley's body will arrive in Potsdam, New York, in a flag-draped casket. Steven's body will be flown to his family in Palos Hills, Illinois.

Shane is medevaced to Germany. He gets mostly patched up, but some things you can't fix with sutures and skin grafts and surgeries. Years later, when he's married with kids and out of the military, I talk to him on the phone once in a while. All I can get out of him about that day is when he's drunk. His speech slurred, he tells me that, after he'd taken up his position away from Riley and Steven, he had taken his armor plates off to cool down. He tells me that before the attack happened, they had all started to nod off. What he doesn't tell me, and doesn't need to, is how the guilt is crushing him.

ABOUT TWO WEEKS AFTER RILEY AND STEVEN ARE KILLED, WE'RE GIVEN ORDERS TO HEAD SOUTH AND TAKE OVER THE SHKIN FIREBASE. The Scouts are hitting battle fatigue and need to swap out. We load up everything we have and drive there in a two-hour-long convoy. Shkin is about two miles away from the Pakistan border. It's close enough that we can walk there and make good time.

Mortars and rockets hit the firebase almost daily. After a week of this, we decide we're putting a stop to it. We drive out of the base to the ridge where we think they're launching the mortars. As we bounce along a rutted creek bed, bullets suddenly rain down on us from the mountain above, plinking off the armor. We stop and shoot back with everything we have, even pounding away with a deafening Russian machine gun we've commandeered and use mostly to terrify the enemy with noise. The fight lasts three minutes. The enemy fire stops, and we realize they've vanished down the other side of the ridge. It was a perfect ambush. We admire it.

The rockets and mortar attacks don't skip a beat. Every day the explosions turn the base into a death zone, forcing us to scramble and huddle in bunkers. The attacks strangle our supply chain, because helicopters won't land when rockets are whizzing into the LZ. Everything comes in on helicopter—ammo, fuel, food, water. At one point, water gets so low that guys are brushing their teeth with Snapple.

We don't get mail for two weeks. And that's when we've had enough. We're fucking pissed. We're going after them. The plan is to push out far enough from base to clear out the Taliban or foreign fighters from Pakistan or whoever we find. We're going to get our supply flights, and our mail, back on schedule.

THE ENEMY'S THERE, AND THEY RESPOND ALMOST IMMEDIATELY. Their mortar fire is very, very accurate. Apache attack helicopters swoop and hover above to identify enemy positions for us. Rockets fly skyward at them as they pass overhead. The Apaches run low on fuel and leave. For three hours we hug the dirt, duck and dodge, as AK-47 bullets and mortars pepper our positions. We call in 1st Platoon for support.

When 1st Platoon finally arrives, the company commander quickly says we're crossing into Pakistan to pursue the enemy. They've already wounded five of our guys. 1st Platoon starts up

Lozano Ridge. Lenny is among them. He's a newbie on his first patrol—it's the first time he's been outside the wire. As he hikes up Lozano Ridge, he takes a sniper round on one side of his pelvis, just below his body armor, and then a second round on the other side of his pelvis. The bullets hit where the femoral arteries converge.

The battle rages for nine more hours. We kill the sniper. Apache attack helicopters have refueled and return, circling above like raptors. We call in A10 Warthogs for strafing runs on the enemy, four thousand rounds a minute tearing into the earth. The sound is overwhelming, a colossal, ragged belch. A C-130 gunship drops thousand-pound bombs called JDAMs. The earth shudders, the shockwaves punch our chests.

When the battle ends, Lenny is dead. We've got numerous wounded. We find several bodies of the enemy. The violence piques the interest of the American media, and Geraldo Rivera of Fox News and Lara Logan of *60 Minutes* chopper into Shkin with camera crews. Geraldo broadcasts a live 30-minute show from the "evilest place in Afghanistan." They tour Lozano Ridge with "the heroes of the day." A Humvee carrying Lara Logan and her cameraman is hit by an IED and blasted on its side. One soldier loses a leg and part of his jaw.

The violence changes something inside us, because we keep going out on patrol, and we go looking for trouble. We're looking for vengeance. All we care about is going out and kicking ass. The Waziri tribe didn't crash the planes into the Twin Towers, but we crash in their doors and knock over chests of drawers in their mud houses, searching for weapons and bombs.

I COULD TELL YOU WE WERE HEROES THE DAY LENNY DIED, BUT THAT WOULD BE A LIE. No one was particularly heroic that day. Very few people are actually heroes in war. For that matter, very few people are cowards, either. Everyone's trying not to die. Mostly, everyone's trying to protect their brothers and sisters from dying or suffering horrifying injuries.

I could tell you that it was one of the worst days of my life, a memory that still haunts me, and that would be true.

Months later, when we're back Stateside, Nathan, one of the guys on Lozano Ridge that day, will get his arm tattooed with a full-sleeve memorial to Lenny. In the story immortalized in ink on Nathan's arm, and recounted during drunken nights, Lenny is a hero who lost his life to a Taliban sniper. But the truth is that, before that terrible day, Lenny had spent his days on base burning shit. He doused our sewage with diesel and set it afire, the Army's age-old solution to sanitation. Lenny's shit-burning duty was punishment. He'd taken a piss test before deployment, but the test results didn't catch up with him until he'd gotten to Afghanistan. He'd "pissed hot"—he'd tested positive for drugs.

He was 19 years old. It was his first time outside the wire. He wasn't really heroic. He died too young because we wanted to get our mail delivered.

Like the rest of us on Lozano Ridge that day, Nathan was awarded the Combat Infantry Badge, the CIB. The *man badge*, they call it. It's prestige, points for promotion. It's coveted. In the stories veterans tell, badges matter. You got a CIB on your chest, guys buy you a beer.

You don't get it for taking mortars on base or dodging incoming rockets. You don't get it if you're a truck driver or a mechanic or a cook. You only get it for "actively engaging the enemy" as an infantryman. You get it for being in a shitty situation, like stumbling into an ambush on patrol. It's a lottery ticket that, if you don't take a bullet in the pelvis or get your legs blown off, pays off with an affirmation of manhood, a medal for valor.

That thin ounce of metal shouldn't validate how much of a man you are, but that's exactly what it does. Badges are why vets spin Hollywood portrayals about battles and what they did. You rewrite the story so you can get the badge.

Nathan got his man badge, but the day that Lenny died from two sniper rounds to his pelvis, Nathan was sitting behind the wheel of a Humvee, weeping. And when the bullets stopped flying, Nathan's beloved 1st Platoon hiked up to the corpse of the Afghani sniper who had killed Lenny. They placed a one-pound block of C4 explosive on the corpse, and they blew the body into pieces. Really fucking heroic.

I don't condemn 1st Platoon for what they did or did not do that day. There's nothing wrong with crying behind a Humvee during a firefight. The truth is, no matter how much the military trains you and attempts to re-calibrate your conscience, you ultimately can't control how you react when someone is trying to kill you. You can't control your own instinct not to kill other human beings. Some guys freeze, some guys piss their pants, some guys break down. Big, brave guys. I've seen it.

Some guys get so overcome with grief and rage that they do horrific things, like desecrate an enemy corpse. That's a fact of war.

But you have to own what you did. You have to own what you did not do. You have to face the truth, come to terms with it. You have to forgive yourself. You have to forgive others. Telling a false story makes you a prisoner of the past. You're trapped. The guilt and confusion eat you, and ultimately will kill you. Combat truths are the hardest truths to face, but you can't come home until you wrestle with your own demons.

THE MAJORITY OF THE GUILT I STILL CARRY IS WHAT HAPPENED AFTER I GOT OUT OF THE ARMY. What happened to my guys once we were all home safe, away from the IEDs and snipers and mortars and rockets.

Matt died from an overdose. Ricky committed suicide by shooting himself in the head. Eric committed suicide by cop—he charged cops with a gun in his hand. They killed him.

And Oscar. Killed in a motorcycle accident. You'd think a guy who survived two combat tours would be smart enough to wear a proper helmet, but he wasn't. He beat the odds—we all had beat the odds—but Oscar couldn't get past that. He was chasing the dragon on his motorcycle, racing for the adrenalin high, until the odds caught up with him, and his skull was shattered because he was wearing an eggshell helmet.

These were my guys. These guys were my people, an extension of myself. An injury to them is an injury to me. It's this communal body. It's family. That's what most of my grief is from—not being there for them.

Their deaths were for nothing. The guys who died over there, they died for you. In a way, they died with a promise to protect you. You owe them a debt of gratitude. But the guys who died afterward, what was it for?

"After I deployed, religion was blown out of the water for me. What it meant, what I was raised with—I abandoned all of it. I couldn't believe anymore. It just felt like God was so ugly over there."

I WILL FOREVER BLEED BLUE

NIKKI DAVIS

ZERO WEEK ENDED, MY FIRST WEEK OF BASIC TRAINING. WHO WANTS TO BE DOING PUSH-UPS ON THEIR 20TH BIRTHDAY? But that was me. I loved it. I thrived. I'm a tough cookie. I've always been that way. I got yelled at a lot in boot camp because I laughed a lot. When the drill instructors were yelling in my face, trying to get under my skin, that stuff tickled me. I went in as a cop. Air Force Security Forces. A lot of people think being an Air Force cop is the shitty end of the deal. It's not the best job you could have. But I made the best of it. I was a kickass troop.

My mom is 4'11" and a single mother. I grew up in the Hilltop 'hood, in a low-income area. My dad wasn't in the picture. He was in the Army. Growing up, all I did was sports. Gymnastics was my first love. My eye was always on the prize, and that was going to the Olympics. I didn't pick up a basketball until 7th grade, but once I did, I never looked back.

After high school, some friends of mine had gone to a recruiter and said we should go into the service together, on the buddy system. I told my granny about it. "Granny, I'm going to go into the Air Force with my friends. We're enlisting together. I'm just waiting on them." I'll never forget what my granny, may she rest in peace, told me. "Don't you wait on them bitches," she said. "Don't you wait on them—you go take control of your future." So I did. I enlisted.

When you're finishing Air Force tech school, you fill out what they call a "dream sheet." You get to list six Stateside bases and six overseas bases where you'd like to be stationed. I didn't put Kirtland Air Force Base, New Mexico, on my damn dream sheet, but that's where they sent me. When they initially told me, I got excited because I thought I was going to Mexico. Then I found out it was *New* Mexico. What the hell? There's a state there? Sure enough, when I stepped off the bus, I thought it was the absolute worst. *Kill me now,* I thought.

I was signing in at the orderly room at Kirtland Air Force Base, and a staff sergeant measures my height. Then she puts me on an old-fashioned mechanical scale. She slides the weights until the scale balances, then tallies up the numbers.

"You're obese," staff sergeant says.

"Excuse me?"

"There are Air Force standards. We're going to have to put you on weight management."

"No, you're not." I was always a little heavy for my height, and I'd gained weight in basic training. But I hadn't gotten fat, I'd *dropped* fat. I'd solidified into solid muscle.

"Yes, *we are,*" staff sergeant says. "You're going on a weight plan.

You're obese. You're overweight."

"Well, you need to do BMI testing on me." Body Mass Index testing. "I'm not fat."

Staff sergeant looks up from her clipboard. She glares at me, hard. "We don't do that here, airman," she says.

"Then we're going to find somebody to do it."

I'm not supposed to be talking like this to a staff sergeant. I'm seriously pushing it. Then my commander comes out of her office next door. She's overheard the conversation. She's a lieutenant colonel. She looks me up and down. "I think I heard about you," she says. "When you get done out here, you come see me in my office."

Oh shit, I'm thinking. My mouth just wrote a check that my ass can't cash, as my granny used to say.

When staff sergeant dismisses me, I go into the lieutenant colonel's office. I'm blunt. "I hate this place," I tell her. "I don't want to be in the Air Force. I want to go home."

She picks up a pen on her desk, clicks it a few times. "You still have an opportunity to get out, if that's what you want to do."

"I don't wanna be here," I say. "If being in the Air Force means being in a place like this, I want out."

She leans forward in her chair. "Listen. You have an opportunity here. You have an opportunity to make something out of yourself."

We talk a while, and she finds out I love basketball. She sends me to the women's basketball camp, and I make the Air Force women's basketball team. A year later, I'm stationed at Aviano Air Force Base in Italy—one of the places I'd listed on my dream sheet—and playing all over Europe for the United States.

That's why she was a great commander. That's why she's been a top cop in the USAF. She saw I had a passion and found a way to incorporate that with serving the mission that I had signed up for. Because at that age, I didn't think about the commitment that I was making, about the oath that I took.

No, I didn't think about going to war when I enlisted. "Well, what do you think you signed up for?" people ask me. It pisses me off. I didn't sign up for war, I just didn't. But I still went from the basketball courts in Italy to the dusty roads outside Tallil, Iraq. Thirty-five clicks outside the wire, where intel has discovered rockets are aimed toward the base. We pull up in the Humvees. Looking at the rooftops for snipers, the doorways for shooters. Praying IEDs aren't underfoot. Your M4 on your shoulder, human beings in your gunsights, the thunder of weapons. The smell of violence, the look of the dead.

The ugliness of war.

You can't feel war unless you've been there.

I GREW UP IN THE CHURCH WHEN I WAS YOUNGER. I ATTENDED ST. JOHN'S BAPTIST CHURCH IN TACOMA, WASHINGTON. I'd already gone through my own revelation about religion. Hell, I've been lesbian all my damn life. I knew that of myself well before I went into the military. But after I deployed, religion was blown out of the water for me. What it meant for me, what I was raised with—I abandoned all of it. I couldn't believe anymore. Because it just felt like God was so ugly over there. I was taught Bible verses that say God doesn't put more on my shoulders than I can bear. And then I am sent to war and I see evil. I feel evil. And I'm a part of it. The things you have to do go against the morals and beliefs you were raised with. *Why do I have to do this?* you wonder. *Why am I here?*

When I got home from Iraq, my mom said to me out of the blue: "You've changed."

"No," I snapped back. "I haven't changed." I didn't want to accept what she said, but it pierced me. It pierced me because it was the truth, and I wasn't walking in my truth.

I didn't think anything was wrong with me. I denied it for the longest time. Eventually I couldn't ignore my anger issues, my temper, the bad dreams. One night I woke up with my hands clenched around my girlfriend's throat. I was choking her in my sleep. She managed to wrench free and wake me up. That's when I realized I needed to go see somebody. I needed to get help. I can't bear the thought of hurting her. I love her so much.

She would watch me as I slept, she told me, and see my trigger finger squeezing over and over, in the grip of a nightmare.

It's a hard transition home from war. I'm supposed to be normal around people. I'm supposed to be the person that people knew before I went to Iraq. But I'm not that person. And I can't get that person back.

I decided I'm going to start being truthful. So now when people say to me, "Yeah, definitely, you've changed," I say, "Yes, I have." It's been rough, it's been scary. It took time to accept that I had changed and that my change doesn't have to be for the worse. As long as I accept who I am, I'll be all right. If I'm okay with my story, I won't be in turmoil. It's not easy, but I can do it. And I want to help other vets know that, too.

My transition from war is forever. I want to be done, I want to be good, but I'm always going to carry the war with me.

I'm always going to carry that darkness within me. It is a burden I will carry until I breathe no longer.

A VETERAN IS A HERO, RIGHT? YOU SERVED. OH MY GOSH, WE SALUTE YOU. THANK YOU FOR YOUR SERVICE. *Thank you thank you thank you.*

Okay, you're welcome.

If you only knew that sometimes I think about killing myself. Not because I can't pay my bills. Not because I had a horrible childhood. But because I went to war and put my life on the line for my country. For love of country.

For a person like me, it's like trying to swallow a sword. You're talking to an African-American lesbian. For love of country. The country that looks at me different. Treats me different. Doesn't accept me. For love of country. I gave my life for people to have their right to freedom of speech. I gave my life for people to hate me for my sexual orientation and for my race. For love of country. I gave my life for the people who make the laws to say I am not deserving of disability from the government that sent me to war. For love of country.

We veterans go to the VA. We tell them that we think there's something wrong with us. They take our blood pressure. They look in our eyes. They look in our ears. They ask us about intrusive memories, traumatic nightmares, hypervigilance. We tell them what's happening to us.

"We don't think there's anything wrong with you," they say.

"No," we tell them, "something's *wrong.*"

They ask us about startle responses, alienation, reckless behavior. They ask us about fear and horror and guilt and shame.

They ask us about dissociative amnesia and negative cognitions and whether we have a persistent inability to experience positive emotions. Again, we tell them what's happening to us.

"Okay, there's something wrong with you," they say. "But we think it's only going to affect you 20 percent." We were willing to give our lives for your right to tell us that we're only worth 20 percent disability? And we have to fight and beg for it?

Imagine a picture of me when I was a little black girl from Tacoma, Washington. You would never imagine that girl's story would be mine. But even though I know the outcome of being willing to give my life, I'd do it again. It's been a tough price to pay, but I love the military. I still love the Air Force. The person that you become. I will forever bleed blue. I will never take back my oath.

"I've lost track of how long I've been in therapy. The most difficult part was looking back and finding the moment that turned me into who I am today. When you finally locate that moment, that tipping point in your life, you don't feel any better. In fact, I started to feel worse."

ONLY THE DEAD SEE
THE END OF WAR

JUSTIN SHULTS

There were mornings when I'd put a gun to my head and say, "Fuck me. I can't do it." I'd disappear for two weeks because my PTSD would get so bad, then just show up one day where I was going to school, another faceless, nameless student among thousands on a college campus. It doesn't matter how many tattoos you have, or if you wear your age on your chest, they're still going to talk to you like a child. Fortunately, we had a veterans' advocate there named Rosa. If it wasn't for Rosa, I wouldn't be here.

"Haven't seen you in a while," she'd say. "How are things going?"

"My meds are bad. I'm going back home." A dozen fucking pills. You'd think they'd get one of them right.

They started me off on prazosin so I could sleep. I didn't dream for nine months because I was on such a high dose. Sleeping for ten, twelve hours, but I would still wake up like I had a two-hour sleep. I was on 10 mg of trazodone. I was on propranol whenever I needed to cut the anxiety. They put me on 100 mg of sertraline, and at one point the sertraline dose was so high that I ended up with serotonin syndrome, shaking like fucking Michael J. Fox when he's all Parkinsons'ed-out. That was me. I had to wake my buddy up, have him drag me to the emergency room. "Get me something that I can't get addicted to," I said. "Just give me something that will knock me the fuck out so I can sleep normally."

So they put me on escitalopram. There were four or five warnings on escitalopram. Loss of appetite. Depression. Increased thoughts of suicide. All the warning signs came up within the first three days. I would go to bed thinking of suicide. I'd wake up angry in the middle of the night thinking about suicide. I would wake up in the morning thinking of suicide. And that wasn't me. I went from a guy who had to go 120 mph on his motorcycle to feel normal to a guy who couldn't get out of bed. I'd lay there, thinking, "I gotta end it today. It's gonna happen today." The only reason why I didn't blow my fucking brains out is that I have a 75-pound bulldog who needs me. Her name's Akira. I couldn't bear to think that she would see me there, dead. She's what kept me from pulling that trigger. A fucking bulldog.

Everyone expects you to be a civilian. Everyone expects you to transition effortlessly into the system once you get back. Everyone expects you not to say *fuck* in a public setting. Well, I had just spent the last ten years getting shot at, and I was going to say whatever the fuck I wanted.

MY FIRST MISSION IN IRAQ WAS LANDING A PAVELOW MH-53 HELICOPTER IN SOMEONE'S BACKYARD. I almost shot a cow. It was the Wild West from there. You're a 19-year-old shoved into that world, and you see a whole bunch of fucked-up shit. I watched a seven-year-old Iraqi girl bleeding to death in front of me because her father had used her as a human shield. The flight medics worked on her next to me as we medevaced her to Baghdad. Her stomach glistened with blood from three American bullets that had hit her and were still embedded in her body. We watched the little girl fight for her life, and after the crew pulled her from the helicopter and rushed her into the surgery ward, the doctors hovering over her, we were relieved. *All right, we did our job.*

No, we learn later. She died.

She was the first of many, but that was the tipping point. My logic about war started to change. You let go of your own humanity to make sense of what's right and what's wrong. There's no turning back on that knowledge. You're never the same person. A bullet doesn't care what uniform you wear, what your ideology is, if you're a small child. Eventually, I would become jealous of that seven-year-old little girl. Her war was over. Mine had just begun. Only the dead see the end of war.

The show goes on, and there's always going to be a child. There's always going to be a woman. There's always going to be an innocent person. There's always going to be another fucking casualty. So you say to yourself, "I don't care what happens today as long as my buddy doesn't get shot." You don't care about *you*. You're only worried about everyone around you.

We're flying over Baghdad at night in the Pavelow, and the bullets start flying up towards us. I'm on the minigun. It can spit six thousand rounds a minute.

"I see tracer fire. What the fuck am I supposed to do?"

"You shoot. You shoot until they stop."

"But what if it's a kid?"

"What about my kids? Think about *my* kids at home. If we crash tonight, I won't see them. If I get shot, I won't see them. You want to be responsible for that?"

No, I wasn't going to be responsible for that. It wasn't just his kids. There's five other guys on my crew, and they all have kids.

You shoot until they stop.

I WAS BORN AND RAISED IN THE PHILIPPINES. MY DAD WAS IN THE AIR FORCE. He died in 1991 after an accident, and we moved to the U.S. in 1993 because of Mount Pinatubo. Here I am, nine years old, dad passed away, my Filipina mom a widow with two kids, and a volcano going off 26 miles away. We moved in with some relatives in California.

The summer of my junior year in high school my buddy starts harping on me to join the Marines with him. "Fuck you, dude," I said. "I'm not made for the military. That's not my life. I'd rather screw off and go to college." But he kept bugging me every week. "I tell you what," I finally said to him. "The next war that kicks off, I'll be right there with you. I'll join the service."

September 11, 2001. I'm driving to school and stop to fill up. A guy at the gas station says I better top off my tank, because gas is soon going to be $5 per gallon. I don't know what he's talking about. "The World Trade Center just got bombed," he says. "We're at war."

When I get to school, the parking lot is almost empty. Half the student body is missing because we shared the school with the military kids, and Beale Air Force Base is on lockdown. I walk into home economics class, and I start catching shit from the teacher for being late. "Listen, the whole world's changing outside us right now," I tell her. "Why are we talking about whether I should buy a can of peas off the top shelf or the bottom shelf? I don't give a shit. New York's being attacked."

Typically a kid acts out like that, the teacher is going to yell at you. But she says nothing. She sits down. She turns on the TV just in time to see the second plane hit.

That's when my buddy turns his chair towards me. I hear it squeak as he swivels 90 degrees, and he just stares at the side of my head. I keep looking forward, watching the planes hit again and again, aware of him staring at me. "You promised," he says.

"What?"

"You fucking promised me. Next war that kicks off, you're joining the service."

It didn't matter whether or not I made that promise to my friend. I had to go. I *had* to join. It was a call to arms. I went to a recruiting office within the week, looked at a big poster of a helicopter, and said, "That's what I want to do." By April, I was in basic training. By October, I was flying. Things changed from then on. The military was my calling.

I SAW MOST OF IRAQ FROM THE SKY. TAKING OFF WHEN THE SUN SETS, FLYING ALL NIGHT, coming home when the sun is already two hours above you. Those were the fun times. Those were the times when you could actually get shot at and shoot back and know you would hit something good. I just wanted to shoot somebody.

Because when your friends die, guys you trained with, the only thing you want to do is get back out there. The first was Jesse Samek, killed during a medevac in Herat, Afghanistan. He was a wingman on his first deployment. JB Lackey was killed in a CV-22 crash near Kandahar. JB taught me what that widget in a Guinness can is for, and that's the first thing that popped into my head when I saw his name on that casualty list. He'd been ready to retire after 24 years in the service. David C. Smith died when his helicopter was hit by a rocket in Helmand while on a medevac mission.

I was always trying to get back out there. I wanted to kill the sons of bitches who'd taken my friends. I was waiting for a motherfucker to start shooting at me so I could go to town. Get me some vengeance. Payback. It didn't matter who. That's why I kept going back—to settle the score. And deep down, I was waiting for my turn in a crash. I figured if I die as a civilian, nothing special. If I die in battle? I'll be remembered forever. That's what I believed. That's why every time one of my friends died, I thought, fuck, Why wasn't *I* on that mission? I kept going back because I chose to. If you die at war, it's probably because you choose it.

Two tours in Iraq. Then a year-long tour in Afghanistan to teach Afghans how to fly helicopters. I was already forged by war. *Bring it on*, I declared. Green-on-blue incidents, when Afghan police or army turned on and killed Americans, were happening. At that point I didn't care if you were supposedly my friend or my ally, as long as you were not in an American uniform, you were a threat. Afghanistan was asking to get in a fight, it really was. I was working in an Afghan compound surrounded by

Afghan soldiers. An Afghan walked into a room, I would've shot him dead right then and there if I thought an American was in danger. I actually pulled my gun once on some Afghans on base. Here we are, training Afghans how to fly helicopters, and my buddies are getting shot and killed. It fucks with you hardcore.

I lived in Afghanistan for almost two and a half years, one year with the Air Force, a year and a half as a contractor doing 90-day rotations. After all the missions in Iraq, after all the trips, after all of it, the only place I could wake up and feel alive and be happy was in Afghanistan. That's where I wanted to live. Life was simple. I didn't have to deal with the bullshit at home. People asking for money. Girlfriend sleeping around on you. In Afghanistan, those things didn't fucking matter, because you're getting shot at. That high level of anxiety becomes natural for you. Here in America, before I was on meds, I would have to ride my motorcycle 120 miles an hour down the freeway just to feel normal. To feel *calm*.

It's the same feeling you get when people are shooting at you. You don't focus on the tracer fire, you focus on your way out. It's a binary system. You either do something, or you don't. You either live, or you die.

I don't know what caused it. I don't know what triggered it. I just remember walking into the VA in San Antonio feeling like shit. It was three weeks after I got out. "This is your veteran service officer," they tell me. I sit down in his office, and he's got a wall full of citations and wears a special ops gray beret. He'd done shit in Panama. The guy's a true operator. I'm looking across the table and suddenly I realize this guy is in a fucking wheelchair. Do you know how much of a piece of shit I felt? Here I am, bitching about PTSD. I'm supposed to sit there and say, "I need help." Instead, I think, whatever my fucking problems are, I'm fine. *I have my legs.*

Before he could say anything, the tears just came down my face. They flowed and flowed. I wept silently and looked at him, mute. I had no idea what was happening to me.

"We're done," he says. "Come on, let's go."

"Don't kick me out, man. I need help."

"I'm not kicking you out. I'm taking you to the ER."

"I don't need to be admitted. I'm fine."

But he takes me over to the ER, him rolling his wheelchair, me right behind him, dejected, head held low, feeling like shit because the guy that's helping me is a lot worse off.

"Everybody goes through it," he says to me. "Whatever your damage is, whatever your issues are, these people are here to help."

They put me in the ER. I'm a mental breakdown case. They said they were going to see me first. I sit for four hours in the waiting room.

Finally they call me up and put me in a room. Five or six different people rotate in and out, each one asking me the same shit. Do you feel suicidal? Do you feel like hurting yourself or others? What caused this? How are you feeling? The same bullshit questions, over and over and over and over. For hours.

A resident walks in. Young girl. She's holding her pen and clipboard. "Do you feel like hurting yourself or anyone else?" she asks me. She's got her pen ready.

"I do!" I snap. She jerks her head up. "I'm going to hurt you if you ask me another fucking question and not get me a goddamn doctor so I can get the fuck out of here." She backs up and leaves the room. Five minutes later she comes back with a doctor and a cop.

"What was that about?" she asks in front of the doctor and the cop.

"You've asked me the same fucking question eight times. You know why I'm here. I've been in the ER for eight hours. Get me out of here, please."

"I'm referring you to a psychiatrist," the doc says.

That was my first experience with the VA. I didn't go back for a long time.

You get to America and nobody wants to hire you. I had eight and a half years of military experience, I had one of the highest security clearances, but I had no degree. "Here's my resume. Pretty impressive, huh?" People look at you, look at your resume, and say, "Yeah. This is great. But you didn't go to school. Sorry."

"I can hold a gun. I can shoot somebody from 800 yards."

"Okay, great. What other experience do you have?"

"I sat behind a gun shooting people and getting shot at, protecting your values and your ideals and your politics. That's my qualification."

I couldn't even get a job at a fucking hotel. "You've got too much experience," they said. You mean to tell me I can't run your front desk because I have *too much* experience, and across the street they won't let me be the manager because I don't have *enough* experience? Maybe I wasn't qualified, or maybe they didn't want to hire a vet. I applied at a big military facility in San

Antonio. Couldn't get a job. I tried to get on with Amazon—but I didn't have a degree. I couldn't get a job as a dog handler.

I traveled around for a few months. I was really battling with PTSD at that point. I didn't know why I was feeling the way I did, why I wasn't able to focus on anything. Why I wasn't able to do a job right. I started doubting myself.

I applied to college. A few months before, I was an advisor to a general in the U.S. Air Force. I was a policy writer for the Afghan Air Force. Now I'm trying to get a passing grade in Accounting 101. I'm ten years older than everyone else.

I take my college acceptance letter to a window in the registration office. There's a woman sitting behind the glass. "Excuse me," I say. "I need to sign up for my classes."

She gives my acceptance letter a cursory glance. "First you have to do these things for orientation," she says. She whips out a pink highlight marker. She starts drawing fat circles on my letter. "This and this and this. Read these things and follow instructions."

That's the first acceptance letter I've ever received to a university, I think to myself, and you just fucked it up with your bright pink highlight marker. I feel like I'm back in high school in home economics class.

"Excuse me?" I say. She stops drawing circles on my acceptance letter and looks up, a slightly bored expression on her face. "I'm a fucking adult," I say. "Talk to me like I'm an adult." She fixes me a brief gaze, looks back down, and runs her highlighter a few more times over the letter.

Veterans need help, they think. They need their hands held. They can't think for themselves. Are you kidding me? Veterans are more than capable. We just don't know the civilian system. And we come from a system where you don't have to ask for help. You say to your brother in arms, "I'm going 50 meters out." You don't ask a brother in arms for help. You don't ask him to cover you. You don't need to say a damn thing. *Got your six*—got your back—it's done. Now we're trying to find the same values in the civilian world. They don't exist here. If they do, they're hard to find.

Veterans are forged by years and years of friendship. Forged by one bullet. Veterans are never going to ask for help. That's what they're bred to do.

THREE TIMES LAST SUMMER I PUT MY GUN TO MY HEAD. The first time I almost pulled the trigger, I had already popped all my anti-anxiety meds. I snuck in a shot of 18-year-old scotch. I was two beers in and I was working on my second joint. I had woken up that morning and thought, "*Oh fuck*. This is it. I can't do it." I sat down on my footboard, my head bent over. My bulldog Akira was with me. I couldn't leave the room. I got back in bed and texted my buddy, who's got severe PTSD, like me.

i can't do it today, bro

i'm leaving in ten minutes, he texts me back.

It's 7:15 in the morning. He's at my apartment by 8:30. He saved my life. When you're about to pull that fucking trigger, you need a brother in arms. The last thing on your mind is calling a stranger at the crisis line. If someone from my call list doesn't pick up, the crisis line might be my lifeline. But otherwise, it's all about being with the vets. That's the people I can walk with. They're my salvation.

I realized I had to do something about my gun. There's no goddamn way I'm getting rid of my gun, so I locked it up with a gun lock. I gave the key to a buddy and said, "Here's my key. If I ask for this in the next couple of months, just shut the door in my face. No questions asked." A couple of times I thought about picking the lock.

If it wasn't for being able to smoke weed, I likely would have pulled the trigger. Weed creates a little joy for me. I can appreciate a blue sky. My psychiatrist doesn't like me smoking weed, but it was a fucking pill that sent me to the ER. I own a 360-pound motorcycle that can go 120 miles an hour in about four seconds. That doesn't scare me, but a pill does. Weed is the only thing that works for me.

4TH OF JULY. THEY'RE SETTING OFF FIREWORKS RIGHT OUTSIDE MY APARTMENT. *Boom. Pop-pop-pop. Boom. BOOM.* There's no time for me to build space. An explosion goes off, I have to sit there and remember: I'm in Seattle. I'm in Seattle. Why would that be happening? Right, because someone is out there blowing shit off. But one firework goes off, and then another one happens, and I think, *Why are there two? Why are there three?* It's stopping my being. It's in my face and I'm forgetting over and over that I'm in Seattle. I'm walking to my fucking tent when the explosions start happening and so I run to the shitter. You're safer in the port-a-potty when the mortars come running in, so you don't move. At least I'm still alive, I'm thinking. If I move, chances are that's when I'll get hit. So I'm just going to stay in the shitter. So I spend an afternoon in the shitter because the mortars come in. I shouldn't have to feel like that in America. When I hear a loud bang, I should just not care. But we're so ingrained. *Incoming.*

I'm trying to heal. I'm upfront about it. The people that I interact with every day know about my PTSD. I have yet to have an episode at work. I just gotta keep my shit in check. That's the goal—just keep it in check. PTSD is a part of you. You can't get rid of it. If you wanted to fix your PTSD, you'd have to go back to your roots and forget about Iraq, forget about Afghanistan, forget about 2003. And if I did that then, fuck, there's no point in living. Because PTSD is a reminder of what it is that we did. For me, PTSD went from being something that was holding me back to becoming my purpose. *It's my purpose.* If I could go back and do things differently, I wouldn't. Despite the last two years of bullshit, despite the times I tried to kill myself, I'm still a better person today. I'm alive. I'm breathing.

My therapy is helping others. Helping others realize that it's okay to be fucked up. In fact, if you came out of Iraq or Afghanistan completely normal, if you keep that shit under cover and keep it contained—I'm afraid of that person. Over there, it's just you and your gun, right? But you can't come home like that. You can't come home feeling that home is Afghanistan.

"Rarely are we told the names of the dead. But sometimes when you're riding away after the coffin has been unloaded, you turn and see the funeral procession in front of you. You face the family, and that's when you know."

MAYBE YOUR PROBLEM IS LISTENING TO SAD MUSIC

JOE JOCSON PORTER

WE'RE SEATED ON BENCHES IN THE BACK OF A DEUCE AND A HALF, THE BIG GREEN ARMY TRUCK WITH THE CANVAS CANOPY. We're wearing our uniforms, boots, helmets. We're all dressed up and ready to go. The cars passing our convoy honk and wave and give us the thumbs-up. Huge smiles. Fist pumps. Shouts of support. Adulation for the soldiers. It feels good.

We're on the way to the Pentagon to help with recovery operations. We're going into the gaping hole caused by the impact of a Boeing 757 and crawl through the debris to find the remains of 189 human beings. It's night, but floodlights illuminate the area like daylight. We're excited. We're fascinated, too, at the thought of seeing death. When it's our turn to head in, our commander warns us what we'll see. He's been in there, and he's obviously disturbed by what he's seen. His face is ashen, his eyes sharp and cold.

The hazmat suits are hot and soon sweat drips down our backs and faces. The masks steam up. We enter ordinary office spaces where computer printers have melted like wax. Sodden papers litter everything. The desks are scorched and crushed. We pick through broken mortar and building rubble and many small pieces of a commercial airliner. Some rooms are completely demolished. In some rooms farther from the impact, people had died in their chairs. But mostly we find pieces of people, not whole people. When we find remains, we call the FBI guys over to recover them.

Everything's coated in dust and dirt. Body parts are hard to recognize at first. I pick up something long and white. *Is this a bone?* I hand it to an FBI guy, who knocks it against a rock to find out. Some of the things we find are obviously pieces of people. Hands, fingers, feet. One guy discovers some flesh that might be a penis. Later on, we'll tell dark jokes about that.

One of my friends finds people still strapped to their airplane seats.

My master sergeant finds a spine with a women's bra wrapped around it. How did that person die? You picture it in your mind. How does that happen? That part of her remains intact. The rest of her did not. Your mind goes there, whether you want it to or not.

There are pieces of airplane everywhere. There's conspiracy theories that there wasn't a plane, that it was just an explosion. As if someone bombed our own people. When I hear those lies, I get angry. I saw the actual remains of the people in the plane. I spent a lot of time digging through the rubble. I saw a lot of bad stuff.

When our shift is over and we stumble out of the Pentagon, they spray us off. We're exhausted—physically and mentally. The first couple days, they give us water and sandwiches. We have cots to rest on. But in the days after 9/11, there's a big rush of support. More and more businesses start setting up camp outside of our area. It's almost a competition. McDonald's starts giving away free hamburgers one day. The next day, Burger King gives away free Whoppers. The next day, a steak chain loads us up with sirloin and potatoes. Free massages to anybody who wants them. When we get out of our hazmat suits, we're all sweaty and gross, but people rush to give us things. "Hey, do you want a sandwich?" they ask. "A bottle of cold water, an energy drink?"

We took a group picture with my friends in front of the collapsed building. We're all kind of smiling, arms around each other, like it was a tourist excursion. How disconnected one is at the moment.

I try not to think too much about what I saw. But it still affects me. All you hear now about 9/11 is how we need to protect the country. Now, it's about how we need surveillance to protect us from terrorists—all that shit. But when I think of 9/11, I see the people who died. They weren't guys like me, guys who joined the infantry, knowing they might die. These were people with office jobs who just went to work one day.

The gruesome work affected each of us in different ways. Maybe it wasn't the same as going to war. Maybe it wasn't the same as killing or seeing your friends killed. But it was still hard.

I was digging through a pile of rubble one day. Small remains of a person—maybe different people, it's impossible to say—kept turning up. Hair and scalp. Some pieces of rib bones. Then

I found somebody's military ID. He was a Hispanic man, and he must have gone to work at the Pentagon that day. He probably kissed his wife and kids that morning and got in his car for his commute on the Beltway. We were about the same age.

To this day, I feel guilty that I can't remember his name. I wish so much that I had ingrained it into my mind.

I HAD TRAINED AS AN AIRBORNE INFANTRYMAN. I JUMPED OUT OF AIRPLANES, RAN THROUGH THE HILLS OF FORT BENNING WITH AN M16. But I spent most of my career as a soldier performing funerals at Arlington National Cemetery. I was a member of the Honor Guard. We lay our nation's veterans to rest. We stand at attention in our dress blues all day in the sweltering summer heat while the families weep and the coffins are lowered into the ground.

Honor Guard is a prestigious posting. There's an intelligence test. You need a clean criminal record. You need to be fairly tall, and you have to be in top physical condition. The Honor Guard recruiter had selected a group of us based on our PT scores. He lined us up, told us to stand at attention. We stood, backs straight and eyes forward. He looked at us and walked around us like he was inspecting a line of horses. He pulled three of us aside. "You guys want to join the Honor Guard?" he asked.

My buddy and I had no idea what he was talking about. "We're not sure what that is, Sergeant."

He talked it up. "You're not stationed on some military base in the middle of nowhere. You'll be in Washington, D.C., honoring our nation's veterans."

We answered the call. I was assigned to Alpha Company and

stationed at Fort McNair, right in Washington, D.C. The War College and National Defense University are there. Air Force One was visible across the water. The chow hall has great food because a bunch of generals and higher-ups work at McNair. We marched in parades and greeted heads of state. We planted flags on the graves for Memorial Day. And almost every day we attended funerals.

Besides honoring the dead, we also performed shows for tourists. I dressed up as a Korean War vet for one production, complete with historical rifle and uniform. Some of the tourists were gray-haired veterans who wanted to talk to us after the show. They'd lean on their canes and tell us about their wars and the weapons they'd carried into battle. I met a few Medal of Honor recipients.

"Spirit of America" was a cheesy stage show with songs and pyrotechnics. *Ladies and gentlemen! This is the story of the Army during George Washington's time,* says the announcer over the auditorium's sound system. We march on stage dressed up in Revolutionary War costumes, firing squibs—fake bullets they use in the movies— so there's the *pop! pop!* of muskets. A guy sings "Time of Our Life," the Green Day song. We're like actors on a movie set.

On the morning of September 11, we were on a bus to Fort Meyer in Virginia to rehearse a follow-up show to "Spirit of America." We see smoke rising in the distance from the Pentagon. Cell phone networks are overwhelmed. We go back to Fort McNair. Nobody had signed off to issue us ammunition, so we don our riot gear, arm ourselves with batons and empty M16s, and patrol the base against whatever might come.

I'm guarding our barracks when my mom finally gets a phone

call through. She's crying. "We're okay, Mom," I tell her. "I'll call you back when things settle down." But things only got more crazy in D.C. We hastily train on how to secure checkpoints, check underneath car chassis for bombs. We uncoil concertina wire and emplace concrete jersey barriers.

Two days after the attack, we were deployed to sift through the grisly debris of the shattered Pentagon.

YOU WAKE AT 4 A.M. YOU WASH THE HORSES, BRUSH THEIR FLANKS, COMB THEIR MANES, SCRUB THEIR HOOVES. You polish the leather tack. Shine the brass. A little to eat before you put on your Honor Guard uniform, yellow pants with yellow stripe, leather riding boots and steel spurs. You load up the horses with the tack. Buckle and cinch the straps, stirrups, halter.

Three pairs of horses pull the caisson. One person rides each pair. Two smaller horses lead the procession, the two following slightly larger, the drafts at the very end. You sit ramrod straight in the blistering heat and control the unruly horses. Keep them lined up and get them to turn the corners without tripping over the lines. You clench the horse with your legs until your inner thighs burn.

The caissons were once artillery wagons in World War I, but now they carry the dead to their graves. Rarely are we told the names of the dead. But sometimes when you're riding away after the coffin has been unloaded, you turn and see the funeral procession in front of you. You face the family, and that's when you know. You imagine the person in the coffin, what their lives were like. They were World War II vets, retirees, dignitaries who served in the military, Medal of Honor and Distinguished Cross recipients.

An elderly widow with a walker, grandchildren grown up, some in uniforms like their fathers and grandfathers before them. As time went on, we started burying the dead from the new wars. A young wife, red-eyed and in a state of shock. Sometimes she has children, some too young to understand what's inside the big box going into the ground. A son, husband and father killed in Iraq or Afghanistan.

I'm an infantryman, I thought, and I'm not over there with them.

After you deliver a coffin to one funeral, another Honor Guard detail may need the caisson for the next. You run the horses from one end of the cemetery to the other. You ride through the history of the dead of America. These men died in Vietnam. These men died in Korea. The Battle of the Bulge. The Argonne. Graves from the Civil War. The pointed headstones are Confederate soldiers—they're pointed so Union soldiers wouldn't sit on their graves, we're told. In the old quarters, the monuments are chiseled with surnames you don't hear any more.

The newer stones are white and repeated in endless rows and bear a symbol of the veteran's religion. Most of them are crosses, but not all. Stars of David. The flaming cross of Seventh-Day Adventists. Buddhists and Muslims. All the different faiths of the United States military. Four hundred thousand graves.

We ride the horses to four or five funerals a day. Between funerals, you find a quiet space in the cemetery for a few minutes. Then you load the next coffin onto the caisson for the next funeral. You get back late in the afternoon. You clean the tack, because the horses have sweated in the Virginia heat and gummed the leather and stained the brass. You clean the horsehair from your uniform for the next day's funerals. You get an hour or two before you sleep, exhausted.

I SERVED AT FIVE HUNDRED FUNERALS. I WAS A GOOD SOLDIER. WE WORKED 14 HOURS A DAY, EVERY DAY. We took care of the horses. We nailed shoes to their hooves. We lathered and rinsed their coats. We shoveled the stables. We cleaned the penis sheaths of the geldings with bare hands. We polished the tack. We trained the horses to stop and turn and gallop and be still. If you want an animal to do what you want, you should coax them along. But the training method we were shown was to be dominant to the horse. If they sense weakness at all, they're going to walk all over you. For some horses, that's true. But some soldiers didn't treat the horses very well. They're stubborn animals, and some guys would react angrily and punch their horses. That bothered me. But there was nothing I could do, especially if they had rank.

There were problems in the platoon. The Caisson unit had the worst DUI rate. "What's wrong with you guys?" the commanders demanded. "Why can't you get your shit together?" The frantic atmosphere, the stress of shitty leadership. Yelling at you when you did stuff wrong. *Why do you have horse drool on your sleeve, soldier?* To be frank, there was a lot of racism, too. I was dating a black girl at the time—and guys threw the n-word in my face. The platoon wore me down more than the horses. I became completely burned out.

Caisson was a prestigious assignment. We were to be thankful for being given that job in the Army. But everybody I knew in Caisson who had planned on re-upping at that point said they couldn't wait to get out.

I was offered a sergeant's stripe if I re-enlisted, but I was through. I left the Army in November 2003.

THEN THE ARMY SENT ME A LETTER. "WE NEED YOU BACK," THEY SAID. SHORT OF SOLDIERS FOR THE WARS, THE ARMY WAS RECALLING ME. I had served four years of active duty, but they had rights to me for four more years in the inactive reserve. "All right, let's do this," I thought. I had just broken up with a girl, and it went badly. I didn't know where I wanted to go or what I wanted to do. Going back into the Army seemed the right thing for me, even if I had no choice.

I was thrown into a leadership position in a National Guard unit. We trained to deploy to Afghanistan. Most of our training centered on IEDs, because that's what was causing most of the deaths and injuries. We were going to pull security on a base. Maybe we'd do patrols.

The unit had deployed to Iraq before, and I kept hearing things. One guy said he was looking forward to shooting dogs. Another guy bragged about shooting an unarmed Iraqi civilian on the side of the road who was videotaping their convoy. I realized the unit was not who I wanted to go to war with. They were undertrained. I sensed that bad stuff would happen. I imagined being over there and feeling pressured to do what your commander ordered you to do, even it meant shooting an unarmed civilian holding a video camera.

The more I was there, the more I fell into depression. It grew darker and darker, and my nights became consumed with nightmares. I wasn't fit for duty. I was in a bad place. I thought about suicide.

I talked to an Army mental health counselor. "I'm having terrible nightmares," I told her. "I had a dream last night where I watched a dog fall to its death."

The lady nodded. "Do you like dogs?"

"Yes."

"All right. So what kind of music are you listening to?"

I named her a couple of songs on my iPod.

"Well, maybe that's your problem," she said. "Maybe your problem is you're listening to sad music."

I was encouraged to talk to a chaplain, but I didn't want to. Whenever I had talked to chaplains, they proselytized. I just needed God, they'd tell me. That was my problem, they said. I'm not religious, and there's a lot of Christian influence in the military. Non-believers are looked down upon. Some chaplains didn't do that—but honestly, the way I was feeling, it wasn't something I wanted to talk to a chaplain about.

Asking to see a psychiatrist is not an easy decision in the military. It goes on your permanent military record.

The darkness closed around me like a curtain. Thoughts of suicide clouded my days. I don't think I really wanted to die— nobody really wants to die. But I worried that if I shipped overseas in my mental condition, if I had to spend a year with these people on a base in the middle of the desert in Afghanistan, it could've been a possibility.

Finally I went to an Army mental health evaluator to see about getting discharged. I sat in a room and waited for my number to be called. The evaluator was a young woman. An older man was there, too, who seemed to be training her. They sat on the other side of the table. She filled out a sheet with checkboxes.

"Do you use drugs?" she asks.

"No, not at all." She fills in a box.

"Are you depressed?"

"Yes, I'm pretty sure I am."

"This doesn't sound serious," she says.

"I feel like I can hardly function."

"Are you faking this?"

"No, it's pretty bad."

"Are you thinking about killing yourself?"

I thought for a minute. "Well, not right now."

The older man leans over and points on her checkbox sheet with his index finger. "All right, so if you see here, if he'd said *yes*," he says, "then we would've moved on to *this form*." He slides a different form across the table towards her. "And then we could discharge him."

She nods her head. They both look at me.

There's a long silence. I'm holding my hands in my lap. I look down at them. Then I get it. "So that's all I needed to say was that I wanted to kill myself? And then I would be discharged?"

Today I get help from the VA close to my home. The hospital is huge, but the psychiatric center is only a tiny section. There's always a crowd of veterans in the waiting room. The doctors seem to care very much, but it's obvious that their time and resources are limited. It's strange and sad how little attention is given to the mental health of soldiers, many of them very young. But I'm thankful for those who take time to help long after the smoke has cleared.

"When you become friends with someone else who was in the military, you know they got your back. Even if you're in the worst spot imaginable, they'll drop everything to come help you out. They'll bend over backwards to help another vet. The biggest thing I miss about the Army is the camaraderie."

TOO MANY MILES IN MY BOOTS

JOE STONE, SR.

I REMEMBER HOW THE AIR SEEMED TO LEAVE THE ROOM WHEN THEY CALLED OUT THE NAMES, ESPECIALLY THE LIEUTENANT COLONEL'S NAME. They had called us to an emergency meeting in the chapel with the wives and the parents and the children.

Lieutenant Colonel Joe Fenty. Good name, you know. Squadron commander. I had just gotten to Fort Drum, New York, and was put on staff duty almost immediately. I was the new guy and didn't know anybody, didn't know who the commanders were, who any of the important folks were. He figured that out as he was getting ready to leave for the day and he came and talked to me.

"You're new here, aren't ya?"

"Yes sir."

It was already seven o'clock at night. Everyone else was already gone for the day. He sat there for a half an hour and just chewed my ear and asked me where I came from and how many kids

I had. He was genuinely interested in what I had to say. I was a sergeant. He was a lieutenant colonel. He talked to me like I was a peer.

He was killed two months later in a helicopter crash in Afghanistan during an extraction off a mountaintop. They were hovering in a Chinook—one of the two-rotor helicopters, the big ones—with the tail down, loading and unloading guys. The pilot thought he saw tracer fire, though it turned out to be embers from a fire that got kicked up in the rotor wash. He thought somebody was shooting at him and he jerked the controls and one of the rotors hit a tree. It was reported that the bird just dropped and tumbled down the mountain and killed ten men, including Lt. Col. Fenty. Fenty didn't need to be there, they had it covered, but he said, "No, my guys are out there." They were kicking off Operation Mountain Lion. He wanted to be out there with his men.

One of the best commanders I ever had. It was gut-wrenching when I found out he was killed. Little did I know his wife was pregnant too, due right around the time my kid was due. I hadn't been deployed yet because my own wife was due in a couple months, and local Army policy delayed your deployment. But he went forward with his men anyway. That was the honorable thing to do. He didn't even get to see his kid.

I COULDN'T WAIT TO GO OVER TO IRAQ WHEN IT FIRST KICKED OFF. I'd been in Cuba a year earlier, and deployed with the 571st Military Police Company to Iraq in January 2004. We were based southeast of Baghdad, on an old Iraqi airbase renamed Camp Cuervo. I was driving convoys, twisting wrenches, a mechanic. The first couple of months were quiet. By March, the IEDs got real bad. Falluja started popping off. Sadr City erupted in a bloodbath. It went from quiet to damn near hell.

The pucker factor was real high. We were mortared every day. You could almost set your watch to it. We were in charge of manning the towers, and one day just as I came off the tower, a mortar round landed right in front of me. *BOOM*. The sparks flew up, dust and gravel flew past my face. One hit the building I slept in, another struck near battalion headquarters. One time dirt erupted fifty feet in front of me, I felt the shock wave hit, and I hit the deck. Mortars usually came in groups of three or four, so I expected the next one on top of me. But the next rounds walked the other direction. One guy had just walked out of the portajohn and a mortar landed right on top of him. He opened the door and was stepping out, and he died instantly.

One morning I planned to be up early to get into the shop before the day turned into a furnace again. I was going to get to the chow hall at 6 a.m., but I overslept. I never oversleep, but I did that day. I'm rushing to the chow hall and a buddy stops me. "Where you going?

"Get some chow."

"Didn't you hear? Chow hall got mortared this morning. We're not getting chow."

The mortar landed at the front of the chow line, struck just as the chow hall opened, and sprayed shrapnel into a dozen soldiers. Grievous wounds. I've had so many close calls. So many.

WE LEAVE AT ZERO DARK THIRTY, AT 3:30 IN THE MORNING, IN A CONVOY OF FIVE VEHICLES—three gun trucks, one empty five-ton cargo truck, and a five-ton wrecker to pick up any vehicles that break down. I'm driving the wrecker, and I'm number four in the convoy. A platoon of ours was operating far to the north, in the Kurdish area of Iraq, one of those missions where we're not supposed to be there. They'd been working with the Kurdish forces, and we're pulling them back down. It's a four- or five-hour trip up there, and we're a couple of hours into it. We're bored. Nothing's going on. Sand dune after sand dune after sand dune. We approach a village.

There's a huge explosion behind me. I look in the rear view mirror and I see a massive cloud of black smoke. I see the Humvee behind me roll through it, and I think, *Oh fuck oh God, that was close*. They're good. They're still moving. I watch the Humvee roll through it, but they don't roll for very long. The Humvee slows to a stop and fire boils off it. I slam on my brakes, bring the wrecker to a screeching halt. The guy sitting next to me is operating the radio. I'm a mechanic, we're not normally running around with guns in charge of the mission. Fuck this shit, I tell him, I'm going. Point your weapon in that direction. I'm going over there.

The Humvee's on fire, licks of bright orange flame and thick black smoke pouring out of it. There's a driver inside, a truck commander next to him, a gunner, and our medic and her medic kit.

The truck commander is okay, he's managed to pull the others out, but they're badly wounded. The driver's legs are peppered with shrapnel, and he's bleeding from all over the place. I take my knife—I remember taking my knife out—and cut away at his uniform, cut his bootlaces off. The gunner has shrapnel in his gut, abdominal wounds. Our medic bag is still in the Humvee.

The Humvee is so on fire that the ammunition is cooking off. Rounds are igniting and flying—*zing! zing!*—all around us. There's grenades in the Humvee, and it's a matter of minutes before they start going off. We pull a truck alongside it to shield us from the intense heat and cooking ammo while we work on the wounded.

The female medic who was behind the driver is the worst off. When the explosion hit, the shock wave caved in her door and snapped her left arm just below the shoulder. She had been sitting right next to the fuel tank. She's got third-degree burns over half of her body from burning fuel.

People are screaming. People are screaming because they're hurt, people are screaming directions, and people are screaming to get bandages out. Our medic bag is in the Humvee that's ablaze, our medical supplies are on fire, so we pull personal bandages out of our utility pockets, little washcloth-sized bandages with straps. You're trained to pull the bandage off the person who is injured, so I pull one off the guy I'm working on, wrap it around his leg, and try to cinch it down to stop the bleeding. And when I do, the fucking strap breaks. It's useless. I pull mine out of my pocket, wrap it around one of his wounds, try to do the same thing. And the same thing fucking happens. The strap breaks. They're garbage.

I turn to our commander, Captain French. "Sir, do you got a bandage?" He looks at me for half a second with confusion and agony in his eyes, then whips out his bandage and hands it to me. That one bandage works, but the guy I'm working on has four or five other holes I still have to plug. I drop my body armor, pull off my fucking uniform top, pull off my tee shirt, and rip the tee shirt into bandages.

While we're struggling to stabilize the wounded, the sergeant in charge of the mission is trying to get ahold of a medevac. But he can't raise them on the radios. It's taking forever. We can't wait much longer. In a few minutes, we're going to load up the wounded in the remaining trucks and haul ass to the nearest post we can find, bouncing over the rutted roads across the desert.

Our female medic is a stocky black woman from the South. She sits there, horribly burned and clutching her shattered arm. She's praying. She prays out loud the whole time. Her name is Staff Sergeant Mitchell.

We're about to load everybody up when they finally raise the medevac on the radio. Got a bird coming in. The LZ is a hundred yards down the road, so we load the wounded onto a truck to drive them there, but the truck gets mired immediately, its tires kicking up sludge. Between us and the LZ is mud, deep fucking mud. So we unload the driver with his bloody legs, the gunner with weeping holes in his gut, our female medic with raw burns over her face and body, and we carry them on stretchers to where the helicopters are coming in. The mud sucks on our boots with every step. We stumble like drunks. It's a long way.

Ten minutes later, we hear Black Hawks thumping in the distance. It is the best sound I have ever heard in my life.

WE HAD SO MANY GUYS GET HURT. SERIOUS INJURIES. THEY ARE INJURED AND THEY ARE ANGRY AT THE WORLD. "*Fuck* the army, *fuck* this, *fuck* that, I'm *fucking* tired of this shit." I met one of them as he came in on a medevac. His leg had been blown off. I went to greet him on the chopper as they unloaded him, and the medics waved me off. "You *do not* want to talk to him right now," they said. I heard him scream at the doctors and the medics that were there trying to help him. He cursed everyone viciously. He seemed to hate everyone and everything.

A gal in our unit was a military policewoman. She had a degree in psychology, and she'd played basketball for Notre Dame. One of the leading scorers on the team, one of the best players. The world was her oyster, but she felt a calling to go in the military and serve her country. She went on a security mission at an Iraqi police station near the Green Zone in Baghdad. She was up on the roof, our guys and the local Iraqis were in a meeting below, and someone fired a rocket at the building. It ripped her arm from her body, her left arm, the one she used to dribble and shoot baskets. After she was medevaced, she pleaded for her wedding ring. The guys in our platoon went hunting high and low and finally found her ring. But that was small consolation. For a long time, she was full of hate. She's overcome her rage now, and has done incredible work for veterans.

A YEAR LATER, I'M STATESIDE. In front of company headquarters, I run into the guy whose legs I'd bandaged up with my tee shirt after the IED blast. It is the first time we have seen each other since that terrible day. We give each other a big hug. He holds me for a long while.

"Thank you," he keeps telling me. "Thank you. Thank you."

He's got a limp and a cane. He's in rehab.

He says, "I don't know what you did out there. But the doc says because of you, I can still walk." His eyes are filling with tears. Mine are too.

I don't know if he's bullshitting me, but it sure feels good to hear him say that.

My contract was up, and they kept trying to get me to re-enlist. "After this tour? No thank you," I said. "I'm done with the Army. I want nothing more to do with this." My family life back home had fallen apart. I came back to an empty house. Divorce. I had a five-year-old child I hadn't seen in a year. I blamed the Army.

I came back and I too was pissed off at the world and the Army. I had PTSD, but I didn't know that at the time. Hypervigiliance. Anger. Dreams. Numb. I was so fucking callous. I had no empathy for anybody. I let everything roll off my back—at least that's the face I put on.

I dreamed a lot about the day the IED hit the convoy. I kept seeing Staff Sergeant Mitchell, horribly burned and her arm shattered, praying as we waited for the medevac. I kept thinking there was something I could have done. I replayed it in my mind all the time, *all the time*, for years. I walked through every instant, from the seconds before the blast to the moment the chopper lifted off with the wounded, over and over and over again.

I'll never stop thinking about it. Was there something I could have done different? If I had been paying attention, could I have seen the IED on the side of the road and waved them off? Should I have seen something, a wire or some fresh dirt, before all that pain and suffering happened?

I got a job as a used car salesman. I hated it. I found another job as a heavy mechanic. I was backing a dump truck out of the shop one day and a tire blew out, there's a thunderous *boom* underneath me, and my PTSD kicked in something fierce.

I shook like a leaf. My blood pressure hit the roof, my heart hammered, I broke into a sweat, I panted for air. I knew what had happened. I knew it was just a tire, I knew I wasn't back in Iraq, but the physiological effects just kicked in. I couldn't help it.

The guys in the shop fucking laughed at me. They were vets too, believe it or not. They were Cold War vets, non-combat vets, so they didn't know. But it was like getting kicked in the crotch by your best friend. I almost fucking quit right there. I worked there a couple more weeks.

I was so fucking lost. Nothing felt right. I didn't know anybody, and I couldn't relate to anybody, either. I felt so alone.

All my buddies were still in the Army. I was the only one who'd left. Everybody else was still experiencing shit and collecting stories to tell. A buddy of mine was on recruiting duty, and I called him up. "I gotta do something," I said. "I gotta get back in." I went through months of rigmarole and eventually got re-enlisted. I felt so much relief when I got back to Fort Drum and ran into somebody I knew who'd been in Iraq as well.

Finally, I thought, I'm home.

I WAS DEPLOYED TO AFGHANISTAN, FORWARD OPERATING BASE NARAY IN THE KUNAR RIVER VALLEY, IN JUNE 2006. A big hot spot in the northeast. We lost quite a few guys. One of the Medal of Honor recipients, Jared Monti, was in our squadron. It was awarded posthumously.

Though I was a mechanic, you're always a soldier first. Instead of having me fix trucks, they loaded me and a squad of guys in a helicopter and dropped us on a mountaintop observation post. Seven guys sitting on top of a mountain for three weeks with a couple of boxes of MREs and a pair of binoculars and a radio. Our security was a couple rolls of razor wire. The crew that went up before us had to walk up the mountain. We were lucky. In wintertime, you'd have to carry so much extra cold weather gear it would've felt nearly impossible.

Six local Afghanis from the valley below lived with us, hired by the Afghanistan National Army. They were armed with AK-47s and camped next to us and gave us intelligence on what was going on below. We'd see a big group of people through the binoculars. "Oh, So-and-So is getting married," they'd inform us, or explain that a funeral was going on. We were looking for smuggling and people planting IEDs in the road by the river.

One time my forward observer spotted four men walking up a spur on the range across from us, and it looked like they were carrying rockets. The Afghanis radioed to see if the local observation posts on that side were expecting resupplies. They weren't. The Afghanis asked for an artillery strike from the howitzers the U.S. had based nearby. I was the guy in charge, so it was my call. The 155 mm shells struck on the side of the mountain, the explosions thundering in the valley. I hoped we didn't kill the wrong people. The thought of this has haunted me ever since. We had friends among the Afghanis.

I grew close with one of the Afghanis in our camp, a man named Daoud. I'd point to something and he'd say it in Pashto. I'd say it in English. We'd write out the words in little notebooks and we'd pass each other's notebooks back and forth. We'd do that all week long. The Afghanis called me *commander* and invited me to meals in their hooch next door. We sat on carpets on the floor. They served the meals in big enameled tin bowls filled with beans and rice and flatbread. Sometimes they served me goat. When you've been eating MREs for three weeks straight, goat tastes pretty damn good. We drank chai tea with goat's milk. The chai leaves floated in the cup and gradually sank to the bottom.

It was a beautiful place. The water and the rivers ran crystal clear. It reminded me of the Rocky Mountains. At nighttime there were no lights, other than perhaps some candlelights or some locals who had a generator. It was so peaceful.

I made good friends with Daoud and other Afghanis. This would be a great place to live, I thought, if people weren't trying to shoot us all the time.

MY ARMY CAREER SPANNED 15 YEARS, TWO MARRIAGES AND FOUR KIDS. I DEPLOYED FIVE TIMES. Now my back is all jacked up. I ripped up my disks carrying the wounded to the helicopter after that IED strike in Iraq. Too many leaps from trucks loaded with gear, too many miles in my boots. I can't pick up heavy tools anymore.

I sleep like a rock, but I only sleep for a handful of hours at a time before I wake up from pain. I don't touch pills. I'll suck it up. Take some Motrin, walk it off, my wife will rub my back. Keep it simple.

The 4th of July is hard for me. They don't allow fireworks on military bases, but where I live now, everybody goes to the Indian reservations and buys gigantic mortars and cherry bombs and firecrackers and lights the shit off all day long. My first 4th of July back from Iraq, all I wanted to do was bury my head in the dirt. I was a wreck for two weeks. I was anxious and testy the whole time. I took it out on my kids. They'd do something silly that kids do, and it just set me off. One time I jumped when a firework popped, and my youngest, my son, laughed at me. I was embarrassed and infuriated. I tried to explain it to them, but it's hard for them to understand. So every 4th of July, I ship them off to their grandma's house. I don't want my kids to see me angry and on edge. I don't want to yell at my kids. I feel humiliated that the fireworks bother me so much. I'm ashamed that I have to send my kids away. I feel weak.

One of my grandfathers was a lieutenant in the Navy in World War II and fought the Japanese in the South Pacific. Another grandfather had been a Marine in the same war. One uncle had been a tank commander during the First Gulf War. Another uncle was a colonel in the National Guard. At family reunions, he'd wear his dress uniform with all his medals. I'd stare at him. I always loved the military, even as a little kid.

I dreamed of being a cavalry scout when I signed up in high school, jumping onto fighting vehicles and running behind enemy lines. But my folks had just divorced. My mom fell on hard times and wasn't working, and I felt I needed to be around to help her. I told the recruiter that I needed to be based close to home. "There's no cavalry spots available," he said, "but you can be a mechanic."

So I was a mechanic in the Army. But I was gung ho. I wanted to be G.I. Joe so badly. You'd think as a mechanic you wouldn't see a whole lot of action, you'd be stuck in camp twisting wrenches, but that wasn't always the case. I volunteered to go outside the wire as much as I could. I guess I got what I wanted.

I've gone through some tough shit. Would I want to go through that hell again? Probably not. But I'm glad I can say I was there. I was a part of it. I can tell my kids, my grandkids, Yeah, I saw some shit. I actually went overseas and did something. All the experiences that I had have made me who I am today. I don't think I'd change any of it.

I miss the camaraderie. I miss the teams. And I miss the discipline, which is funny. Who wants to get yelled at all the time? Who wants to have to be in a certain place, at a certain time, every minute of every day? But I miss it, I really do.

"I don't always know if I mourn the passing innocence of my generation or the death of a man I dreamt of being."

A PRISON LIKE MINE IS A QUIET PLACE

ADAM CAJIUAT POSADAS

WHEN I WAS YOUNG, I SPENT TEN MONTHS IN AN IRAQI PRISON. It was the middle of war, as if War can be the name of another season. If that is the case, for me it is a hot season, endless and dry, and every day is the day before, repeated. A prison like mine is a quiet place, nearly peaceful in my memory. Long hours marked by the shuffle of slow, shackled steps across a dusty, sun-drenched courtyard. There is violence in that soft sound.

I'm older now, though still a young man by any measure. More familiar seasons continue to turn, but my eyes seek solace in shadows cast by that relentless sun. I was twenty years old in the season of war. I was an interrogator in the U.S. Army. I ran operations in a prison northwest of Baghdad. I did not survive. None of us did. Nobody does.

The past five years have offered many lessons in living, but there is no teacher for this grief in me. It took a year staring at a lake surrounded by mountains to perceive that grief is the thing at the center of my healing. Even now I don't always know if I mourn the passing innocence of my generation or the death of a man I dreamt of being. If they aren't the same thing, surely I can't tell. Whichever the case, now we know something of what our parents knew, or our grandparents. The same things can haunt our vacant eyes, and we can understand a little better their regrets.

We are not so different from the ones who came before, and there is nothing new about this thing we must confront. No matter how technology advances, no matter how battles are fought, people do not win wars and people do not lose wars. The only proper verb for war: we suffer it.

Only the dead have seen the end of war. I find it notable that some people still quibble over whether it was a Greek philosopher from the fifth century BCE or a Spanish one born twenty-two hundred years later who first uttered that truth. Over two thousand years of conflicts and you still care to argue who said it? Then go to war!, I say. Like so many other things, it won't matter anymore.

Whatever the name for its lingering effects, I suffer the symptoms survivors share. I have trouble sleeping. I have trouble sitting quietly with my thoughts. I have trouble trusting others. I have trouble trusting myself. It doesn't trouble me at all if I can't affect conversational niceties or social graces sometimes. So much for not sweating small stuff—as hot as I felt in the season of war, I don't sweat much of anything now.

I try to talk about it sometimes, with distant acquaintances and passing strangers, but who else could understand?

"I just cannot imagine!" a friend says to me. I can't imagine it either, but I do remember it. That's the real trouble I have: remembering some things so clearly. But I can't forget. We cannot any of us afford to forget.

I am afflicted with a poet's metaphors, Trickster's truths, a storyteller's mythic reality, and Raven's memory of the way things were. It's verse that enlivens me. Stories bind me into my form while freeing me to wander a dusty spiral track through a thousand new worlds.

There are shadows at the crossroads of trauma and healing, and no map through the darkness save what we manage to put down ourselves while we wander. I have gone into combat, a warrior, and returned from battle with wounds long in mending. I discovered myself scattered across an inner landscape suddenly made harsh under the boots of marching armies—fleshy bits of me hung from dead branches, were mixed in with scree under thorny, desiccated scrub. I collected each moldering gobbet from wherever I could find them, made a pile of my own remaining viscera, and began the slow sorting process, sifting through my leftovers to see what could be salvaged.

From the garbage heap of me I found a worn-down fragment of the large chip formerly occupying my shoulder. It could serve as my strong right heel, if I ever stood again. There were all the shiny tracks my tears had made, which I carefully set to new courses carrying on the work of veins. My skin I found in ragged, mismatched strips. I did my best to mend them back, rougher than before, and thicker where I had to double over the material—I'd have to curl in a little to fit again.

I have made my way back from death, but I am not who I was at the beginning. If I'm no longer so wounded, I am also not the Warrior I was. That was such a good version of me, though! And I so enjoyed that life. What's left for me? What life do I lead at the other end of healing?

Adam Posadas took his own life on March 7, 2016.

A PRISON LIKE MINE IS A QUIET PLACE

"What would our life be like right now? Where would we be? What would I be doing? So many decisions I've made are a result of what happened. So many things are different now."

I ALREADY KNOW
WHY YOU'RE HERE

DANIELLE VILLANUEVA

THAT DAY, SOMETHING WAS WRONG, SOMETHING WAS BADLY WRONG. I COULD FEEL IT. Mark didn't call me, and he called me almost every morning. Real quick, just to say hi honey, love you, gotta go now. He called on the satellite phone from base. It'd be nighttime for him in Afghanistan, around 9 a.m. my time. About two weeks earlier, Mark had told me they were getting ready to go out on a mission, clearing IEDs for convoys, and he was really unhappy about it. Very dangerous area. He didn't really agree with what they were doing. He was exhausted. He'd lost a lot of weight.

Maybe he just couldn't get time to call, I thought. He's in a war.

He would be coming home soon. The night before, I had shopped for a homecoming dress, an outfit to wear at the formal ceremony when his unit was welcomed back. I was looking for a pin-up style dress.

But that day, I just tried to keep myself busy. Washed a load of clothes. Swept the front walk. Played Legos with Finnegan, a year and a half old. I needed to get out, so I went over to my parents' house in the afternoon. We ate some lunch. I tried to read. I tried to hold a conversation. I tried to act like everything was normal.

My cell phone rang. It was my neighbor. A nice couple. They liked Finnegan. They knew my husband was in Afghanistan. "Hey, where are you?" she asks. "There's these men walking around in uniforms asking for you. They were at your door."

I thanked her and hung up. After a few minutes, I told my parents I needed to go back to my house right away. I asked if they would watch Finnegan for a little while. He was napping. I got my keys and drove home.

I was eight months pregnant, living in Chandler, Arizona, and waiting for my husband to come home from Afghanistan.

We met in Mililani, Hawaii. I was in the Navy, a Chinese linguist, a little white girl from Arizona. I was miserable and stuck in the barracks. At a party one night somebody steals my purse and keys, and my car gets stolen, my Honda Civic. I go through Craigslist ads looking for a new car. I get bored and start poking around in the personal ads. And I see an ad—it's actually in the platonic friends section—that Mark had posted.

A couple weeks later, we meet at the Starbucks in Mililani. His name is Mark Wells, Mark Christopher Wells. He had just come back from a 14-month combat tour as a medic near Hawija, Iraq. He was there in 2004 and 2005. Not a good year. A lot of death. To me he seemed lonely and lost, and at the time I didn't really think about it, but now I can see that's what brought us together. He had been married, and his marriage had dissolved while he was in Iraq. He had been on anti-depressants for a while and was sick of those and wanted to get off them.

He'd learned how to save people, but he'd also watched so many die. He was tired of being a medic. He wanted to switch over to Explosive Ordnance Disposal, EOD, the guys in the bomb suits who defuse bombs and IEDs. I thought, God, you're an adrenaline junkie. I'm just this cubicle monkey. I don't get it.

He always wanted to go to culinary school. He played the bagpipes, and had played at soldiers' funerals in Iraq. One of our first dates was on St. Patrick's Day. He played the bagpipes and cooked an Irish meal of corned beef and cabbage for me.

We fell in love. Before he runs off to the military's EOD school at Eglin Air Force Base in Florida, he says, "I want to marry you." He didn't have a ring, but that didn't matter. For the first time in my life, some guy is telling me he wants to marry me, and I want to marry him, too. I'd never met someone like him before. He was sent to Florida for training to become a bomb tech. I flew down nine months later, and we were married.

You come to that moment with somebody when you realize you have something to lose.

PHOTOS ON HIS FACEBOOK PAGE. THAT'S HIM IN THE BOMB SUIT. IT LOOKS HORRIBLE, HOT AND HEAVY. This one's at EOD school in Florida. Here he is in Iraq, the first time, as a medic. This is in Hawaii. You can tell from the red dirt. More Iraq stuff—they're posing with their rifles and the Girl Scout cookies someone had sent them. You see how much younger he looks? This one, in

Japan with other Japanese medics he was training. They're all drunk. This one, when he went to Sri Lanka and trained Sri Lankan military officers how to de-mine their own fields. This is him in his younger years, head shaved boot camp-style, he's got a baby face. This one was taken in Afghanistan. He's doing EOD now. A lot older. He was almost totally gray. This one's Finnegan, our son. Mark was a really, really good dad. He was a wonderful father.

Before his last deployment, we took a trip to Ireland. I wasn't planning on getting pregnant. We already had a toddler, Finnegan, and we didn't want to have any more kids until after he got back. But we were in Ireland and I guess babies are made in Ireland. Three weeks before he left for Afghanistan, I found out that I was pregnant. I stayed in Chandler, Arizona, my belly swelling with his child, waiting for him to come home.

THEY DON'T SEND MEN TO YOUR DOOR TO TELL YOU THAT YOUR HUSBAND'S SICK. They don't send men to your door to tell you that your husband's been wounded and is on the way to Walter Reed. The only time they send someone to your door is to tell you that your husband is dead and coming home in a coffin. We all know it. But for some reason, we tell ourselves, "That's not why they're here. It can't be."

I drove back from my parents' to our house. The men in uniform were gone. It was three o'clock in the afternoon on a Saturday. I stared out my window in Chandler, Arizona, waiting for the men in uniform to return.

HE DIDN'T HAVE TO GO TO AFGHANISTAN FOR ANOTHER TOUR. He could have chosen a duty station in the States, but he chose to deploy with the people he knew and whom he had trained with, and whom he cared about like family. He deployed with them because he couldn't live with himself if he wasn't there with them.

They told me it was a long, dusty road in Helmand Province, Afghanistan, and they saw something that looked suspicious. Just a piece of debris on the road that maybe shouldn't be there. The convoy halted. Mark dismounted from his truck and went down to look. Everybody else stayed behind in the trucks. That's the rule—the team leader goes down by himself. If something happens, no one else gets hurt.

Maybe, Mark thought, this isn't a big deal. It's just trash. I don't really need to worry about this. Maybe that's why he didn't get into his bomb suit before he bent down for a closer look.

He had responded to countless instances like this on countless missions. He had defused hundreds of bombs. He was one of the best bomb techs they had—that's what they all said. Mark was one of the smartest, one of the most careful, bomb techs in the Army.

I was told that he knelt down to look at it. I was told he barely brushed his hand onto the dirt when it went off. The blast hit him in the face, throwing him back, and he collapsed immediately, his blood flowing onto the dust on the road.

The last time we had talked on the satellite phone, he said he was burnt out, overworked. He said he didn't want to go on that mission. He just wanted to go home. That's all he wanted, to go home. That's all I wanted, too.

I WAITED FOR THE MEN IN UNIFORM TO COME BACK TO MY HOUSE IN CHANDLER, ARIZONA, TO TELL ME THAT MY HUSBAND WAS DEAD. I watched the shadows lengthen outside as the afternoon wore on. I was in the desert in Arizona, Mark was in the desert in Afghanistan, we were both in deserts, half a world apart. I sat in my living room in silence, staring out the window.

A knock, three hard raps. I look toward the door. I wonder for a moment if I can just sit there until they go away.

Three more knocks. Sharp, measured. And then I realize I'm opening the door and I can feel the warm air outside and see the sun on the front walk. Two men stand there in pressed uniforms and polished shoes, backs straight, their arms hanging at their sides, hands clenched. They wear black berets on their heads and medals on their chests and grim faces. One of the men looks down at my pregnant belly, the great curve of our unborn child inside me. I can see the panic in his eyes, and I suddenly feel this deep pity for him.

The other man looks at me, fixes his eyes on my eyes, a sad, determined expression on his face. "Ma'am, are you Mrs. Danielle Wells?"

I don't answer, I don't make a sound. I look back into his eyes and nod my head, slowly, once.

"Ma'am, the Secretary of the Army regrets to inform you that your husband, Staff Sergeant Mark C. Wells, was—"

I just cut him off. "I already know why you're here," I said. I felt a wave of nausea wash through me. "I already know." I put my hand on my forehead. "Thank you. I don't need you here. You guys can leave. You guys can go. Thank you. Thank you for your service."

They asked me if I needed to sit down. I said no. They asked if I had family to support me. I said I did. I asked them to leave and they said, "Yes, ma'am." They straightened their coats and they turned and walked to their car and drove away.

They maintained their composure, but I could tell it was devastating for them to wake up on a Saturday morning with orders to notify a pregnant woman that her husband has been killed by a bomb in Afghanistan.

I WAS URGED NOT TO HAVE AN OPEN CASKET. "Oh, you're pregnant," people said to me. "Just remember him as he was." So Mark's casket was closed, draped with a flag. I hated it. I never got to see him again. That was him in there, in that casket, but I never quite believed it to be true.

I asked for the autopsy report from the Army. I read it carefully from beginning to end, every word. I read the graphic details of his injuries, the medical description of how the blast had destroyed his face, the destruction of the tissues of his brain, the anatomical terms of the parts of the skull and blood vessels. It was clear there was no hope of him surviving. And if he had survived, he would not have been Mark anymore, the man who loved to cook and read books to his son, the man who played bagpipes, the man who had been my husband. Mark had vanished forever in a fraction of a second.

The report listed the wrong age for Mark. I was very upset. A wave of doubt crept over me. I'm eight months pregnant, I've been waiting for months for my husband to come home, and why am I getting this autopsy report? Is that really him they're describing? They sent me an amended report, correcting his age.

Yes, the Department of the Army assured me, the man in the casket had been my husband.

Some of Mark's friends were wounded on that deployment but came home alive. One lost his eye. Another lost his hearing. They come home with parts of their bodies gone or destroyed. I wonder if they labor under the weight of a guilt they do not deserve. His brothers, who came home with injuries to their bodies, injuries to their minds, injuries to their souls, do they suffer even more because they made it home and Mark did not?

I was so angry with Mark. I wanted to scream at him. Why weren't you wearing a bomb suit? What were you thinking? How could you leave us?

MOTHER'S DAY 2011. TWO MONTHS AFTER MARK DIED. Mark had always made me feel special on Mother's Day. He sent flowers and cards. He made me feel how proud he was that I was the mother of his children. His new baby daughter, Caitlynn, was three weeks old. Mark had chosen her name, but had never gotten to see her. I was alone in the house with an infant and a toddler. I was deeply depressed.

I had gone full circle. I was born at Williams Air Force Base in Chandler, Arizona, the daughter and granddaughter of veterans. I left Chandler to get away and see the world. I had become a Navy linguist. I had left the Navy to become the wife of a soldier. Now I was back in Chandler, Arizona, receiving my husband's body off a plane at Williams, a war widow with two children.

I started drinking that day because I was sad, and drank most of the day and kept drinking for a long time afterwards. I numbed myself with alcohol. It was my way of coping. As time went on, I wondered if I was drinking because I was sad, or just sad because I was drinking. But no one really noticed. In the military, people only notice if you're not drinking.

I wasn't awake. I wasn't *present*. I'd get up and do the day-to-day routines of life, grocery shopping and playdates and walks in the stroller around the block, but I felt nothing inside, I felt empty, like all the joy I might have ever known had been torn out of my life by that bomb in Afghanistan.

STEVEN WAS MARK'S CLOSEST FRIEND FROM HIS TIME IN HAWAII. THEY WERE BROTHERS IN ARMS. Steven loved Mark, and Mark's death devastated him. They were both bomb techs. They'd deployed together to Afghanistan in the same unit, and while I grieved in Arizona, Steven was still there, on the base, sick with loss. The missions had largely ended, and they were idling away the days, waiting to come home. Caitlynn was a newborn, I was home a lot, and my days felt empty.

We started communicating on Facebook and email, just as friends, supporting each other. Steven returned Stateside with the unit in July. We talked a lot, and we grew closer and closer. Two years after Mark was killed, Steven asked me to marry him. I said yes. I said yes because my children needed a father. I said yes because I was lonely. I said yes because I wanted to love and be loved again, and I had found that person.

Maybe people think that I leapt into someone else's arms, that I ran to take solace in a man who does the same job as my husband once did. Maybe they think Steven lost his best friend on a dusty road a world away, so now he's marrying his best friend's wife and raising his best friend's children out of some sense of duty. What a great guy, they may think, to marry Mark's widow and take care of her.

That's not what happened. The marriage is real, the love is true. But you're judged by others, especially in the EOD community. You always wonder who's judging you for not remaining the grieving widow in black, or the haunted and lonely best friend, as if Mark would want an endless sadness to follow his memory.

Mark's urn and his bagpipes rest on a table at home. Finnegan looks at pictures of his father and asks about him. Was my daddy brave? Do I look like him? We're at the grocery store, picking up a gallon of milk, and Finnegan blurts out, "My dad is dead and he died by a bomb." The ladies in the checkout line gape at Finnegan, at a loss for words, as disturbed and dumbfounded as the men who came to our door in their uniforms that day. I've gotten used to these awkward moments. What does one say to a woman with an infant and a toddler in a checkout line whose husband was killed in a war? I smile at them. "He's okay," I reassure them. "He'll be all right." I don't know what else to say.

Steven and I argue about how to raise the children. I never had a chance to have those fights with Mark. He only got to be a dad for eighteen months.

I AM TRYING TO UNDERSTAND MY IDENTITY. FIRST I WAS AN ACTIVE DUTY SERVICE MEMBER OF THE U.S. NAVY, a Chinese linguist. Then I left the Navy and became a military wife. Then I was a mother. Then I became a widow. I was kicked out of those worlds and into another very swiftly. Now I'm trying to understand this new identity, what it means to be a veteran, a military wife, a daughter of military parents, a military widow. For better or for worse, I embrace who I am, but it can be lonely. You think nobody could possibly understand. Then it becomes a self-fulfilling prophecy. You think no one can understand, so you don't talk to anyone else and give them a chance to try and understand. But when you do reach out, you start finding people who've been there. You find people who actually do understand. And sometimes you realize that's all there is. Just because you lost your husband too doesn't mean you and I are going to be friends.

That's been part of my grieving process—finding a new self. A new identity. There's more out there. I can't be defined by this one event in life. I don't want to be stuck, to never see past the loss. I'm trying to build a different side of me. Maybe a side Mark would never have gotten to see.

Some people tell me to try to put the past behind me. But I can't do that. I think about everything. What would our life be like right now? Would Mark like how I'm raising his children? Would he like who I've become? Would he still love me?

"We didn't know much about PTSD coming back because, in the Marine Corps, you're trained to be mission-oriented. You're conditioned to carry on. You contain your emotions. All the stuff lingers there—the good, the bad, and the ugly—until it comes to a head and you have to address it."

THE ONE THING SHE WAS PUT ON THIS EARTH TO DO

BRANDON MITALAS

MY BATTALION LANDED IN IRAQ ON SEPTEMBER 11, 2004, THREE YEARS TO THE DAY AFTER THE FALL OF THE TWIN TOWERS. From there, the Marines Corps sent me to Kuwait, where I was one of a handful of guys who ran an airport. We rolled thousands of pallets of food and ammo and equipment into military aircraft headed into Iraq. Planes came in from Baghdad and other bases full of Marines headed home after their tours. Military jets, and sometimes civilian airlines, landed with fresh Marines for the war. We could get them off the plane and unload twenty tons of gear in under an hour. We knew how to run a flightline.

We also received the dead, and we sent them home. The remains of every American and coalition troop killed in Iraq came to our airport before being sent to their next of kin. They arrived from Iraq on battlefield transport and then were flown to Dover Air Force Base, where the final, official autopsies were done. Then they'd be sent to their home towns, wherever they came from, to their parents or wives or families.

226 is the number of Marines and sailors and airmen that I carried on and off the planes. 226 men and women who had been killed. 226 *Fallen Angels*. That was their call sign on the radio—*Fallen Angels*. We'd get a call relaying that ten Fallen Angels were inbound on a bird. Soon after, ten flag-draped coffins would come in on a KC-130. Sometimes the dead came in body bags.

We conducted a meticulous, formal ceremony every time a Fallen Angel was unloaded from a plane. A detail of Marines would enter the flight crew's door on the side of the aircraft. They'd unstrap the transfer cases, which were large coffins made of polished aluminum, from the cargo deck. The ramp would be lowered, the truck would be waiting, and two lines of personnel awaited below, standing stiff at attention. On the order, we stooped down and grasped the handles of the coffin. On the order, we lifted the coffin. On the order, we carried the coffin step by step down the ramp to the waiting truck.

When the coffin was loaded on the truck, we made an about-face. We marched in formation back into the plane. As the ramp went back up, the detail gave the funeral salute, a precise, six-second sweep of the arm, like a salute in slow motion. Then we brought our arms in a six-second sweep down.

When I got back to the States and left the Marine Corps, I tattooed the Roman numerals for 226 on my right arm, *CCXXVI*. I had the numerals covering a tattoo of a broken heart, like a Band-Aid. The number 226 kept popping up in my life. I'd push pause on a DVR recording and it stops at 2:26.

My initials added up to 26. My girlfriend's too. I didn't regard the appearances of the number 226 as coincidence.

I got a lot of other tattoos, too—the Gates of Heaven, with a Marine silhouette standing guard, the pillars of the gates formed by the Twin Towers. I got an hourglass, the sands of time trickling down, with an angelic wing on one side, a demonic wing on the other. The phrase in Latin SI VIS PACEM, PARA BELLUM, which means, "He who desires peace, prepare for war." The date *01-26-05*, the worst day of my life, when thirty coffins came in one day.

The tattoos and the man who did them, Jerry, are one of the things that saved my life after I came home. A few years ago, I had Jerry start a new series of tattoos on my right arm: a therapist's couch with a tattoo machine on it. A jigsaw puzzle covering up desert camouflage. The ongoing story, told in symbols, of me putting my life back together. When I got home from war, I had lost my innocence. I had lost the ability to feel normal.

THE ATTACKS ON SEPTEMBER 11 GOT UNDER MY SKIN. THE PLANES CRASHING, the burning towers, people leaping to their deaths. Deep down in my core, I burned with anger, and I felt the need to do something bigger and be a part of something bigger. I was 19, going to classes, playing college soccer, and working part-time delivering pizzas.

A few weeks after September 11, I delivered a pizza, and the guy who opens the door is a Marine recruiter. He's got the high-and-tight haircut and he's well built. "You look like a big athletic kid," he says to me. "You ever thought about joining the Marine Corps?"

I look at him. "Nope, but I'll take a free tee shirt." He doesn't give me a tee shirt on the spot, but he gives me his business card. "Come in tomorrow and we'll talk and get you a shirt." I said I would, but I told him he wasn't going to sell me on anything.

The next day I went to the recruiter's office and got my tee shirt. He gave me a bunch of brochures. Then he sat me down and showed me a fifteen-minute video on boot camp, the obstacle courses, the weaponry, the look of pride and determination on the faces. I loved every minute of it. I was hooked. But I didn't sign any papers.

One day a couple of months later, I went to my college classes in the morning, then drove home. I lay down for a quick nap. My mom peeked in on me, and she figured I'd skipped school that morning. That night, after I got home from soccer practice, my parents and I got into it. We had a big fight. They laid down their ground rules: "If you're going to live here for no rent, you're going to get a full-time job." I stormed out and I drove down to the elementary school a few blocks from our house. I sat there for hours thinking and crying, and that night I decided I was going to go talk to the recruiter.

The next morning, as I was heading out the door, my mom pushed one more time. "Don't come back unless you have three full-time job applications," she said. I went straight to the Marine Corps recruiting office after classes. I think he knew he'd see me again. I gave him my stipulations: I needed to go into the reserves, I needed to be back from all my training by August so I could play college soccer, and I needed to get out after four years so I could pursue professional soccer. I was pretty good, and that was my dream.

"No problem. You can leave in three weeks," he said.

I reached for his pen. "Where do I sign?"

I took my contract and I went back home, and before I'd gotten ten feet in the door my mom asked if I had gotten three full-time job applications. "No," I said, "I got *one*."

"Well, I told you to get *three*." I was arrogant and spiteful and a nineteen-year-old punk, and I slapped the signed contract committing me to the Marine Corps onto the kitchen table.

"What's that?"

"It's my contract with the Marine Corps. I leave for boot camp in three weeks. *Thanks, Mom*." She looked at it, and then an awful expression came over her face, and she started sobbing.

But I was too young and pissed off to let her tears move me. I just kept pushing. "I'm going to be a Marine."

Part of me knew I'd be going to war some day. The war had already begun in Afghanistan. We didn't yet know we'd be invading Iraq. I just wanted to become a man.

You're supposed to stay in a hotel the night before you leave for boot camp. But the recruiter was a Marine named Staff Sgt. Brownfield, and he played indoor soccer with my uncle. Because he knew my uncle, Staff Sgt. Brownfield pulled some strings for me, and instead of staying in the hotel the night before boot camp, I got to sleep in my own bed. He picked me up at 4 a.m. the next morning at my parents' house to take me to the airport.

He pulled into the driveway and kept the car running, his door open.

No time for long good-byes. Hug and a kiss to Mom, hug and a kiss to Dad. Love you, love you. My mom managed to hold it together, at least in front of me. "Do well," my dad said. "Keep in touch when you can. We'll see you when you're done." My dad is a first-generation Greek-American raised in a very strict household. Grandpa we called *pappou*, Greek for "grandfather."

My brother and sister were still sleeping. I'd given them a kiss goodbye while they slept. And that was it. I was gone.

But I was scared. My world was really small and contained. I'd never really been away from home. All that changed really, really quick.

You see videos and hear stories about how bad boot camp is. People who've gone through it tell you it's even worse than that. It is.

The first two weeks I was writing my dad, begging him to rescue me. "Get ahold of our congressman! Find a way to get me out of here!" The drill instructors always yelling in your face. Nothing is ever good enough. You're tired. Bad food. But once I settled into the routine, once I embraced the challenge, it became an amazing experience. I figured out a way to solve the problem of homesickness, and it was to turn everything into a competition, even if it was getting my socks on faster than the guy next to me. And I started to love it. I fell in love with boot camp.

You see the transformation happening in yourself. Things you couldn't do the day before, now you can do them. It's not just gaining physical strength—it taps something deep inside you, releases this sense of courage and power. I went to boot camp with a fear of heights. But you've gotta go climb a rope that's fifty feet high and you've gotta rappel off of a hundred-foot tower, just you and the rope. It was terrible in the moment—the fear was overwhelming me—but once I got on the ground, I looked back up and thought, "I just did that."

That sense of invincibility. That's one of the main things the Marine Corps instills in you in boot camp. You come out of boot camp with the sense that there's nothing you can't accomplish. You have that strength to stand up and do what's asked of you. You have an indomitable will.

After boot camp is the Friday graduation ceremony. The families come on base. I was raised Roman Catholic—Catholic grade school, first communion, confirmation, the whole thing—so my parents and I went to mass at the chapel at the University of San Diego the following Sunday morning, me in my U.S. Marine dress blues. After the service, we talked with the priest.

Your dress blues. Talk about that sense of invincibility. The dress blues feels like a cloak of armor.

I LOST 35 POUNDS IN BOOT CAMP. I WAS GAUNT. I LOOKED EMACIATED. The last two weeks of boot camp aren't quite as physically demanding, and they start to let you have a little fun. They took our whole company of six platoons to a San Diego Padres game for Military Appreciation Day. We wore our camouflage. We sat high up in the bleachers in our own little section, isolated from the civilian fans. And they let you bring a little money, which most guys splurged on junk food. Oh, man, I had nachos. I had a chocolate chip cookie ice cream sandwich. I had one of those king-sized Snickers bars. We were loving it. It felt like heaven.

When we get back to base, they put on a big feed for us, chicken-fried steak, and we all just got to stuff our faces.

We each got two steaks and pasta and rice and potatoes. Most of us stuffed ourselves silly.

And then the drill instructors took us outside afterwards and they just hammered us. They call it "smoking" you with PT. Wind sprints, push-ups, sit-ups, until everybody is puking like dogs.

It was to teach us a lesson, like everything in boot camp. Even if you can indulge, don't. Don't ever let your guard down. Never let your guard down.

NATHAN RAYMOND WOOD, A GUY I NEVER MET WHILE HE WAS ALIVE, WAS KILLED ON MY PARENTS' WEDDING ANNIVERSARY IN 2004. It was November 9. He was killed during the Second Battle of Fallujah, which kicked off with house-to-house clearing. The bodies of over 100 Marines were shipped to our airport in Kuwait that month. When the body of Nathan Raymond Wood came off the C-130 in a flag-draped coffin, our chaplain gave us a few details about him. I found out that he was from Bothell, Washington, and he went to Juanita High School, ten minutes away from where I grew up. Because of that, and because he was killed on my parents' wedding anniversary, I felt a connection to him. The next day I read the press releases in the newspapers back home. Our chaplain gave me the flag that had covered his casket on his flight from Iraq to our base in Kuwait. He knew it meant something to me.

I still have Nathan's original flag, and it still has everything written on it from the day he came in—his name, date of birth, Social Security number, blood type—along the band of white canvas on the edge of the flag, where the flag attaches to the pole. I have the flag mounted in a case in my living room, high atop a bookcase, the highest item on the wall.

A year later, I was home for my parents' wedding anniversary. I reached out to the Marine Moms Network and asked if they could get me in touch with Nathan's family. I gave them my story. They gave me his mother's email address. I sent her a short email—I didn't know if the one-year anniversary of his death was going to stir up a lot of emotion, and I didn't want to cause them any more grief. But a few hours later, I got a call on my cell phone. It was his mother, and she invited me to a family dinner a couple days later.

Later on that day I got dressed up in my dress blues and went out to Nathan's gravesite. I pull up and get out of my truck, and there's two people standing there, his two best friends from high school and childhood. I planned on saying my respects and leaving quickly, but I ended up staying two hours. They told me a bunch of stories about him—having fun in high school, good times they had together. I told them my experience carrying his casket when he came through my airport. I told them about the flag. We hugged and cried.

When I went to his house where he grew up to have dinner with his family, I didn't wear my uniform. I didn't want to stand out—it wasn't about me. The extended family was there, uncles, cousins, some friends. After dinner, they shared stories and asked me about who I was and what I'd done and why I felt the need to reach out to them. We planted a tree in his front yard in memory of Nathan. I got to dig the hole. I felt very honored.

Nathan's dad gave me pictures from his deployment that he had sent home, even a video of a firefight that he was in the night before he was killed.

I still have them, but I've never watched the video or gone through the pictures. I know exactly where they're at, though. They're in a box in my closet, on the top shelf, on the right side.

THE PLANES LANDING WITH THE FALLEN ANGELS SMELLED OF DEATH. The aluminum coffins were heavy, filled with what had been a Marine, often a big man, and the gear he'd been carrying when he was killed. But some coffins were not heavy enough, and when you lifted them, you could tell that only a part of a man was inside, that they hadn't been able to collect all of the body. Some Fallen Angels arrived in body bags from remote combat zones in Iraq where they didn't have the aluminum coffins. The body bags lay on the steel pallets. You could see the shape of the body, the drape of the plastic over the head and chest and legs and feet, the body unnaturally still.

After we unloaded the aluminum coffins from the planes, the bodies were taken to the morgue. They documented the contents, confirmed the identity, took notes on wounds and burns. Then the coffins were stored in a refrigerated van. The remains were packed with ice for the flight to the United States.

I only cried twice. Once was in November. We had loaded many flag-draped coffins. Nathan's was among them. The flags were draped over each of the dozen coffins and ready for the flight home, but I went back inside the plane. I stood there for a long time. I adjusted tiny imperfections in the draping of the flags. I trimmed a thread hanging off one of the flags. I went through every flag on that plane, as tears ran down my cheeks. I cried again on January 26, 2005. Thirty Marines and one sailor had been killed in a helicopter crash the day before. We loaded their remains and the remains of yet another eleven Fallen Angels who needed to be sent home. I got off my shift and went back to my room. I grasped Nathan's flag and I wept.

For months after I got home, I couldn't bear the sight of an American flag. Once when I saw a flag-draped coffin in a movie, a sickness spread instantly inside me, bringing me to my knees.

I WAS LIVING IN PORTLAND. I WAS LIVING ALONE. I HAD GOTTEN HOOKED UP WITH A SOCCER CLUB and started coaching at the youth level. I had no idea I had PTSD. I'd fallen into a pattern of self-medication. For me, it was a lot of drinking. Four, five, six nights a week. I'd drink myself to sleep, trying to forget everything and trying to avoid the nightmares and waking up in the middle of the night, breathless, sure that somebody was about to bust through my door and kill me. I kept seeing the coffins and the body bags. My dreams, the demons of the subconscious, were terrifying. I learned that when I didn't remember falling asleep because I had a bottle of vodka or whiskey next to me, I didn't dream as much. And it became this crazy, destructive, downward spiral.

What triggered it was just an ordinary evening, an errand I'd run a hundred times before. I was driving to a convenience store a few blocks away. I felt a car following me too closely, his headlights menacing me from behind, and I could feel my flight-or-fight kicking in. When I changed lanes, he changed lanes. When I pulled into the parking lot at the store, he pulled in. I stayed in my car and watched him open his door and get out and enter the store. I watched him browse the aisles through the store windows. I waited until he paid for his things, left the store, and pulled away. Then I went in and bought my stuff.

On the drive home, a block up the road, I passed a Kentucky Fried Chicken. A yellow floodlight shown in front of their fryer chimneys. A plume of smoke or steam rose into the air. And the floodlight and the smoke immediately took me back to the yellow floodlight we'd walked under as we carried coffins between the refrigerated van and the morgue in Kuwait.

It took me back to somewhere I never wanted to be again, and in seconds I was sobbing, tears streaming down my face. I kept driving, blinking crazily through the tears. To my core, I was sobbing. The floodgates had burst.

I sat for hours on the front stairs of my apartment, thinking. I wasn't sure whether I wanted to live another day, or if I should end my life. To live or die. To escape the constant bombardment of bad memories, the darkness that permeated my life. I held a knife in my hand, tracing the blade on the skin of my wrist. I wondered what it would feel like to end it all. I wondered if it would hurt. I wondered what people would think if I did it.

My mom was long asleep up in Seattle, two hundred miles away, when I called her. It was after 1 a.m. The phone rang and rang, and then she answered, said, "Hello, what's going on, Brandon?" There was no hiding the trembling in my voice. I told her about the car following me on the way to the store. About the yellow floodlight and the cloud of smoke and how that put me back at the airport in Kuwait among the Fallen Angels, alone in their aluminum coffins. I told her I was struggling, bad. I told her I wasn't sure I was going to make it through the night.

She said she was getting her keys and coat. She was coming to get me. She was driving to Portland right then, in the middle of the night. She'd be at my apartment before dawn. She was on her way.

But the sound of her voice brought me back somewhere I could hold on. Talking to her took me off the metaphorical ledge, at least for the moment. I told her that I'd be okay for the rest of the night, and she convinced me to go talk to somebody for the first time. And I did. I woke up the next morning and drove straight to Seattle and met her at the VA emergency room and had my first psych appointment. That was my path. That was my crossroads.

She saved my life that night. If that was the one thing she was put on this earth to do, I'm still here because of it.

At the time, I didn't believe I would see my twenty-fifth birthday. I'll be thirty-five years old in August.

WHERE THEY'RE AT NOW

AS OF MARCH 2017

DESHAUN CAPLES

I LIVE IN WESTERN WASHINGTON WITH MY WIFE AND KIDS. Honestly, every day I just want to get better at being a father. The crying is still a high-stress trigger for me. At this point, my oldest daughter has a rough understanding of what's going on. My kids work with me as I try to teach them why Dad gets so mad about little things.

I have a five-month-old son. When he cries, it still brings me back to that medevac in Iraq. I still fight that reality every day. Sometimes I feel my life would be easier if I could just forget Iraq altogether, but it always creeps back, usually with a vengeance. I'm trying to accept that.

I find myself not wishing to be the *old me* anymore. Now I focus more on being the best version of my true self *today*. And my wife helps me be the best father I can for my kids.

My goal is to continue to push my kids to become successful and happy, each in their own way. I help them become the best versions of themselves. If anything, I feel like I have the tools to teach them to push and learn through adversity.

I look to history to find answers to problems I don't fully understand. I realize I am a character in one of man's oldest stories: war.

DOMINIC WILKERSON

RIGHT NOW I'M JUST TRYING TO MAKE IT. I'm trying to balance my health with my career and school. It's tough. School work is going downhill while I try to work more hours. Every month I'm in the VA trying to fix my leg and other health issues—I've started to have chronic migraine headaches. I'm down to budgeting the bare minimum now, just enough for food, house, utilities. I love taking photographs and had an excellent camera, but I ended up selling most of my camera equipment to pay my bills. I put off opening my own business until I can fix everything. I'm sorry, but right now it's grim.

ROBIN ECKSTEIN

I'M STILL TRYING TO FIND HOPE. SOME DAYS I WAKE UP AND THINK *This planet sucks.* Other days I wake up feeling good. I'll go out and feel like I'm part of the world. Then I catch myself. I'll notice I'm having fun and enjoying myself, and realize I shouldn't. I'll feel like I should have died in Iraq. It's like a slap in the face.

But I feel there's been a shift. For the last 13 years, I was waiting to get hit by a bus. I didn't care about myself or my life. I started changing that and started caring more about what happens to *me*. I lost a hundred pounds and decided to stop putting garbage in my body. I'm trying to clean up 13 years of not caring about myself. In order to have a life, I have to care. Some days I still wake up and wish I'd get hit by a bus. But more and more I say, *No, I'm going to keep pushing.*

I'm trying, and I'm going to keep trying. If there's anything I can say to other veterans, it's just keep trying. I don't know how many treatments I sought for PTSD. Most of them didn't do anything for me. I eventually found something that helped a little, and then something else that helped a little more. All of us veterans are stumbling

through this. The VA doesn't know what to tell us. They don't have a cure. They don't have something that works for every veteran and makes them better. So you just keep trying and ride the roller coaster.

I'm living in Southwest Portland. I'm involved with Mission Continues, which is a volunteer organization for veterans. I'm still seeking treatment. I'm going to take a comedy class, try to get myself out there a little more. You don't know until you try.

MIGUEL ESCALERA

I'VE BEEN MARRIED TO MY WIFE ANGELICA MAY FOR SEVEN YEARS. We have two beautiful kids, nine-year-old JaevinMiguel, and Ava Liana, who's turning two. They're growing like weeds. They have taught me so much about bringing a life into the world.

I'm a full-time student in a physician assistant program. I'm also a Navy reservist. I've been doing that for six years, and I want to continue. I really, really enjoy being in the military. I work with veterans through AmeriCorps. I get veterans connected to services, help them continue their educations. I help them find housing or even a meal.

Everything I've done since my war experience has been an effort to try to live my life to its fullest in order to honor my fellow Marines and corpsmen who weren't able to come back, like Doc Mendez. I would feel guilty if I didn't do well in life and honor him by helping other people, raising a good family, and being a good person. Because Doc Mendez *was* that person. He was a great man.

Sometimes I have good days, sometimes I have bad days. Anxiety and sleep are the biggest things. I don't suffer from depression, but I'm not out of the woods yet. I know it can still affect me in the future.

The war changed me.

I've never told my story to anyone before. This is my first time. It's been immensely therapeutic in a way that I never expected it to be. I've been able to self-seek and realize where I came from and what I've done. I hadn't really had time to stop and think. With life going on, it's hard to take time to pause.

Telling my story opened up old wounds and memories, pulling me back. At times as I was telling my story, I was getting vivid feelings of warmth and chills and cold, and even as I tell you this now, my skin gets raised up, as I imagine, even briefly, my wartime experiences. But telling the story has been extremely therapeutic.

I've seen my Marine brothers and fellow corpsmen on Facebook, but I've kept my distance so far. I worry about my experiences and haven't known what to say. But I want to reconnect now.

My wartime experiences have shown me that we live in a great country. Other countries suffer war and poverty. I want to raise my kids to be aware of that and respect our good fortune. Don't waste your time, and your life, on nonsense. I want to go overseas and do mission work and help countries that suffer from disease and war.

I'm telling my story so my children can read it someday. I might not be able to tell my story to them. They weren't yet born when I went to war, but I'll have this book on my shelf if they ever want to dive in and understand what my life was like before them. My experiences have driven me to where I am today—and even to them. Like listening to Grandfather or Grandmother tell you stories about their lives, powerful stories mold and shape us. Hopefully my children can read this story and make their own inferences about life.

KEVIN CHOSE

THEY SAY A MAN DIES TWICE. He dies once physically, and he dies a second time when the last memory of him is forgotten or no longer spoken.

Some men go to the ends of the earth and erect statues to preserve their memory. Others have a ton of sons in order to immortalize themselves. I'm the latter, with two sons to carry on my family name. We ask the meaning of life only to be answered, quite matter-of-factly, with *I love you, Dad*.

It is my hope that my two sons may perhaps read my story one day and better understand why I wasn't there. I hope that the events told here explain why I was gone, and never truly came home.

The unwritten rule of "don't talk about what happened in the war" has created a divide between veterans and their families. I hope that through these stories we find this common ground. Perhaps then fewer men would be unnecessarily immortalized on silly walls that only their real brothers go see.

DENNIS ELLER

I'M STILL TEACHING CHEMISTRY AT A HIGH SCHOOL. I'M ATTEMPTING MY SECOND ASCENT ATTEMPT OF MOUNT RAINIER THIS SUMMER. I'm still raising my three awesome daughters as a single dad, and I'm dating a wonderful woman.

My combat experiences affect me every day. I catch myself losing my temper. The things that keep me going are my daughters and my students. I look at my students and think: the shit that they go through is the shit I went through—they just have a different way of going through it. They experience homelessness or drugs. But they keep going. They give me a little bit of hope.

There are still dark days. That shit doesn't go away. Some of the worst is watching news and social media networks cover the combat in Mosul. How they glamorize soldiers now. They all look like Special Forces operatives. Now every veteran has a beard and skinny jeans and massive tattoos. That's not how it is. It bothers me, because half the people who are glamorizing it didn't fucking live the life. It brings back memories of the hypocrisy.

I'm still dealing with all the economic ramifications of divorce and coming home to an empty house. It makes life really hard.

Every time I think I get past all the bullshit, I get sucked back in.

Most days are good. More laughter than darkness. But it's tough sometimes. One of my friends is a police officer. He's on the honor guard, and he stood watch over his slain friend all night. Days like that are tough. They bring back a lot of memories of watching good people die.

As far as whether my story means anything, I don't think it does. I did what I had to, I did what I thought was right, and I did my job. That's really all you can say.

EMMANUEL WRIGHT

I'M ENROLLED IN A GRADUATE DEGREE PROGRAM FOR MENTAL HEALTH COUNSELING. I hope to continue using ecotherapies for healing and growth from trauma. I have begun to find voice in advocating for social justice, particularly in regards to working with Syrian and Iraqi refugees. Some day I may work with refugees abroad as well.

My experiences in Iraq are my moral compass. They have shaped my worldview in such a way that everything I do on a daily basis in some way relates to Iraq.

In particular, the Iraqi girl.

I manage symptoms I have related to major depressive disorder and PTSD. Some days are easier than others. Over the past year or so, I have developed psychotic features stemming from depression. I see things and have flashbacks. Mostly I see people, sometimes the girl, or I hear them speaking to me. The voices usually say something negative about my worth, my intelligence, or even my guilt. Most of the time, I manage these voices with ease, but other times the voices can be jarring and the experiences intense. I like to think, however, that these challenges show my resilience. Despite having a disability, I can do good things and be a positive influence in my community.

The war affects everything I do, every day, in every interaction I have. I see my life as two parts: my life before the war, and the life I have now. In many regards, I cannot recognize the person I was before the war. That person seems to be a myth, someone who probably never actually existed to begin with.

Telling my story has given voice to my voicelessness. I have often resorted to writing as a way of expressing myself. Each time I write, the burden is lessened. Mostly I write bad poetry. I read one poem [about an incident in the story] in front of a group of people. First I was terrified, then I was overcome with grief. Then I felt empowered, because I knew that the people in the poem were not forgotten. Others now know what happened and, in their own way, they too will have a memory of that man in Iraq who was trying to provide for his family but was taken from them much too soon.

ZONG HER

I<small>T WAS</small> 3 <small>A.M., AND THE</small> B<small>URGER</small> B<small>RASSERIE IN</small> L<small>AS</small> V<small>EGAS WAS</small> <small>OPERATING AS IF IT WERE A NORMAL LUNCH HOUR.</small> Brightly colored lights flashed with the beat of a blaring Top 40 song, a tune I had never heard, since only two weeks before I'd come back from Afghanistan.

Scattered groups of loud drunks ate fancy American cheeseburgers and drank 20-ounce milkshakes. Many were rude, one man even yelling at his waitress. I bit into my bacon blue cheeseburger, ignoring the ungrateful people who surrounded me.

Greasy food like this was what I missed about being in the United States. I sipped some water from my glass, appreciating that I could actually drink water from a tap. Red ketchup dribbled out of the burger onto my white summer jumper. The layers of makeup I'd caked on my Afghanistan-tanned face had withstood the tears from the argument earlier with my girlfriends.

I was sitting alone at the bar. Vegas was not what I would have chosen as a relaxing vacation after a nine-month deployment to Afghanistan, but the girls pressured me into it and I had put down a huge deposit. I kept reassuring myself that I would love it and that I could handle the loud, crowded Vegas lifestyle.

But the truth was, I hated everything about the trip.

Even though I came back safe and sound, I had changed. I was different somehow and, for the life of me, I couldn't be who I used to be.

I didn't belong. Everything I had felt about my career, my friends, my social life had completely changed. The social butterfly everyone remembered had died. I stopped being friends with most of my social network. My old friends probably hate me because they can't understand why I pulled away.

And it hurt. It hurt because it felt like I failed at being *me*. Worse yet, I hated feeling I had failed everyone who knew the *old me*. It was easier to make new friends who didn't know me before. Dating relationships became harder. I felt that men were intimidated by my military experience.

That first year back, I attempted to have a smooth transition. But the shame and secrets I kept to maintain an image of an ordinary life were heavy and unbearable at times. I fell into an addiction to shopping at thrift stores. In Afghanistan, I only had access to secondhand items. Something about buying used things brought me comfort. I spent all my money, and I couldn't stomach going back to my former job. I was evicted out of my apartment.

I realized I couldn't keep trying to be the old me. I had to embrace my new self.

One of my biggest personal achievements in Afghanistan was connecting with people through yoga and listening to them. I decided I would go back to school and apply to a PhD program in psychology. I want to serve military veterans and the prison population with a focus on mental health.

It's been three years since that deployment. I've completed several psychology classes. A year ago I decided to accept a military contract position in Afghanistan to pay off my school loans, apply to graduate schools, and use my free time to write. As I write this, I'm still in Afghanistan.

MIKE FARNUM

I RETIRED FROM THE ARMY AFTER 23 YEARS OF SERVICE. I tried law enforcement and armed security, but I really hated it. I worked for Veterans Conservation Corps, then as a biologist. I went back to school and served as the VetCorps representative on campus. On more than one occasion, I was told I had saved a veteran's life. Now I'm Director of Military Outreach at a university. I'm still trying to save lives.

Recently two guys ran full speed in front of my office window, one chasing the other. There was loud yelling. It turned out one of the guys was a car thief. *What if one of the guys was armed?* I wondered. *What would I do if bullets started coming into the window?* I'd get away from the window so I'm not a presentable target. I'd move to a safe spot in the building. I already know where that is, and I know what to do, even though I've never been instructed on that.

I've already thought all about it. That's what soldiers do. We think about *scenarios*. We see what's going on, and we make a plan. We'll always have that.

I knew people who died or were killed or committed suicide during my wartime experiences. I have photographs of them on my desk. They're ten inches above my computer screen, so I see them every day, all day. I think about them—often. What am I doing here, in my job? Am I doing it in a way that would bring honor to their sacrifice? They gave their lives so I could continue doing what I'm doing. That means something to me. These gentlemen are my moral compass. They keep me on track. They're the people I need to live up to. I want them to know I'm not going to waste my life.

If anybody says that telling their story has not been meaningful, they're telling a lie. Yes, it's meaningful. To tell your story, you have to reflect on it. When you reflect on it, you learn about yourself. Some people might wonder if they should embellish their story. But you realize you don't really have to. The experiences you have had are unique. No one else has been in the same places, talked to the same people, operated in the same conditions. Telling my story has been educational. It's been humbling. It's been enlightening.

I hope that, in the telling, somebody out there will be able to learn from my experiences. Maybe it will help them get past something. If we can keep veterans from committing suicide, or becoming drug addicted or homeless—if we can do that for just one person—that's a legacy.

JEFF RADCLIFF

I'M WORKING CONSTRUCTION, RESIDENTIAL REMODEL STUFF. I LIKE IT. I've got two dogs and am starting to save for a down payment on a house. I have a few veteran buddies I try to hang out with on a regular basis. I am up in the woods hunting and camping every weekend I can.

When I was in Afghanistan, I was pretty bigoted and closed-minded. I hated all Muslims and Middle Eastern people. My friend Zach always joked that I would marry a Muslim, and so it's ironic that my girlfriend now is from Iran. We've been dating for two years. Zach still calls me up to give me shit about it.

I'm the type of person who tries to bottle everything up and not talk about it. About every six months I have a pretty serious breakdown. I don't think it's so much from trauma or PTSD, but just thinking about the whole experience, and what a waste of almost six years of my life it was. I get pretty depressed sometimes about where I could be now if I hadn't joined. I feel sad for guys who get killed over there, because it isn't changing anything. It's just such a waste of a life.

I'm still dealing with physical injuries and the insane amount of frustration that comes with trying to deal with the VA.

I don't have nightmares, but I do have one specific memory that sticks with me and comes to mind every single day. We were running a convoy somewhere near Shirghazi, and two Afghani guys flagged us down. I hear on the radio that they want the corpsman to come and take a look at a little kid. The older guy is carrying a baby. Our terp [interpreter] is telling us that he's saying his baby won't wake up. I take a look, and the kid is dead and has been for a while. He wasn't killed from battle or collateral damage or anything—the infant was just dead. I was 20 years old at the time. I had no idea what to do, or what to tell this guy. So I gave him some Motrin and told him to give it to the baby with some water and he would wake up tomorrow.

I feel horrible about that every day.

It's been a long time since I've talked about a lot of this. It would be meaningful to me if people could read the stories in this book, and somehow see the pain and damage, and realize the problems the war has caused people, and understand it's all over nothing. I hope people understand that the everyday normal American has more in common with most Iraqis, Afghanis, Iranians, North Koreans, Cubans, and whoever else, than they have in common with the people of our government, the people in charge, the people who start these wars where people go to die, killing foreigners who are just like them.

TIMM LOVITT

THE SKY IS A DEEP DARK BLUE, THE SUN IS HOT AND HIGH OVERHEAD, AND THE WATER IS REFRESHINGLY FRIGID; it's perfect for cooling down after a brutally steep hike. The best part about this place is that there is no one around. I pull out two lukewarm beers. I open one and place the other in the water, knowing that it will only take a few minutes to cool down. I take a sip and I feel like I could stay here forever.

It has been a little over ten years since I transitioned out of the Army. I have a family: a beautiful wife, two funny and smart boys, and the sweetest golden retriever. I worked my way through an associate, bachelor, and master degrees and now have a career in higher education. I have overcome a lot and things are really starting to turn out very promising.

With all that in mind, it is hard to deny that I could stay here for the rest of my life. The water is absolutely still. The sun warms my skin. There are no distractions. I have the space and time to think back to some of those crazy times in the Army. Life was much simpler back then. I only needed courage and, at times, my humor to get me through.

Who am I kidding? The sun is starting to fall now and I realize that I need to hit the trail if I am going to make it back in time to pick up my oldest son from his sailing lessons. I finish my beer and put it into my pack. I grab a rock and throw it out into the water. The ripples break the surface of the perfectly still water and now I have one more reason to leave. I start off in the direction that I came, but quickly turn around and run back to the lake. I bend over and grab the second beer. It has to be cold by now, and I know that I should not leave a trace in this place where I could have stayed forever.

NIKKI DAVIS

THE ONLY THING THAT SEEMS TO BE A CONSTANT IS MY TRANSITION FROM MY OLD LIFE TO MY NEW. Some days are better than others. I've learned through both the good and bad days that the war will forever be a part of my journey, but it does not define it. Going back to school was the first step in a positive direction. While in school, I was able to reconnect with other veterans. I found my new mission: helping my fellow veterans any way that I can. To do this, I had to work through some of my own personal challenges that I had suppressed. Back then, I helped veterans be successful in college. Now I help veterans with moderate to severe traumatic brain injury (TBI), spinal cord injury or other neurological conditions. I help these veterans gain their independence. I wouldn't trade my journey for anything. This is my new mission. Like my past missions, I will give my all. The veterans I work with gave their all.

My journey has been filled with twists and turns and hills and valleys. I've had a great support team: my wife Ginette, "The Executive Team," and close family and friends. Without their support, I don't know where I would be. With their support, I have endless possibilities.

JUSTIN SHULTS

RECENTLY, ONE OF THE AFGHANI GUYS I HAD TRAINED DIED IN A HELICOPTER CRASH IN AFGHANISTAN. Shortly after, one of my student veterans here [at the school where I work] committed suicide. It's been a tough week. I'm trying to hang in there.

I've been trying to decide whether I need to focus on *me*, or focus on helping other people. Luckily I've been working with my therapist. "Why choose between the two?" he said. I can do both. So I'm starting a new job teaching people how to fly drones. I'll get back into the military mindset, but still be a civilian. And I'm going to continue to help veterans.

I'm still trying to figure out my transition. Thank God for therapy and everything else that got me here. I've been able to gain a difference in perspective. I've become able to consider the shittiest feelings of my life and understand that *this will pass.* That's where I'm at. I'm still trying to find my way, but at least there's an outlook for tomorrow. Before, I had so much suicidal ideation. It's still there, but it's more of a fight at this point to make sure that I take those feelings and learn from them. Now my task is to teach what I learn and prevent more veterans from taking their lives.

JOE JOCSON PORTER

AFTER GETTING OUT OF THE SERVICE, I MOVED ACROSS THE STATES TO SEATTLE TO RECONNECT WITH MY BIRTH MOTHER, WHO WAS HAVING HEALTH PROBLEMS. It was a big change after spending my life living and driving up and down the East Coast, from Maine to Florida.

My mother died of heart failure a few months after I moved. But in that time, I'd begun to set down roots. I found a job as a bookseller and met some great people. I began to fall in love with western Washington. My love of books led me to my wife, who was also working at the bookstore part-time. So I decided to stay.

Washington is a lot like Maine, once you get away from the city and see the small towns and the sprawling forests along the roads. There are so many natural places to explore. City life takes its toll on me sometimes, so to keep sane I go on long hikes with my friends and Astro, my dog. I'm working to become a professional illustrator/designer and writing a novel.

JOE STONE, SR.

THOSE TIMES I WAS DEPLOYED TO IRAQ AND AFGHANISTAN— THOSE WERE HARD TIMES. You go over as a young guy believing you're invincible. When people start dying and getting horribly injured, it really shocks you. You start questioning your morality. You question your spirituality. But those experiences made me a better person, and they made me understand that what's important in life is the people around you. Not just your family, your blood, but the people in your life and community. Those relationships are the most important things in life.

I joined the Army to be involved in something bigger than myself. That's essentially why we join the military—we want to be part of something bigger. We want to serve our country. But I'm glad I got out. I'd been in for fifteen years. I did five deployments, and three of those were combat tours. For the sake of my family, and my body, I was okay with leaving the Army. After another divorce, I remarried. My wife and I live in Vancouver, Washington. I just got accepted at a university. In all my days, I never thought I'd be enrolled in a university. It's a huge accomplishment.

One of the things I've missed most after I got out was that sense of camaraderie. I found a good replacement through volunteering. I joined the VFW and got really involved. I was invited to speak at Veterans Day on the history of "Taps." For me, "Taps" isn't a history lesson. It brings me back to those memorial ceremonies that we seemed to have way too many of. Talking about "Taps" meant a lot to me. It was a great experience to get in front of people.

If my family hears a loud bang, they immediately look to me to see how I'm going to react. My first thought is *something bad*. A loud bang takes me back to Iraq or Afghanistan for a split second. I know it's not mortars or rockets—I know that. But still your heart races and you become ultra-alert. You check your surroundings for a few seconds. You see what's going on. This is all subconsciously. Ninety-nine percent of my days are fine. I joke around, I laugh with the kids. But there are times when a car backfires or someone slams a door in the house—and that takes me back.

I have buddies who are drinking themselves to death. It's horrible. It's fairly common too—a buddy died of alcohol just this last year. Every year is an anniversary when someone was killed. Those days can be hard. Rather than distracting myself, I try to channel those feelings. I can't ignore those memories and not give them the respect they deserve, so I try to deal with them head-on and hopefully become a better person. There's a right way and a wrong way to deal with your struggles. I've made a conscious effort to do the right thing. I went to counseling to deal with PTSD. I play my guitar. I work on my writing. Volunteering also helps you deal with those issues.

My military experience is something I'm proud of. Even if I don't agree with the reasons we were there, I'm glad I was a part of it.

ADAM POSADAS

WHERE IS MY BROTHER NOW? I DON'T KNOW.

What I do know is that on March 7, 2016, just as 0600 rolled around, Adam was last seen here: 47.2690° N, 122.5517° W —the coordinates of the center of the Tacoma Narrows Bridge. I know that Adam was sitting on the rail of the westbound bridge, 188 feet above the water. I know that the last person who laid eyes on my brother happened to be a former Army chaplain who was travelling east when he witnessed my brother fall backwards from the rail into the cold waters of the Puget Sound.

I know that the Puget Sound is a hook-shaped, quickly-moving body of water that eventually dumps out into the Pacific Ocean.

I know that after an exhaustive search by the Coast Guard and four other agencies, the body of my baby brother was not recovered on that dark and gloomy Monday, nor has it surfaced since.

I also know that Adam had struggled for a decade since his discharge from the Army. The Army, as much as it had been a place for Adam to belong, was also a place that caused him deep hurt, abused him, battered him, and finally rejected him. I know that Adam was imprisoned by PTSD not only from the trauma of war but from the trauma of being betrayed by his "battle buddies" in the most horrific of ways. I know now that Adam was a victim of military sexual assault. Now you know, too.

These are the things we know that bring us to just before 0600, March 7, 2016: Adam had just completed 14 weeks of intensive VA-administered therapy to unpack his life before and after the Army: a tragically beautiful story that served to craft my brother into the survivor that he was—headstrong and graceful all at once. At the end of the program, Adam was given an official diagnosis of complex PTSD. I don't know this for sure, but given the events that followed, I believe that this diagnosis served as a life sentence for my 30 years, six months, and one-week-old brother.

Adam's body is certainly lost in the water, but his soul is found in every word he ever poured onto a page and in every song he sang. Adam is etched in every single memory that he shared with those who loved him and with those who hurt him. That is where Adam is now, and where he shall remain forever.

— Christine Posadas

DANIELLE VILLANUEVA

LIFE GOES ON, BUT EVERY TIME SOMEONE WALKS THROUGH MY FRONT DOOR THEY SEE A GIANT PAINTING OF AN EOD BADGE WITH A BLACK LINE PAINTED OVER IT. The black line indicates that someone has died. Their eyes will look below and see a flag case along with an urn, a picture of Mark, and a framed certificate for the Purple Heart medal. The kids keep pictures of Mark in their rooms, and we honor him by hanging mementos and memorabilia. It would feel wrong not to put things up.

Mark wanted his ashes to be scattered overseas, but I have hung on to his urn for now. I wanted the kids to be old enough to participate in such a trip. We may head back to Ireland to honor his Irish roots and scatter him over the Cliffs of Moher. On our trip to Ireland before he deployed, we drove for hours to see the famous cliffs, but there was so much fog we couldn't see three feet in front of us. We looked at each other and laughed.

The kids are not immune to grief, despite them being so little when Mark died. They tend to be blunt and honest—Finn moreso than Caiti. He announced to his first grade class that his dad "died fighting in a Afghanistan." He loves it when I say things like "Your dad liked this song," or "You have your dad's hair."

Caiti knows she was born after he died, and things come up every day as she gets older. She's now at a point in her life where she seems to understand the abstract concept of death. She can sometimes get jealous of Finn because he has photos of him and Mark, and she does not. Because of this, she has developed a strong relationship with Steven as her father. She used to only call him "Steven," but more recently has started calling him "Daddy." In my heart, I do not believe that Mark would object.

Grief is sneaky. You never know when it's going to rear its ugly head. In a four-person household, it's often striking one person at any given moment while the other family members are fine that day. There are days when I don't want to be in a particular emotional place, but suddenly my children take me there anyway. Finn comes home from school and asks Steven about his dad, bringing Steven to tears. Caiti suddenly hides her picture of Mark in a drawer, and when asked why, she says, "It's hard to look at." Caiti tells her grandfather that she has no pictures of her and her father together, and it makes her "heart hurt." How do you explain to a five-year-old how much she was loved and wanted by a person she's never met?

My days are hit or miss. I can't go too far down the black hole of "what if" anymore, because I have to live in the "what is." Since losing Mark to war, my politics have shifted and I've become very anti-war. In 2012, I got a tattoo on my upper back/lower neck of two arms breaking a rifle with red poppies surrounding it. The symbol of the broken rifle is a condemnation of war itself. The current political climate is uncertain and has me on edge. I worry about Steven and where he could possibly be sent. There's a lot of rhetoric that this is what you chose, so you deserve whatever is coming to you. But you can be a military family and still say you don't want more war and conflict.

BRANDON MITALAS

Four months after returning from the Middle East, I went back to college and resumed my goal of playing professional soccer. I injured my Achilles tendon, which ended my playing career. Now I'm the assistant coach for women's soccer at a university.

Not a single day goes by that I don't think about what we did over there—carrying the Fallen Angels. Not a day goes by I don't think about Nathan, and his friends and family. I drive by Nathan's grave just about every week and visit at least once a month. I give it a salute and run my hand over his initials on my arm with the tattoos. I say, *Oohrah, Nate.* Love you, buddy.

The other day I heard "November Rain" by Guns N' Roses playing in a store, and it stopped me in my tracks. At the airport in Kuwait, a cassette tape was passed down to us by the previous unit. It had just two songs on it: "November Rain" and "Sweet Child O' Mine." Since it was our only cassette tape, we listened to those songs a lot. Those two songs have always affected me, and still do, obviously. The irony of those two songs is glaring to me, too. The worst month for us came in November 2004 with the Battle of Falluja—"November Rain" takes me back to that time. "Sweet Child O' Mine" strikes a deep chord. It makes me think of my story with my mom.

When I visited the Midwest, driving along country roads and passing small towns, a song by John Michael Montgomery called "Letter From Home" came on the radio. It brought me to tears right away. I can move on from the negative emotions that certain songs like that evoke by saturating myself with them. That night, I looked up the song on YouTube and listened to it over and over. That's kind of my tactic dealing with things that stir up emotions that may have been dormant for a while: I expose myself to them again and again. I use that process to help me if things pop up. Because things do pop up.

Telling my story, and talking about these things, is not an easy task. I have found it increasingly difficult to separate the emotion from the process of telling the story. Unloading everything that first time, face to face—it was powerful, it was meaningful. But it was also difficult. It brought a lot of things to the surface that I had consciously and unconsciously suppressed for a long time. Vulnerability is scary. It's also liberating. I gave a keynote speech to a large audience at a high school. It was terrifying, but you can see that, when it's over, you're okay. The world is still spinning. The sun is still rising in the east and setting in the west. And you still have a purpose. You don't have to be afraid of your past.

Everyone has their own unique story, and I don't understand how mine can affect others in a meaningful way. I know it does, but I still can't fully grasp why. These memories of things I've done and seen and experienced—they almost ended me. Multiple times. Part of me does not understand how those same things also have the power to save a life or positively affect change in another human being who doesn't know me.

But the fact is, if indeed my story has the power to save a life, or change a life for the better—and if I can help just one person by talking about my struggles, my experiences, my demons, and my ascending path to success and happiness and joy—then it's worth it. The pain of telling the stories, the pain of remembering the sights and sounds and smells and moments—it's all worth it.

AFTERWORD

JEB WYMAN

I KNOCKED ON THE DOOR TO ROBIN'S THIRD-FLOOR APARTMENT. I was breathing hard. "Did you run up the stairs?" she asked. I nodded. It was a lie. The truth was that my heart was hammering because I was anxious. Thirty minutes earlier, I'd given her a copy of her story to review. I said I'd leave her alone to read and consider it, and went downstairs. She should text me when she wanted me to return. Now I was about to find out her reaction. I wondered if reading her story would open old wounds, and I'd find her deep in grief. I worried she'd be angry that the intimacy of her pain was being told.

But Robin was smiling. "It's good," she said. "It's hard to read, but it's the truth." The draft went through small changes and corrections over several months. Like all the stories, it had been edited from the transcript of our talks. The first time we'd met, she'd talked for almost three hours. She had more to tell me, she said. I returned a week later for another three hours. She admitted that the first time we'd met, she'd had a can of mace stashed in her chair. "But when I saw you, I figured

I could handle you if you'd tried anything." I'm sure she's right. She's tall. She's a soldier.

That was the first of seventeen times I met with the veterans in this book to review their stories. Each time I worried whether I had done justice to their story. Each time I worried if reading their stories would be painful. They are not easy stories to tell, much less share publicly. I had told the veterans that I would craft the stories as honestly as they had told them to me. I came to realize that there was just one thing I hoped to achieve, and that was writing a story that each veteran embraced.

All the veterans reviewed their stories. All of them said yes.

THE FIRST POST-9/11-ERA VETERAN I MET WAS A YOUNG MAN NAMED ELLIOTT. He was a student at the community college where I teach. In October 2003, about six months after the invasion of Iraq and just as the insurgency began years of bloodletting in Baghdad, Elliott came up to me after class. "I'm being deployed to Iraq," he told me. "I need to withdraw from all my classes." The institution was unprepared. He had to petition the school so his deployment wouldn't ruin his grade point average. He returned a year later and re-enrolled in my class. He was smart as hell, a terrific writer, and earned a perfect grade. We didn't talk about his time in Iraq.

The veterans kept showing up in my classes. Guys like Rudy, who like so many other veterans sat in the far corner of the room, back to the wall, exits and entrances carefully in sight. He sat silently in class with dark circles under his eyes. I didn't understand at the time, but now I realize that he probably slept little. Rudy said almost nothing until the last day of class, when he stood up and told his astonished classmates how his Humvee had been hit by an IED. The blast killed the three others in the vehicle, people very dear to him. He was the only survivor. Rudy took a nonfiction writing class with me the following quarter. He wanted to visit the widow of his sergeant, who had been killed in that Humvee, as well as his grave. He wanted to write that story. But a few weeks into the quarter, Rudy disappeared from class.

Adam also sat with his back to the wall. For that class, I'd assigned a course reader with a bright orange cover. Adam came to class with a purple cover on his course reader. "I'll come talk to you in your office," he said when I asked about it. He explained that for a year in Iraq he'd interrogated prisoners in bright orange jumpsuits. Any bright orange hue now made him sweat, panic, and reel. In Texas, a troop of school kids in identical electric orange tee shirts had sent him fleeing.

And Tony. An Army medic, Tony was in my first-quarter English class and wrote about the day in Iraq when his Humvee hit an IED near Falluja. He was pulled from the wreckage and into a fierce ambush. Injured from the blast, Tony crawled over to a gravely wounded soldier and put a tourniquet on him. The man did not survive. The story ended with Tony's medals in a drawer, gathering dust, and his failure to find meaning in it all.

Tony's story inspired this project. This book is dedicated to both him and Adam.

THEY HAVE DATES. JANUARY 26, THE DATE BRANDON CARRIED THIRTY COFFINS OFF A PLANE. April 6, the date Doc Mendez was killed in Ramadi. March 5, the date Mark C. Wells, Danielle's husband, died in Afghanistan. They remember the dates, and the dates surface every year. They remember the dates because of unbearable loss. Life changed forever.

At the end of Tim O'Brien's short story "How to Tell a True War Story," the narrator has read his story to an audience of civilians, perhaps at a local library. A well-meaning woman in the audience comes up to him afterward and says it was such a sad war story. Hopefully he can put it behind him, she says. O'Brien says nothing, but he's angry. She doesn't get it. "It wasn't a war story," he tells us. "It was a *love story*."

Most of the stories in this book are about love, too. They're about the guilt and grief we feel when the people we love are killed or horribly injured. The stories are about moral injury, the invisible wound caused by witnessing something profoundly wrong, like the deaths of civilians, particularly children. Human beings are hard-wired to recoil from killing, even in war, even when the ones who die are the enemy. Superb training makes men and women effective in battle, but it does not change the moral center of their identity. No matter how much physical and ideological armor you give to your soldiers, war ravages the human heart.

I KNEW WHEN I STARTED THIS PROJECT THAT I WASN'T LOOKING FOR NARRATIVES OF BATTLES AND BRAVERY. I wasn't looking for "war stories." What I wanted were accounts by veterans like the students in my classrooms, ordinary individuals who enlisted, trained, and served. They had been infantrymen, corpsmen and medics, mechanics and truck drivers, and they did not regard themselves as heroes. I knew too that I wanted stories with the honesty of speech. But I did not know ultimately where this project would lead.

I met Miguel Escalera at the student vets center of a local community college. He was studying to get admitted to a physician assistant program. He was the VetCorps representative on campus, helping other student veterans find their feet in higher education and the civilian world, both of which are bewildering to so many veterans. Miguel is soft-spoken and a little shy. He was clean-shaven, his hair was neatly trimmed, and he was dressed in a starched collared shirt and slacks. Any observer would envy his self-possession, his good looks, and his impeccable professional appearance. You would not guess that he had served as a Navy corpsman for the U.S. Marines during the fighting in Ramadi in 2004.

He asked the other veterans in the room if any wanted to talk to me. When no one volunteered, he said, "Well, okay. I guess I can talk with you." He showed me to a small back office. I turned on the recorder and asked him where he had grown up.

He spoke for two hours. He did not betray any emotion as he talked, though his story shook me. When we were done, I asked him if telling his story had stirred up difficult memories. I worried that I could be responsible for opening painful feelings and old wounds, and that I was causing grief for the veterans who shared their experiences. I worried about that for a long time.

But Miguel said that telling his story had helped him. It was therapeutic, he said. He was glad he'd done it. I would hear the same thing from other veterans after they'd told their stories, even when it took hours and they soaked their shirts with sweat.

I came to regard Miguel's story, and the other stories I heard later, as sacred. The storytellers had shared with me the depths of human experience, the experience of war. I felt an intense obligation to the storytellers and their stories. I now believe that veterans must tell their stories in order to come home, and that we must listen to their stories. I believe that, insofar as civilians can understand, only veterans can teach us what it means to go to war. The only way to understand is to sit in the presence of veterans and hear their stories.

After Miguel's interview, I drove home in silence. I turned off the radio that day, and I drove in silence for the next year and a half. The noise of the car radio seemed to profane the stories that were now in my head. I had to sit with them alone.

Miguel's story changed the course of the project.

I FIRST MET DESHAUN OUTSIDE THE LIBRARY OF A COLLEGE WHERE HE WAS TAKING CLASSES. He was dressed smartly and looked like any other college student, though he had a presence, a maturity, that distinguished him from the younger people around him. There's a warmth and magnetism about Deshaun. He is instantly likeable. You want to spend all day with him. We made our way to a private study room that he'd reserved.

He pulled out souvenirs from Iraq, photos, maps. He pulled out deployment books, which are like yearbooks—the history of the tour and photos of everyone in the unit. He pointed to the portraits in the books, telling me the stories of the individuals. Fifteen minutes after we'd sat down, as we came to a photo of a young Marine who'd been killed, he broke down and wept openly, unable to speak for a long time. He apologized and composed himself. During the three hours we spoke he broke down twice more.

 Months later, Deshaun called me up out of the blue. I was driving and pulled over. He was at a hotel, waiting to go downstairs to meet a co-worker. He was attending an employee training for a large national delivery company. During his interview, he'd been asked if he had PTSD. He wondered how his answer would affect his chances for employment.

We talked on the phone for forty-five minutes. I was elated to hear from him. I'd completed a draft of his story weeks before and was getting anxious, since he wasn't returning my texts and emails. Eventually I accepted that many of the veterans I was working with would go out of touch for long stretches, responding again when they were ready. They have times when the noise of the outside world is just too much.

Deshaun invited me to come to his house to review the story. His wife Kitearia, who worked a night shift at a hospital, was asleep. I gave Deshaun the draft and he disappeared downstairs to read it. I waited, again full of anxiety how he would respond. He had been reluctant to reveal how his war still affected him. But when he finally emerged he was smiling broadly, and my worry melted away. Kitearia woke up and joined us, and Deshaun immediately put the story in her hands. "I want you to read this," he said. The kids were up, and so was Nike, the young husky, who bounded over everything. Kitearia sat on the couch and started to read.

I wondered how Kitearia would react to her husband's story. I wondered if she would be angry with me or insist that the story not be published, that she would not have her husband's experiences revealed. She read silently amidst the noise and chaos of the kids and the dog. Deshaun played with them, thoroughly enjoying the commotion, smiling all the time. Kitearia finished the story. She wiped some tears from her eyes. I held my breath. Then she said, "It's really good." Then she said, "Deshaun, honey, you didn't tell me all these things."

Kitearia later told me that reading Deshaun's story had helped her understand his experiences and brought them closer together. If there is one thing about this project I am proud of, that is it.

When we talked, Justin quoted the well-worn phrase "only the dead see the end of war." War changes the soul forever. War is never forgotten. You're never the same person, as Justin says.

"War is hell" has become a vapid cliché drained of meaning. It's attributed to William Tecumseh Sherman, who laid waste to swathes of Georgia on his march to the sea. Few people know the rest of Sherman's famous quote: "It is only those who have neither fired a shot nor heard the shrieks and groans of the wounded who cry aloud for blood, more vengeance, more desolation." The truth is that war is *literally* hell. Over and over, veterans reach for the word "evil" to name their experiences.

All of us share the responsibility when our men and women are sent to war. In our recent wars, we seem determined to care for the physically wounded warriors who come home. Partly because of a profound collective shame over the treatment of Vietnam veterans, we also seem to care about soldiers with PTSD, which is the lingering psychological effects that result when a human soul faces imminent destruction. Keep troops in combat for 200 days, and 100 percent of them will experience post-traumatic stress. We kept troops in Iraq for tours of up to fifteen months.

We don't think so much about the weight of war on the human heart, however, nor the burden of memory. We fetishize heroism, and we want to believe that heroes aren't darkened by grief, gnawed by guilt, or pierced by moral injury. But of course they are. They are our sons, daughters, brothers and sisters, mothers and fathers. They are us.

Of course, there is no forgetting, either. The only way forward is embracing the memories and the new person born from those experiences. That means creating the story—and sharing it. I hope these stories move other veterans to tell theirs. I hope these stories help light the space between those who have been to war and the society that sent them. They need to be part of the community. They need to belong. They need to be understood.

Seattle
April 2017

ACKNOWLEDGEMENTS

To Rose Slaton and Catherine Sutthoff Slaton for their many emotional hours typing transcripts. To Matthew Miller, Mary Sanford, and Anne Wyman-Allen for advice on early drafts. To the Veterans Training Support Center for excellent and free trainings for veteran service providers. To these mental health professionals who shared their knowledge of healing war trauma: Matthew Jakupcak, Mark Fisher, Scott Michaels, Matt Dowling, Emmett Early, Thor Ringler, and Mary F. Wyman.

To Peter Schmidt for his steadfast mentorship, counsel, and invaluable friendship. To Timm Lovitt, Chris Szarek, Mike Farnum, Jaime Yslas, Jerimiah Meyer, Seth Peterson, Rosa Lundborg, Demetrius Hatcher, Vickie Bell, Jason Schlegelman, Lt. Col. Dave Millet (ret.), and Deanna Sleep for graciously introducing me to their brothers and sisters. To veterans Samantha Powers, Rebecca Murch, Will Schwab, Jason Alves, Tristan Riesen, and others for support and encouragement. To the veterans too numerous to name who shared their stories with me.

To John Phillips (USMC), Luciano Marano (USN), and Adrianna Moore (USN) for their fine portraiture work done pro bono. To Bob Hereford (USAF) for giving this book professional photo editing and photography. To Christopher Dollar (USN) for expert design and layout of this book. To Ethan Casey of Blue Ear Books for believing in this project and seeing it through. I'm grateful to Seattle Colleges and Jill Wakefield, chancellor, for sabbatical support of this project.

Finally, with love, to Darci, Levi, and Jaspar for enduring my absences, physical and emotional, for the last two years.

PHOTO CREDITS
AND PERMISSIONS

Deshaun and Nevaeh Caples, page i, courtesy of Kitearia Caples

Deshaun and Nevaeh Caples, page xiv, by Bob Hereford

Dominic Wilkerson, page 18, by Adrianna Moore

Robin Eckstein, page 32, by Bob Hereford

Miguel Escalera, page 46, by John Phillips

Kevin Chose, page 64, by Bob Hereford

Dennis Eller, page 90, by Luciano Marano

Emmanuel Wright, page 110, by Bob Hereford

Zong Her, page 124, courtesy of Zong Her

Mike Farnum, page 136, by Luciano Marano

Jeff Radcliff, page 150, by John Phillips

Timm Lovitt, page 168, by Bob Hereford

Nikki Davis, page 182, by John Phillips

Justin Shults, page 190, by John Phillips

Joe Jocson Porter, page 204, by Bob Hereford

Joe Stone, Sr., page 216, by John Phillips

Adam Cajiuat Posadas, page 230, courtesy of Christine and Jeremy Posadas

Danielle Villanueva, page 236, by Luciano Marano

Brandon Mitalas, page 248, by John Phillips

Photos in "Where They're At Now" courtesy of the veterans; photo of Adam Cajiuat Posadas courtesy of Christine and Jeremy Posadas

"My Prison is a Quiet Place" published by permission of the estate of Adam Posadas

FURTHER READING

There has been a surge of literature born of the post-9/11 wars. Among books by veterans, *My Life as a Foreign Country*, by poet and soldier Brian Turner, is a beautiful and moving memoir. *Kaboom: Embracing the Suck in a Savage Little War*, by Matt Gallagher, recounts his year of patrolling the streets of Baghdad. Brian Castner, who served in Iraq as a bomb tech, lays bare his challenges of coming home in *The Long Walk: A Story of War and the Life That Follows.*

Phil Klay's *Redeployment*, a collection of short stories, was the winner of the 2014 National Book Award. Other notable works of fiction include *Fives and Twenty-fives* by Michael Pitre, David Abrams' dark comedy *Fobbit*, and *The Yellow Birds* by Kevin Powers. *Green on Blue* by Elliot Ackerman, *The Knife* by Ross Ritchell, and *The Watch* by Joydeep Roy-Bhattacharya are novels of the war in Afghanistan. *War of the Encyclopaedists*, by Christopher Robinson and Gavin Kovite, tells its story from the perspective of the generation who fought it. *Billy Lynn's Long Halftime Walk* by Ben Fountain, a superb novel and now a film by Ang Lee, critiques America's hero culture.

The Corpse Exhibition and Other Stories of Iraq, by Hassan Blasim, is a harrowing series of metaphorical stories of post-invasion Iraq through the eyes of Iraqis. Dexter Filkins spent years as a reporter witnessing the piteous descent of Baghdad into sectarian violence, and his book *The Forever War* is haunting. David Finkel followed up his excellent book *The Good Soldiers*, which documents an Army battalion during the 2007 troop surge, with *Thank You for Your Service*, a harsh chronicle of these soldiers battling post-traumatic stress back home. Evan Wright accompanied the Marines during the Iraq invasion, recounting that odyssey in *Generation Kill*, which was made into an HBO series.

Outstanding books about the psychological impact of wars others than those fought by America include *My War Gone By, I Miss It So*, by Anthony Loyd, a memoir of covering the horrors in Bosnia and Sarajvo, and the fierce addiction of war. *Aftershock*, by the British journalist Matthew Green, expertly examines war trauma in UK troops from that nation's conflicts in Northern Ireland, the Falklands, the Balkans, and Iraq and Afghanistan. The human cost of Russia's war in Afghanistan in the 1980s is recorded in *Zinky Boys: Soviet Voices from the Afghanistan War* by Svetlana Alexievich, who was awarded the 2015 Nobel Prize in Literature.

Literature about war trauma reaches as far back as humanity has recorded the experience of war. Jonathan Shay's brilliant *Achilles in Vietnam: Combat Trauma and the Undoing of Character* analyzes the impact of war in the *Iliad*, Homer's epic poem. *Odysseus in America: Combat Trauma and the Trials of Homecoming*, also by Jonathan Shay, examines the universal challenge of coming home from war as portrayed in Homer's *Odyssey*.

The Body Keeps the Score: Brain, Mind, and Body in the Healing of Trauma, by Bessel van der Kolk, and *Trauma and Recovery: The Aftermath of Violence*, by Judith Herman, discuss the impact of trauma on human psychology. Edward Tick's *War and the Soul: Healing Our Nation's Veterans from Post-Traumatic Stress Disorder* and

Warrior's Return: Restoring the Soul after War draw on decades of work in healing Vietnam veterans. A powerful self-examination of the trauma of combat is *What It Is Like to Go to War* by Karl Marlantes, who served with the Marine Corps in Vietnam.

THE EDITOR

Jeb Wyman teaches writing at Seattle Central College. He is the academic director of the Clemente Course for Veterans at Antioch University, a six-month program in history, philosophy, art, and literature to help veterans gain insight into their experiences, prepare them to pursue further higher education, and build community with other veterans. In the summer, he and his family operate a commercial salmon vessel in Bristol Bay, Alaska. He lives in Seattle.

MORE TITLES
FROM BLUE EAR BOOKS

www.blueearbooks.com

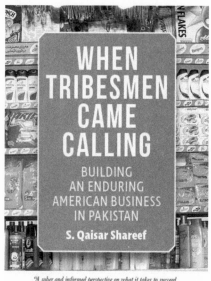

WHEN TRIBESMEN CAME CALLING

BY S. QAISAR SHAREEF

"Qaisar Shareef tells the story of the development of Procter & Gamble's business in a highly engaging way, revealing business principles and the importance of understanding and respecting local cultural sensibilities and political developments. Qaisar's narrative, grounded in real-life stories, offers a sober and informed perspective on what it takes to succeed in a challenged part of the world, while providing a window into the political and economic challenges and opportunities in Pakistan today that I believe readers will relish."

– **John Pepper**, retired CEO of Procter & Gamble Company

THE EXPERTS

BY CLYDE EDWIN PETTIT

Long out of print, *The Experts* is Clyde Edwin Pettit's masterful selection of self-damning words from the men who led America into a disastrous war in Vietnam. Includes the full text of Pettit's prescient January 1966 letter to Sen. J. William Fulbright, warning of the "ever-present possibility of catastrophe."

LIVE AT THE FORBIDDEN CITY

BY DENNIS REA

A singular look at the rapidly evolving Chinese popular music scene, by one of the first progressive Western musicians to perform extensively in both China and Taiwan. Includes a rare eyewitness account of the little-reported June 1989 massacre of protesters in Chengdu.

THE DESCENT INTO HAPPINESS

BY DAVID HOWELL

"*In the tradition of such contemplative travel memoirs as* Zen and the Art of Motorcycle Maintenance *and* Blue Highways, *Howell makes discoveries about America – and himself.*"

— **Jim Higgins**, Arts and Books Editor, *Milwaukee Journal Sentinel*

HOME FREE: AN AMERICAN ROAD TRIP

BY ETHAN CASEY

"Ethan Casey listened hard and well in his books on Haiti and Pakistan. Now he's listening to an America that's dealing with uncertainty, division, and change."
— **Paul Rogat Loeb**

BEARING THE BRUISE: A LIFE GRACED BY HAITI

BY ETHAN CASEY

"As an eyewitness, Casey gives readers an informed perspective on many of the political and social complexities that vex those who seek to make common cause with Haiti."
— **Paul Farmer**

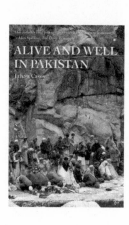

ALIVE AND WELL IN PAKISTAN

BY ETHAN CASEY

"Compulsory reading for anyone visiting Pakistan"
— **Harvard International Review**

"Wonderful ... a model of travel writing"
— **Edwidge Danticat**